CRYPTOPOLITICS

Anthropology of Media

Series Editors: Mark Peterson and Sahana Udupa

The ubiquity of media across the globe has led to an explosion of interest in the ways people around the world use media as part of their everyday lives. This series addresses the need for works that describe and theorise multiple, emerging, and sometimes interconnected, media practices in the contemporary world. Interdisciplinary and inclusive, this series offers a forum for ethnographic methodologies, descriptions of non-Western media practices, explorations of transnational connectivity, and studies that link culture and practices across fields of media production and consumption.

Recent volumes:

Volume 12
Cryptopolitics: Exposure, Concealment, and Digital Media
Edited by Victoria Bernal, Katrien Pype, and Daivi Rodima-Taylor

Volume 11
Digital Archives and Collections: Creating Online Access to Cultural Heritage
Katja Müller

Volume 10
Theorising Media and Conflict
Edited by Philipp Budka and Birgit Bräuchler

Volume 9
Media Practices and Changing African Socialities: Non-media-centric Perspectives
Edited by Jo Helle-Valle and Ardis Storm-Mathisen

Volume 8
Monetising the Dividual Self: The Emergence of the Lifestyle Blog and Influencers in Malaysia
Julian Hopkins

Volume 7
Transborder Media Spaces: Ayuujk Videomaking between Mexico and the US
Ingrid Kummels

Volume 6
The Making of the Pentecostal Melodrama: Religion, Media and Gender in Kinshasa
Katrien Pype

Volume 5
Localizing the Internet: An Anthropological Account
John Postill

Volume 4
Theorising Media and Practice
Edited by Birgit Bräuchler and John Postill

Volume 3
News as Culture: Journalistic Practices and the Remaking of Indian Leadership Traditions
Ursula Rao

For a full volume listing, please see the series page on our website: https://www.berghahnbooks.com/series/anthropology-of-media

Cryptopolitics

Exposure, Concealment, and Digital Media

Edited by

Victoria Bernal, Katrien Pype, and Daivi Rodima-Taylor

berghahn

NEW YORK • OXFORD

www.berghahnbooks.com

First published in 2023 by
Berghahn Books
www.berghahnbooks.com

First paperback edition published in 2026

Library of Congress Cataloging-in-Publication Data

Names: Bernal, Victoria, editor. | Pype, Katrien, editor. | Rodima-Taylor, Daivi, editor.
Title: Cryptopolitics : exposure, concealment, and digital media / edited by Victoria Bernal, Katrien Pype, and Daivi Rodima-Taylor.
Description: New York : Berghahn Books, 2023. | Series: Anthropology of media ; Volume 12 | Includes bibliographical references and index.
Identifiers: LCCN 2023004599 (print) | LCCN 2023004600 (ebook) | ISBN 9781805390299 (hardback) | ISBN 9781805390336 (ebook)
Subjects: LCSH: Information society—Political aspects—Africa. | Digital media—Political aspects—Africa. | Power (Social sciences)—Political aspects—Africa.
Classification: LCC HM851 .C7823 2023 (print) | LCC HM851 (ebook) | DDC 302.23/1096—dc23/eng/20230414
LC record available at https://lccn.loc.gov/2023004599
LC ebook record available at https://lccn.loc.gov/2023004600

British Library Cataloguing in Publication Data

A catalogue record for this book is available from the British Library

EU GPSR Authorized Representative

LOGOS EUROPE, 9 rue Nicolas Poussin, 17000, LA ROCHELLE, France
Email: Contact@logoseurope.eu

ISBN 978-1-80539-029-9 hardback
ISBN 978-1-80758-104-6 paperback
ISBN 978-1-80539-030-5 epub
ISBN 978-1-80539-033-6 web pdf

https://doi.org/10.3167/9781805390299

Funded by the FWO (Fund for Scientific Research in Flanders) through the Odysseus Grant (FWOG.A005.14N).

Contents

Figures

Introduction

Cryptopolitics and Digital Media

Katrien Pype, Victoria Bernal,
and Daivi Rodima-Taylor

Under President Joseph Kabila it became a criminal offense in the Democratic Republic of the Congo to have a SIM card that was not formally registered at the telephone company. In Kinshasa, rumor had it that this law was prompted by death threats the president had received via an *appel masqué* (phone call with a hidden ID). Anonymous threats were totally in line with the politics of intimidation that the Kabila regime enacted on its citizens via the secret service (ANR) and its network of spies who issued indirect warnings via text messages and were responsible for the disappearances of anti-Kabila protestors. Kinois (residents of Kinshasa) explained to Katrien Pype that someone most likely had bribed a telephone company employee to obtain the president's personal phone number.

While it is difficult to verify the accuracy of these statements, we take them seriously because crucially, these discourses involve contemporary imaginations of power as entanglements of unseen forces, including tech companies and state surveillance apparatuses that infuse communications with secrecy and suspicion. These power relations are steeped in mutual distrust between the parties involved such that communication is understood as a means of manipulation. The stories spun around the new law in Congo furthermore showed that citizens do not solely imagine themselves as subjects but also as agents in power games that rely on ambiguity, confusion, and deception.

We propose the term "cryptopolitics" as a way to draw attention to the significance of hidden information, double meanings, double-crossing, and the constant processes of encoding and decoding messages in negotiations of power relations. These manifest as secrets, hidden knowledge, allusions, insinuations, suspicion, obfuscation, ambiguity, skeptical interpretations, and conspiracy theories, which are at the heart of social and political life.

Cryptopolitics is based on the premise of "depth," the assumption that there are various layers of meaning hidden beneath that which is said or shown (Barber 1987: 61–68). It involves the management of communication in ways that play off ambiguity and the distinction between concealed and overt information. It involves twin processes of encrypting and decrypting, the agentive practices of ambiguity, obfuscation, and dissimulation, and the engagement in practices of decoding, of trying to apprehend what is hidden, discerning the meaning, and the intentions and motivations behind the covering up.

The gap between the overt and the covert is a murky terrain; it is like a black box. Some may know what is actually hidden, while others do not. Secrecy and decoding are deployed to produce boundaries of exclusion and inclusion. Cryptopolitics, thus, are intimately entangled with inequality and difference. One of the basic underpinnings of any cryptopolitical agency is that some people are "in the know," while others are not, and should remain in the dark. Yet no one fully controls the meanings and interpretations others ascribe to the hidden and the obscured. That gray area is a subjunctive space: a space full of possibility and opportunity, but also of danger and risk as the chapters in this book show.

Cryptopolitics is not new, but it takes novel forms and has new consequences when it enters society through digital media. While digital media seemed to promise a new age of transparency and open access to information, it has also created new sources of ambiguity, opacity, and deception. The recent rise in fake news, conspiracy theories, and uncertainties about truth claims and science draw attention to powerful ambiguities manipulated for political ends. For example, the use of so-called dog whistles (secret symbols and words) by white supremacists in the United States and other extremists shows the complexity of the public and private because the public can be filled with hidden signs that constitute a form of private, secret communication (Am 2020; Drakulich et al. 2020, Weiman and Ben Am 2020). The internet and social media, moreover, increase possibilities for people to live fragmented, compartmentalized, or secret lives: they can appear as different people and inhabit different worlds online and offline. Digital media also introduce new layers of technological opacity; what goes on behind the screen as data is collected, transmitted, and stored, is invisible (Bernal 2020). The workings of algorithms and machine learning can produce results through processes that remain obscured even to those who designed them. As the 2022 crash of various cryptocurrency platforms shows, even the ostensibly robust transparency of blockchains did not prevent swindling and theft, and perhaps even contributed to it as the claims made by cryptocurrency promoters created a false sense of security among buyers/investors.

Secrecy, deception, and ambiguity are not novel activities nor new objects of analytical inquiry (Simmel 1906, Taussig 1999, West and Sanders 2003), but cryptopolitics brings these kinds of activities into view under a unified conceptual framework that reveals how they are deployed politically. Cryptopolitics, thus, focuses attention on the workings of the hidden and the deceptive in relations of power. By "crypto" we draw attention to activities of concealment and revelation, and to the skills of encrypting, decrypting, coding, and decoding. By "politics" we highlight the power relationships and dynamics associated with secrecy, dissemblance, clandestine activities, and exposure. "Cryptopolitics" then encompasses the practices of producing confusing or ambiguous communication for specific purposes, and the hermeneutical strategies, practices of exegesis, and efforts to make sense of signs and forms that obscure, shield, and hide.

New forms of cryptopolitics emerge with digital media, including the veiled, complicit partnerships between states and technology companies, enabling surveillance or internet shutdowns in times of elections or other tense political moments, as happens frequently in Africa and throughout the Global South. A growing number of states rely on telecommunication and technology companies to help limit the circulation of information that threatens their political power. States also seek to use data collected by tech companies for various political ends. In both these efforts the official rationale is often that of "security," a paramount contemporary domain of cryptopolitics since threats and espionage produce and are produced by secrecy and suspicion.

Encryption and decryption have gained prominence as technological issues, but through cryptopolitics we analyze them as cultural phenomena. In the contemporary world, the skills of concealment, ambiguity, and subterfuge as well as the skills of discernment and interpretation are both social and technological. Political conflicts, elections, repression, and revolt, along with other political flashpoints bring cryptopolitics dramatically to the fore. Everyday interactions and interpersonal relationships are also fields for cryptopolitics as people increasingly manage their relationships with others through revelation and concealment, especially as they conduct their lives across online and offline worlds. What needs to be hidden from whom, and what gains power or protection from being hidden, and who is able to decipher ambiguous communications depends on the social and political context. Ethnographic research and anthropological perspectives thus are key to understanding the dynamics of cryptopolitics in any given context.

Cryptopolitics is a lens that helps bring into focus a dynamic of power and communication that operates in a wide array of settings. This anthology explores cryptopolitics in diverse African contexts through ethnographic perspectives and in-depth qualitative studies. The authors situate their work at the intersection of cultural anthropology, media studies, and African studies.

Cryptopolitical Perspectives in Anthropology and African Studies

Cryptopolitics means strategically saying one thing, but meaning another, or showing one thing, while concealing something else. Strategic, enigmatic locutions are "thick" (multilayered), where meanings lie beneath the surface for those who have the skills to interpret and read between the lines, while the naïve may take them at face value. Cryptopolitics foregrounds these processes whereby information is hidden or made ambiguous, and communications contain indirect, symbolic, and secret meanings to be interpreted. These processes are entangled with power and powerlessness, with political intent or consequences.

While the issues of secrecy, deception, allusion, and hidden meanings are central to much of anthropology, the concept cryptopolitics is not. To date the term has only appeared in anthropology in a 2012 publication of *Arizona Anthropologist* authored by Raymond Orr who was a graduate student at the time (Orr 2012). He writes about the Isleta Native American community where he conducted fieldwork: "Isleta politics are well-hidden. Individual and group bellicosity takes the form of crypto-politics. These types of politics express themselves non-politically through forms of social subterfuge. Disagreements, hurt feelings, desire and senses of injustice are part of Isleta communal life but the particular community norms allow bellicosity to be expressed openly only at high cost to participants" (Orr 2012: 61). Orr adds that "conflict and where it is (and is not) acknowledged is complicated for both those in the communities themselves as well as the scholars who study them" (Orr 2012: 61).[1]

Orr mentions the influence of political science on his approach but does not cite any source for "crypto-politics." The earliest usage and perhaps the coinage of the term dates from a 1965 article by political scientist T. H. Rigby. Rigby (1965) used "crypto-politics" to describe the political system in the Soviet Union where public politics were state-orchestrated or suppressed, and where processes of official decision-making were hidden behind a façade of institutions. As anthropologists, both Orr and the contributors to this volume extend cryptopolitics beyond the state to encompass a broad range of power relations.

Orr goes on to suggest that Isleta's initial "tranquility," which he depicted at the essay's outset, is possibly enforced by secret forms of conflict such as slander, rumor, and even accusations of witchcraft. Orr thus captures the very essence of cryptopolitics that we have conceived here. It is about deceptive appearances, secret and ambiguous communications and "politics" that takes indirect and unconventional forms. As James Scott (1985) has pointed out, besides overt acts of resistance such as organized rebellions, the less powerful often turn to subtler acts of non-cooperation. These everyday forms of resistance may include evasion, strategic ignorance, or non-compliance, and frequently contest the "public transcripts" of formal hierarchies through a "veiled discourse of dignity and self-assertion" (1985: 137; see also Scott 1990). While such "weapons of the weak" are often cryptopolitical in character, cryptopolitics are employed by the powerful as well.

A few works outside the discipline of anthropology have used the concept of cryptopolitics. Ananya Kabir (2014) rather uniquely connects cryptopolitics to the crypt in her analysis of Kashmiri resistance and cultural production around the body, the grave, and martyrdom. But scholars have usually understood this concept in a much more literal manner to mean the politics surrounding digital encryption and/or the internal power dynamics in the blockchain developer community (e.g., Groos 2020; Monsees 2019). There is a history of conflict over the uses and spread of encryption, sometimes referred to as "cryptowars" (Hellegrean 2017; Jarvis 2020). Such struggles show, as we explore throughout this volume, that concealing and revealing both involve power. The controversies surrounding Julian Assange, WikiLeaks, Chelsea Manning, and the revelations by Edward Snowden are indications of the global significance of hidden knowledge, clandestine communication, and the powers of revelation associated with the digital (Hintz, Dencik, and Wahl-Jorgensen 2017). In that sense, we may inhabit a particular cryptopolitical condition—one that is facilitated and amplified through digital media.

Our chapters all share a focus on Africa. There are compelling reasons why ethnographies of African digital cultures provide fertile ground for the exploration of cryptopolitics. The first is that in certain African contexts indirectness and the cryptic have been preferred forms of communication. For example, in her seminal article on popular arts in Africa, Karin Barber (1987: 8) writes that "works which appear conservative . . . may conceal criticism of, or reservations about, the status quo which people have good reasons not to express openly. They often reveal doubts and anxieties; and possibilities of an alternative view appear in textual loopholes, fissures, and silences." Second, conspiracy theories thrive in postcolonial Africa, where citizens have a long history of distrusting their leaders, and where they struggle to make sense of political pronouncements and events that they find confusing or suspect. Third, Africanist anthropology has an enormous archive on the occult and the invisible realms in cosmological worldviews, in which believers can only try to understand the world by interpreting signs. Fourth, digital media, consumed mostly through smart phones, has rapidly become central to African politics and social life. As is the case in the rest of the world, African states, private companies, humanitarian organizations, religious communities, families, and other networks rely on digital technology in one way or another.

Furthermore, sorcery and magic, two key rubrics in africanist anthropology, are cryptopolitical behavior because these actions depend on a deliberate manipulation of material reality by invoking hidden, occult powers. The complexities of studying the political dimensions of the hidden and the occult in the current era of neoliberal globalization can be illustrated by the example of the "occult economies" of post-apartheid South Africa (Comaroff and Comaroff 1999). As the impoverished masses witness vast wealth passing to the elites through the hidden speculations of the neoliberal market, some people resort to novel magical means in pursuit of their goals. Their practices, often parodying the free market, find expression through a variety of contemporary media—including "dial-in diviners" and multimedia ritual technologies. The proliferation of "mystical arts" in postcolonial Africa should not be viewed as a retreat to the traditional past, however, but rather as employing culturally familiar tropes and technologies to produce new ways of coping with contemporary inequalities: a "new magic for new situations" (1999: 284). Such populations that are disenfranchised or marginalized politically as well as economically seek sources of power in the occult while also suspecting that elites use such powers to achieve the positions they hold. Witchcraft accusations are closely related to practices of decoding, where signs must be deciphered to uncover hidden, spiritual machinations. Yet clearly cryptopolitics is not solely an African phenomenon. Practices of encoding and decoding are part and parcel of social life anywhere around the world.

Cryptopolitics is not a new phenomenon that has only emerged with digital media. Rather, discussions about encryption, fake accounts, deep fakes, and disinformation remind us that deliberate confusion, double-speak, allusion, suspicion, distrust, and deciphering are often part of human interaction, and are always embedded in strategies of power. At the same time, we should keep in mind that cryptopolitics is foundational to the digitized world, as technologies amplify the duality of concealment and revelation, and also magnify the scale, scope, and set of stakeholders associated with any particular instance. With this book, we introduce the concept of "cryptopolitics" as an analytical space that is fruitful for new investigations in contemporary power configurations. We hope that the chapters of this volume can serve as an inspiration to engage in similar research beyond the African continent.

Secrecy and Cryptopolitics

Our lives are made up of relationships, moments, utterances, and experiences in which ambiguity, doubleness, and indeterminacy may be cultivated, appreciated, and explicitly sought after. In other instances, these same characteristics are considered threatening and deceptive, prompting suspicion and efforts to decipher hidden truths. Navigating powerful institutions and everyday social life means constantly calibrating the desirability of transparency or opacity, of disclosing more or less information, and, on the other hand, continually assessing the real import of information one is given. Scholarly attention to cryptopolitics thus brings nuance to the study of secrecy, which very often seems to be understood as the radical opposition of full transparency or full opacity. We consider these two modalities to be opposite ends of a continuum, with most of life taking place between them, where concealment and revelation work together in a range of informational practices depending on the context.

Secrecy, ambiguity, and dissemblance mediate nexuses of power and knowledge. There is power in keeping things hidden and power in gaining access to what is hidden, as well as in being able to interpret what lies beneath the surface. Regulating exposure is essential for constructing "intersubjective and institutional life" (Manderson et al. 2015: 183), yet hiding and concealing are practices that leave traces. The existence of secrets or hidden agendas is often known, suspected, and made manifest either willfully or inadvertently. It is important therefore to view encoding and decoding practices through their performative aspects, with attention to the ways valued information and knowledge are concealed, imparted, or deduced through increasingly diverse communicative practices and interpretive skills. This underscores the processual dimension of such concealed content—the establishment of secrets and the occasion of their revelation invest them with social force (Jones

2014; see also Herzfeld 2009). Instances and practices of disclosure and of interpretation should therefore be seen as political, in fact, as cryptopolitical.

Secrecy is also sometimes described as silence—as if keeping secrets just means not talking about something. With our notion of "cryptopolitics," we want to unsettle that taken-for-granted correlation between secrecy and silence. An analytical focus on cryptopolitics shows that much is actually said while hiding something else. People use veiled language, speak in indirect fashion, and downplay one thing by emphasizing another. In many of our interactions, we are constantly producing partial truths. The notion of "partial truths" has gained particular salience in anthropology to refer the fact that claims and narratives always come from a particular positionality (Clifford and Marcus 1986). But it is also the case that certain utterances are purposely chosen in order to avoid other, riskier statements, and thus keep that information, those experiences, emotions, and opinions hidden. Here we draw attention to the fact that certain statements, testimonies and confessions, and other narratives may disclose specific parts of significant data, while the speaker may choose to obscure other parts. The calibration of transparency and opacity that makes up a significant part of any cryptopolitical action occurs in intimate lifeworlds, in political communication, in economic transactions, in religious practices, and in artistic expressions. It involves the speaker's agency, their assessment of the communicative context, and their repertoire of communicative resources and skills, and triggers the agency of the audience in determining what is being obscured and why.

Cryptopolitics can take many forms (see below). Apart from the deployment of irony, figurative speech, and other discursive forms, gestures can also be mobilized in cryptopolitical activity. Within anthropology, the wink is probably the best-known symbolic gesture. Generations of students have been trained in our discipline's signature method of participant observation by learning about Clifford Geertz's distinction between the blink of an eye and the wink (1973). The latter is a socially significant act that differentiates within a group of people by bodily communicating common knowledge and a shared perception. The shared understanding of a wink among those in the know could be considered cryptopolitics on a micro level.

Whispering, in its literal and its metaphorical sense, is another cryptopolitical gesture. Just like ironic utterances and the wink, the whisper materializes the double layering of how information is often managed. The whisper produces sound that is only intelligible to a limited group of people, and thus makes audible the boundaries between those who should know and those who should not know. The act of hiding is made manifest in a very sensuous way.

The whisper has become a powerful sign in the Global North where various idioms emerged around it, for example a neologism such as "whisper networks" (Babel 2018). Commonly, whisper networks reference chains of informal information-sharing among women, who exchange knowledge about marginalization, violence, and vulnerability, in an attempt to provide protection against male abusers. Whisper networks highlight a form of resistance through hidden disclosure; they arise from an uneven distribution of the power to speak along gendered lines. They are thus manifestations of cryptopolitics in a society where powerful men dominate not only many industries but also formal systems of justice.

Distrust, Duplicity, and Discretion

Cyptopolitics is always a social practice, embedded in relationships, and therefore it is the privileged terrain of anthropological inquiry. Overall, cryptopolitics is deeply entangled with trust and distrust. Hiding and obscuring information, intentions, and affects may be inspired by a lack of trust toward the receivers, whether they are intimate others, political agents, or non-identified actors of global power configurations.

Relations of distrust are often characterized by duplicity. Double speak, fake accounts, and disinformation may at once be symptoms of distrust toward certain authorities or audiences. At the same time digital media itself generates distrust. There is growing global desire to share information in end-to-end encrypted environments evidenced by the massive growth in Signal and Telegram accounts in early 2021 after WhatsApp announced that it would share data with Facebook (WhatsApp started in California in 2009 and was acquired by Facebook, now Meta Platforms, in 2014). This backlash against WhatsApp seemed to be inspired by distrust in Facebook, which had been sharing users' data with other private companies and sometimes with repressive states.

Yet, distrust often governs interpersonal relationships and relations to and among institutions as well. Experiences of doubt about other's intentions and motives generate suspicion and conspiracy theories. This plays out strongly in Africanist research, where uncertainty, confusion, and distrust have become tropes in the study of social and political life (Cooper and Pratten 2015). Unstable economies, authoritarian regimes with whimsical political leaders, and lingering civil wars have instilled a distrust between people and their leaders, and also among citizens themselves (Bernal, this volume). Practices of hiding and shielding have been explored in urban Africa, where pretense and bluff, for example in Inhambane, Mozambique, and Abidjan, Ivory Coast, are applauded as necessary strategies for social advancement (see Archambault 2017; Newell 2012).[2] Furthermore, social codes that hide uncomfortable truths reign.[3] Such contexts instill a basic sense of doubt and skepticism toward what is said and shown, as people expect that others are actually hiding difficult truths.

Efforts to hide uncomfortable truths have also been observed where certain medical conditions are stigmatized. People may engage in a wide range of cryptopolitical strategies to conceal health problems. Relatives and friends may cooperate in these efforts to dissimulate as research on HIV care in Burkina Faso and Zambia has shown (Hejoaka 2009; MackWorth-Young, Bond, and Wringe 2020; Rhine 2014). Vague language, figurative speech, and other indirect locutions may signal the desire to be discrete. Crucially, in such contexts, people may understand and therefore refrain from asking questions.

In contexts where taboos, stigma, and repression are most heavily felt, cryptopolitics plays a larger communicative role. In such instances, duplicity is not linked to treachery, but to discretion. Whispers, winks, and coded language manifest complicity, a relationship thriving on shared knowledge, while outsiders do not have access to that information. Duplicity may be a way of avoiding the power of others or a way of exercising power over others.

Exposure and Disclosure

Of course, where there is discretion, there are also restricted groups or communities of people where the secrets can be aired. For example, in Bedouin worlds (Abu-Lughod 1993), women's songs reveal their "veiled sentiments" through indirect expression not every listener comprehends. They engage in doublespeak to protect dominant power hierarchies, while nevertheless expressing their opinions and feelings. Ethnographies of mental health draw attention to practices of information management that border on cryptopolitics. Central to the care of the self are processes of sharing private emotions, traumas, and anxieties with others suffering from the same affliction or with therapists. Therapeutic support groups work in part by allowing hidden knowledge to be expressed in a ritualistic context (Kitanaka 2015).

Privacy, or the identification of the boundaries between the private and the public, is one of the social domains where cryptopolitics comes to the fore. Ultimately, social life resides in a paradox: insofar as secrecy produces social boundaries, the very existence of the secret is public knowledge. Boundaries between "those who know" and "those who do not know" (or "those who ought to know" and "those who should not know") thrive in any society. These boundaries are policed: practices are put in place in order to protect them, while protest, contestations, rumors, and leaks challenge these boundaries. Anthropological work often involves trying to understand how such boundaries are materialized, preserved, and transgressed or transformed. Cryptopolitics offers a purchase on these relationships and processes with particular attention to their power dimensions and to the significance of ambiguity and double meanings.

Several African societies have idiomatic expressions addressing the necessity of only partial transparency. In Kinshasa, the proverb *toyebi motema ya batu te* (we can never know what is in the hearts of others, Pype, this volume) warns that relatives, friends, neighbors, or strangers may not always have the best intentions, and full disclosure is risky. In Burundi, the term *ubgenge* denotes cleverness in indirection or dissimulation, a strategy of "hiding just enough" and "revealing just enough" of one one's own intentions and/or the intentions of others (Turner, this volume). Such ethnographic examples show how cryptopolitics works through a balance between opaqueness and disclosure.

The #metoo movement that spread across the globe in recent years is another testimony to the power relations that often compel secret-keeping and pretense on the part of the vulnerable (Chandra and Erlingsdóttir 2020). It can be seen as a cryptopolitical phenomenon in that it not only revealed how widespread the practice of secrecy surrounding sexual abuse was but also called for the unveiling of negative truths about powerholders. All these observations show that in private and public life full transparency or exposure means vulnerability.

The affordances of digital media and social platforms are significant here because of the ways they allow users to scale between full exposure and discrete communication. Parameters within platforms such as WhatsApp, Facebook, and other apps require users to think about their publics and social networks and to deliberate about the scale at which they want particular content to circulate online (though these controls themselves obscure the ways Facebook uses people's data). Digital media also make it easy for people to secretly make audio/video recordings of conversations or activities and to share these fully or in snippets (whether edited or not) online. In order to avoid context collapse (or the possibility that non-addressees also read a particular post), users sometimes post "images with references comprehensible to some of the viewers but not others" (Miller et al. 2016: 175). People may also manage their images and reputations or seek to manipulate audiences through the use of pseudonyms, fake accounts, and doctored images. VPNs (virtual private networks) are sometimes used to hide a person's location, while the Tor network can conceal a person's browsing activity. Digital media, moreover, (from social media content to the Google search function) offers people access to a highly curated, subjective slice of data and information—which is frequently presented as objective and understood to represent the full picture.

Though, as Cambridge Analytica so dramatically revealed, the control people think they exercise over digital information is often illusory (Hinds, Williams, and Joinson 2020). The encryption practices advanced through social media platforms, when linked for instance to fintech and banking, may create exploitative invisibilities such as data capture and "Ponzi" schemes, as shown by Daivi Rodima-Taylor (this volume). The compilation and use of big data is creating new opaque zones of power and establishing potent invisibilities embedded in growing disparities of expertise and access, which may lead to new social inequalities (Nuttall and Mbembe 2015).

As cultural anthropologists, we are mainly interested in people, communities, and institutions that are engaged in processes of encoding and decoding. Yet, several of our contributors draw attention to the nonhuman actors in cryptopolitics. Lisa Poggiali (this volume) describes how new biometric technologies of population regulation encode and decode information about bodies, citizenship, and belonging. These biometric data do not always result in transparency, however, but lead to new forms of concealment or evasion. The risk of ethnic and racial discrimination arising from limited inputs that create bias in software programs is well known. The fixing of identity through biometrics can also have dire political consequences for affected groups. While technologies can sometimes work to solidify and fix identities to negative effect, other times they can be used to construct more fluid and multifaceted identities. Such technologically mediated identity creation is cryptopolitical; seeking, on the one hand, to exercise political power through revealing what is viewed as an essential identity, and on the other hand, engaging in political resistance by manipulating and subverting assigned identities. Peter Chonka (this volume) draws attention to the algorithms used by search engines that through their autocompletion features suggest clan identities as search terms for any search involving a Somali name. In doing so, search engines may influence perceptions and constructions of Somali identity.

Infrastructures of Cryptopolitics

Diverse material and immaterial infrastructures undergird cryptopolitics. Digital media has enabled transparency, but it has also enabled opacity, anonymity, the dark web, and new forms of deception and manipulation (Bernal 2020; Beshiri and Susuri 2019; Coleman 2014). Institutions are both material and cultural, including big technology companies, startups, universities, research institutes, local governments, and states. All these are mobilized by social and political actors engaged in hiding or exposing data and information, while technical affordances, skills, and access vary—thereby contributing to exclusions and inequality. The specific constraints and affordances of applications, platforms, algorithms, mobile phones, and modes of digital media such as videogames, and various other devices and infrastructures can be seen as providing material bases for cryptopolitical activities. Our anthology therefore contributes to the broader study of communicative infrastructures as socio-technical assemblages with their material, ideational, and peopled dimensions (see also Bernal 2021; Rodima-Taylor and Grimes 2019, Rodima-Taylor 2021).

While European governments enforce some data protection measures on digital communication providers, various African countries often create regulatory carveouts that undermine the use of encryption. Security—whether national or public—is often the stated reason for legislation that limits anonymity and the use of encryption so as to combat terrorism and crime, but such measures also squelch protest and political opposition and limit freedom of speech and assembly. In various African countries and beyond, the use of encryption is restricted in order for states to monitor political opponents, journalists, and human rights defenders. Registration and licensing of encryption service providers are mandatory in many African countries, and failure to hand over secret encryption codes to state authorities, or using prohibited encryption tools can lead to enormous fines and imprisonment. Regulators and other government agencies thus easily gain access to decryption keys and encrypted data (CIPESA 2021).[4] Digital technologies have also fostered new surveillance and security measures used by states and private companies. The stockpiles of data are powerful public secrets that are known yet hidden from citizens, a form of cryptopolitics. The objection of African governments and the US government to the encryption of communications is testimony to the power that rests in information and in data. Struggles over who controls what is known, what can be revealed, by whom and to whom are being waged globally.

Such new power formations lead to new power struggles, as the tensions between the European Union and American platform companies show. They also generate new strategies and tactics of resistance. All over the world, to varying degrees, people engage in new, digital, and non-digital practices in efforts to escape repression and retain some privacy—whether they are responding to the state, other authorities, or surveillance capitalism (see also Couldry and Mejias 2019; Zuboff 2019).

Cryptopolitical Aesthetics

The digital world offers new terrains for engaging in strategic play with the gap between the said and the unsaid, the surface and the depths. The ongoing proliferation of new media affords new strategies of secrecy and doublespeak, and new grounds for suspicion, while demanding greater skills of encoding and decoding. These have multimedia dimensions as they are manifested across a variety of domains and materialities—highlighting the need to explore them across a variety of media and in the contexts of both social and material realms of particular cultures and societies (Jones 2014; see also Ferme 2001; Rajewsky 2005). Digital encryption itself, or the translation of plaintext into ciphertext (unreadable by a human or by a machine without the cipher), may be understood as privacy or may be understood as clandestinity, a means of keeping secrets that could be dangerous.

One of the most inspiring discussions of "digital depth" is Jennifer Deger's analysis of Yolngu digital practices (Deger 2016). Yolngu mobile phone users produce "spectral depth" by creating digital images with Greenscreen software, montage and GIF effects. These generate layered images and allow Yolgnu people to "creatively participate in a profoundly synaesthetic and sentient world, a world enlivened by uncanny encounter" (2016: 111). Key here are the "inside meanings" in a world "that far exceeds the registers of what the eye can see, the camera can capture, or indeed, what the anthropologist will ever know" (2016: 116). The ostensible factualness and truthfulness of a photographic image that is often assumed turns out to be an illusion.[5]

Digital tools such as cropping, zooming in, adding markup text and arrows, and bringing photos together in a collage allow digital users to draw attention to the hidden and to read different layers of meaning into a political event, text, or performance.

Humor and public secrets may provide one of the most surprising infrastructures of cryptopolitics. Both genres of social communication draw on a collective understanding that there is a gap between the said and the unsaid; there is something that for one reason or another cannot be expressed explicitly. Postcolonial African regimes thrive on doubleness (see Bernal, this volume; Mbembe 1997), and cultural formats that cultivate doubleness may therefore flourish in such political cultures. It may not be a surprise, therefore, that humor and rumor (see Bernal, this volume) have been major themes in African studies (Barber 1987; Obadare 2016; B. White 2007; L. White 2000). Insofar as many postcolonial African regimes have tried to suppress antagonistic voices while broadcasting their own propaganda, citizens deploy humor and rumor, cultural genres that thrive on anonymity, insinuation, and double meanings, as means of alternative storytelling. It is through humor and rumor that other "real" versions of events can be exposed.

Conspiracy theories are another genre associated with cryptopolitics. The premise of any conspiracy theory is that certain realities are hidden and need to be made manifest to larger publics. The digital sphere becomes an additional space in which citizens can expose the various forms of hiding and obscuring of their state or where subalterns can contest their leaders anonymously. It is probably no coincidence that humor, rumor, and conspiracy theories make up large parts of digital content. Several of our ethnographies indicate that African citizens are profoundly aware of how their states perform a politics of deception. Citizens respond by communicating in hermeneutical genres such as rumors and conspiracy theories.

Cryptopolitics may also work through religious culture and genres. Many religions cultivate a variety of genres of decryption and disclosure that engage with notions of doubleness. Religious leaders and practitioners often understand their worlds as bifurcated between a visible and an invisible world. Mediation between the two spheres is often the privileged province of religious leaders, who thus obtain much power and influence over their community. In addition, many religious communities have installed experts, rituals, and cultural genres to safeguard the boundaries between the visible and the invisible, the material and the transcendental. Pentecostal-charismatic Christianity, which has gained much prominence in Africa since the 1990s, thematizes exposure and revelation. Witchcraft films in Ghana (Meyer 2015) and evangelizing TV-serials in Kinshasa (Pype 2012) are genres that foreground processes of decoding. Filmmakers construct plots that revolve around the identification of evildoers, after they have caused mishap and distress in the lives of the protagonists. Sermons, another genre of Pentecostal-charismatic Christianity, often contain decryption of biblical verses or tales, and pastors engage a discourse in which they claim to reveal messages that are hidden in the Bible (Pype 2011). Sermons and confessions are embedded in power hierarchies. Confessions involve strategic revelations as the confessees, marginal figures in the community, admit their transgressions while announcing they have changed in order to be accepted in the Pentecostal community. All of these examples suggest the range and diversity of contexts in which cryptopolitics play a part.

Overview of the Chapters

This anthology brings together original research on diverse countries in Africa and diasporas, including Somalia, Eritrea, Burundi, Kenya, Tanzania, Mali, South Africa, and the Democratic Republic of Congo. All of the chapters examine the role of emerging digital technologies and platforms in mediating knowledge production, with a focus on cryptopolitics—the coding of messages and unveiling of hidden meanings in negotiations of power, identity, and legitimacy. A common theme is the relationship between the state and society with particular attention to conflicts, migration, ethnic rivalries, and authoritarian systems. The diasporic and transnational dimensions of belonging and governance are another focal point of the anthology. The analyses are based on original empirical material and demonstrate the multidimensional aspects of cryptopolitics that transcend and interweave online and offline, public and intimate socialities, and formal and informal spaces. The chapters demonstrate how political and social practices are always anchored in local sociality, and show that the analysis of the role of social media in contemporary Africa is frequently crucial for understanding the cryptopolitical dynamics between the powerless and powerful.

Katrien Pype presents an analysis of the cryptopolitics embedded in the tension between the visible and the hidden in Congolese digital media. The local concept *benda bilili* or "pulling images" conveys a specific "aesthetic of ambiguity" that characterizes the digital universe of Kinshasa. Cryptic communication among Kinois involves socially conditioned strategies of limiting the amount of information conveyed and interpreting the limited information provided by others. Concealment constitutes an important strategy for managing personal relationships. The enigmatic online posts that are rapidly becoming a norm in Kinois digital and social media space also provide new tools to deal with the "vulnerability of human sociality" in offline realms.

Simon Turner reveals the increasing role of social media in the culture of cryptopolitics in Burundi, where selective concealing and revealing of information has long been part of social and political strategies. Digital media have afforded new forms of interaction between the state and its citizens in a context where ethnic conflict and contestation simmer under the surface of the country's politics. The practice of concealing emotions and information, peculiar to Burundian royal courtiers of the past, fosters an online culture where people search for what is hidden, and engage in strategies to sound out adversaries. Social media afford public visibility to debates and critical opinions, enabling protagonists to elicit responses from the public and force people to take a stand on contentious issues. Digital media thus serves as an important cryptopolitical tool of unveiling the hidden in this context.

George Ogola examines cryptopolitics in the exchanges among Kenya's online publics, arguing that digital platforms like Twitter have disrupted the economies of control that have traditionally governed the circulation of information in the country. Ogola traces the hashtags of "Kenyans on Twitter" as they draw from the "disorder" of everyday life and shape new debates and practices of engaging with institutional politics. Calling for a broader view of politics as "dispersed and infra-institutional," Ogola reveals how Twitter conversations assemble novel "pockets of indiscipline" that incorporate more inclusive discursive practices. Yet digital platforms also create opportunities for the establishment of a new repressive information regime by the Kenyan state.

Marie Deridder and Olivier Servais address cryptopolitics in their analysis of the video game *Muslim Mali,* which was set and being played in the context of an ongoing conflict in Mali. The game positions the player as a Muslim Malian shooting down French fighter planes. The game played into the growing social unrest and rejection of elites and a surge in Islamic groups and militants. The chapter explores how Western media reactions to the Muslim Mali game drew on narratives of African otherness. In contrast, Deridder and Servais present a detailed analysis of the complexity of political events and actors in the Malian conflict. Instead of a simplistic opposition between African Muslims and the West, the analysis reveals the complexity of regional and global power assemblages with their geopolitical interests.

Peter Chonka focuses on the political interactions of the conflict-ridden Somali state and its global diaspora with the virtual digital publics mediated by an array of local and global media networks. Chonka's detailed analysis of the actors mediating Somali conflict in physical space considers national and regional militias, international recruits from the African Union's Mission to Somalia, as well as diverse "media producers" such as local public and private broadcasters that are intertwined through global social media platforms such as Facebook and Google. Tech platforms not only play a role in cryptopolitics through the circulation of conspiracy theories, but also through their auto-completion features that often suggest clan-related keywords for searches involving Somali names.

Daivi Rodima-Taylor explores the cryptopolitics of digital chat apps that have become widespread in Africa. The apps accommodate large groups as well as enable private, encrypted chat messaging on their platforms. Such apps are increasingly central in mobilizing online savings groups and migrant remittances; they are also used for fundraising for a variety of causes. Drawing on empirical material from South Africa and Kenya, the chapter explores the paradoxical partnership between WhatsApp as a BigTech platform and these informal economic initiatives. Rodima-Taylor discusses the novel questions this poses about digital media and civic spaces in Africa. She analyzes the cryptopolitics of these emerging pathways of digital mutuality that, while building on vernacular organizational templates and facilitating alternatives to formal banking, also create exploitative invisibilities and foster data capture, while giving rise to scams and Ponzi schemes.

Victoria Bernal analyzes the ways people in Eritrea and among the diaspora regard the dictatorship of Isaias Afewerki through a prism of humor. She argues that the double meanings and ambiguities of humor resonate with the cryptopolitics of dictatorship. Reflecting on questions of political repression and the limits of internet freedom, Bernal suggests that such humor and mistrust are products of extreme repression. The pervasive sense of surveillance produces a constant awareness of the need to conceal and of the presence of duplicity. The political humor in people's everyday conversations and in online media that is out of the reach of the state constitute diverse forms of politics. Humor unveils the ambiguities and inconsistencies in official narratives and figureheads and exposes these to public scrutiny and questioning.

Lisa Poggiali examines the emerging strategies of digital governance that seek to render refugee identities legible to security systems in Kenya. The Kenyan state presents biometric identification measures as necessitated by threats posed by Al Shabaab, for example. The state faced international pushback when it tried to implement overt policies restricting refugees, so it has turned to indirect strategies of control through procedural measures, including the registration of refugees' sim cards and biometric technologies of identification. Poggiali also explores the digital strategies used by refugees to evade or redirect the gaze of the Kenyan state. New technologies of population regulation enable new ways of encoding and decoding information about bodies and citizenship, often limiting refugees' movement and legal status, but also providing novel ways for refugees to create alternative configurations of security and sociality.

Victoria Bernal is a cultural anthropologist whose scholarship in political anthropology contributes to media and IT studies, gender studies, and African studies. Her work addresses questions relating to politics, gender, migration and diaspora, war, globalization, transnationalism, civil society and activism, development, digital media, and Islam. She is Professor of Anthropology at the University of California, Irvine. Bernal's articles and chapters have appeared in various collections as well as in anthropological, African Studies, and interdisciplinary journals, including *American Ethnologist, Cultural Anthropology, American Anthropologist, Global Networks, Comparative Studies in Society and History, African Studies Review*, and *Political and Legal Anthropology Review.*

Katrien Pype (associate professor at KU Leuven, Belgium) is a cultural anthropologist, mainly exploring media, popular culture, and technology. She has written about the production of television serials, television news programs, TV dance shows, and long-distance communication, all in the context of contemporary Kinshasa. Her work is published in edited books, and in journals such as *Africa, Ethnos, Journal of the Royal Anthropological Institute, Journal of Modern African Studies, Journal of African Media Studies*, and others. Her monograph, *The Making of the Pentecostal Melodrama: Religion, Media, and Gender in Kinshasa*, was published with Berghahn Books (2012). Pype also co-edited, with Jaco Hoffman, *Aging in Sub-Saharan Africa: Spaces and Practices of Care* (Policy Press, 2016).

Daivi Rodima-Taylor is a social anthropologist and researcher at the African Studies Center of the Pardee School of Global Studies of Boston University. Her research focuses on African informal economies, financial technology and social media platforms, and migration and remittances. She has conducted longitudinal field research in East Africa and published in journals including *Africa, African Studies Review, Global Networks, Social Analysis, American Ethnologist, Journal of International Relations and Development, Environment and Planning: Politics and Space, Geoforum, Global Policy*, and *Review of International Political Economy.* Her recent publications include the co-edited volume *Land and the Mortgage: History, Culture, Belonging* (Berghahn Books, 2022) and the co-edited special issue *Fintech in Africa* (*Journal of Cultural Economy*, 2022).

Notes

We are grateful to KU Leuven where this project is part of a longstanding collaboration between Katrien and Victoria, which started while Victoria held a Senior Research Fellowship there. Earlier versions of all chapters but that by George Ogola have been presented at panels organized by Katrien, Victoria, and Daivi at ECAS 2019 (Edinburgh) and the annual meeting of the ASA 2019 (Boston). Ogola's chapter was first presented during a workshop on infopolitics organized by Katrien and Victoria at KU Leuven (February 2019). The order of the names of the book co-editors is alphabetical.

1. Orr considers cryptopolitics reflexively in relation to Native American Studies where he found a "taboo" on researching intratribal conflict as opposed to conflict between Native Americans and "whites" (2012: 64). He argues that "Power processes that exist on reservations are overlooked and the dynamics of political change go unaccounted for and part of native lives remains peculiarly caged" (2012: 65). It is thus important to acknowledge that certain disciplinary "cages" and informal taboos shape knowledge production.
2. In Abidjan, for example, Sasha Newell (2012: 65) noted that his Ivorian friends "were loath to admit" to work at low-level, part-time jobs, which was "so demeaning that it had to be avoided or hidden from one's community." In postwar Inhambane, most young residents have "more to hide than to display, whether it is what they did—such as their involvement in criminal and sexual activities—or what they lacked—that they slept on the floor for want of a bed, skipped meals, or wore trousers with missing buttons and a broken zipper" (Archambault 2017: 60).
3. For example, in Kinshasa, a common saying is that "not all truth needs to be told."
4. "How African Governments Undermine the Use of Encryption." 2021. CIPESA, October. Retrieved 5 January 2022 from https://cipesa.org/?wpfb_dl=477.
5. This category of "inside meanings" did not appear with digitalization, of course; Aboriginal bark painting harbors similar inside and outside meanings. "Inside meanings" then refer to "the dimensions of stories and images that cannot be made public—or can only be revealed through ceremony." Visual effects may be sprinkled on digital photographs in order to suggest a "shimmering effect," a sense of the emergence of the ancestral land. On the glimmering surface of the screen, discursive and affective realms bring together "personal biographies, ancestral stories, and family" (Deger 2016: 125). Similarly, "deep or inside" ancestral knowledge will not easily be conveyed in the public arena, and it may be protected by sorcery or other means.

References

Abu-Lughod, Lila. 1993. *Writing Women's Worlds: Bedouin Stories*. Berkeley: University of California Press.

Archambault, Julie Soleil. 2017. *Mobile Secrets: Youth, Intimacy, and the Politics of Pretense in Mozambique*. Chicago: Chicago University Press.

Babel, Anna. 2018. "The Invisible Walls of the Whisper Network." *Anthropology News*, 10 May 2018. https://doi.org/10.1111/AN.859.

Barber, Karin. 1987. "Popular Arts in Africa." *African Studies Review* 30(3): 1–78.

Bernal, Victoria. 2020. "The Aesthetics of Cyber Insecurity: Displaying the Digital in Three American Museum Exhibits." In *Futureproof: Security Aesthetics and the Management of Life*, ed. Asher Ghertner, Daniel Goldstein, and Hudson McFann, 33–62. Durham, NC: Duke University Press.

———. 2021. "The Cultural Construction of Cybersecurity: Digital Threats and Dangerous Rhetoric." *Anthropological Quarterly* 94(4): 611–38.

Beshiri, Arber, and Asim Susuri. 2019. "Dark Web and Its Impact in Online Anonymity and Privacy: A Critical Analysis and Review." *Journal of Computer and Communications* 7(3): 30–43.

Chandra, Giti, and Irma Erlingsdóttir, ed. 2020. *The Routledge Handbook of the Politics of the #Metoo Movement.* Abigdon: Routledge.

Clifford, James and George Marcus. 1986. *Writing Culture: The Poetics and Politics of Ethnography*. Berkeley: University of California Press.

Coleman, Gabriella. 2014. *Hacker, Hoaxer, Whistleblower, Spy: The Many Faces of Anonymous.* New York: Verso Books.

Comaroff, Jean, and John Comaroff. 1999. "Occult Economies and the Violence of Abstraction: Notes from the South African Postcolony." *American Ethnologist* 26(2): 279–303.

Cooper, Elizabeth, and David Pratten, ed. 2015. *Ethnographies of Uncertainty in Africa.* Basingstoke: Palgrave McMillan.

Couldry, Nick, and Ulises Mejias. 2019. "Data Colonialism: Rethinking Big Data's Relation to Contemporary Subject." *Television & New Media* 20(4): 336–49.

Deger, Jennifer. 2016. "Thick Photography." *Journal of Material Culture* 21(1): 111–32.

Drakulich, Kevin, Kevin Wozniak, John Hagan, and Devon Johnson. 2020. "Race and Policing in the 2016 Presidential Election: Black Lives Matter, the Police, and Dog Whistle Politics." *Criminology* 58(2): 370–402.

Ferme, Marian. 2001. *The Underneath of Things: Violence, History, and the Everyday in Sierra Leone.* Berkeley: University of California Press.

Geertz, Clifford. 1973. *The Interpretation of Cultures: Selected Essays.* New York: Basic Books.

Groos, Jan. 2020. "Crypto Politics: Notes on Sociotechnical Imaginaries of Governance in Blockchain Based Technologies." In *Data Loam: Sometimes Hard, Usually Soft; The Future of Knowledge Systems,* ed. Johnny Golding, Martin Reinhart, and Mattia Paganelli, 148–70. Berlin: De Gruyter.

Hejoaka, Fabienne. 2009. "Care and Secrecy: Being a Mother of Children Living with HIV in Burkina Faso." *Social Science and Medicine* 69: 869–76.

Hellegren, Isadora. 2017. "A History of Crypto-Discourse: Encryption as a Site of Struggles to Define Internet Freedom." *Internet Histories* 1(4): 285–311.

Herzfeld, Michael. 2009. "The Performance of Secrecy: Domesticity and Privacy in Public Spaces." *Semiotica* 175: 135–62.

Hinds, Joanne, Emma Williams, and Adam Joinson. 2020. "'It Wouldn't Happen to Me': Privacy Concerns and Perspectives Following the Cambridge Analytica Scandal." *International Journal of Human-Computer Studies* 143: 102498.

Hintz, A., Lina Dencik, and Karin Wahl-Jorgensen. 2017. "Digital Citizenship and Surveillance Society: Introduction." *International Journal of Communication* 11: 731–39.

Jarvis, Craig. 2020. *Crypto Wars: The Fight for Privacy in the Digital Age; A Political History of Digital Encryption.* Boca Raton, FL: CRC Press.

Jones, Graham. 2014. "Secrecy." *Annual Review of Anthropology* 43: 53–69.

Kabir, Ananya. 2014. "Cryptopolitics and Cyberpoetics: Facebook Pages as Memory Portals." *MLA Profession.* Retrieved 13 January 2023 from https://profession.mla.org/cryptopolitics-and-cyberpoetics-facebook-pages-as-memory-portals/.

Kitanaka, Junko. 2015. "The Rebirth of Secrets and the New Care of the Self in Depressed Japan." *Current Anthropology* 56(S12): S251–62.

Mackworth-Young, Constance, Virginia Bond, and Alison Wringe. 2020. "Secrets and Silence: Agency of Young Women Managing HIV Disclosure." *Medical Anthropology* 39(8): 720–34.

Manderson, Lenore, Mark Davis, Chip Colwell, and Tanja Ahlin. 2015. "On Secrecy, Disclosure, the Public, and the Private in Anthropology." *Current Anthropology* 56(S12): S183–S190.

Meyer, Birgit. 2015. *Sensational Movies: Videos, Vision, and Christianity in Ghana.* Berkeley: University of California Press.

Miller, Daniel, Elisabetta Costa, Nell Haynes, Tom McDonald, Razvan Nicolescu, Jolynna Sinanan, Juliano Spyer, Shriram Venkatraman, and Xinyuan Wang. 2016. *How the World Changed Social Media.* London: UCL Press.

Monsees, Linda. 2019. *Crypto-politics: Encryption and Democratic Practices in the Digital Era.* London: Routledge.

Newell, Sasha. 2012. *The Modernity Bluff: Crime, Consumption, and Citizenship in Côte d'Ivoire.* Chicago: Chicago University Press.

Nuttall, Sarah, and Achille Mbembe. 2015. "Secrecy's Softwares." *Current Anthropology* 56(S12): S317–S324.

Obadare, Ebenezer. 2016. *Humor, Silence, and Civil Society in Nigeria.* Rochester, NY: University of Rochester Press.

Orr, Raymond. 2012 "Notes from the Field: Regarding Iron Cages; Crypto-Politics and the Hidden Conflicts of American Indians." *Arizona Anthropologist* 22: 59–65.

Pype, Katrien. 2011. "Confession-cum-Deliverance: In/Dividuality of the Subject among Kinshasa's Born-Again Christians." *Journal of Religion in Africa* 41(3): 280–310.

———. 2012. *The Making of the Pentecostal Melodrama: Religion, Media, and Gender in Kinshasa.* Oxford: Berghahn Books.

Rajewsky, Irina. O., 2005. Intermediality, intertextuality, and remediation: A literary perspective on intermediality. *intermédialités*, (6), pp.43-64.

Rhine, Kathryn. 2014. "HIV, Embodied Secrets, and Intimate Labour in Northern Nigeria." *Ethnos* 79(5): 699–718.

Rigby, T. H. 1965. "Cryptopolitics." In *The State of Soviet Studies*, ed. Walter Laqueur and Leopold Labedz. Cambridge, MA: MIT Press.

Rodima-Taylor, Daivi. 2021. "Digitalizing Land Administration: The Geographies and Temporalities of Infrastructural Promise." *Geoforum* 122: 140–51.

Rodima-Taylor, Daivi, and William Grimes. 2019. "International Remittance Rails as Infrastructures: Embeddedness, Innovation and Financial Access in Developing Economies." *Review of International Political Economy* 26(5): 839–62.

Scott, James. 1985. *Weapons of the Weak: Everyday Forms of Resistance.* New Haven, CT: Yale University Press.

———. 1990. *Domination and the Arts of Resistance: Hidden Transcripts.* New Haven, CT: Yale University Press.

Simmel, George. 1906. "The Sociology of Secrecy and of Secret Societies." *American Journal of Sociology* 11(4): 441–98.

Taussig, Michael. 1999. *Defacement: Public Secrecy and the Labor of the Negative.* Stanford, CA: Stanford University Press.

Weiman, Gabriel and Ari Ben Am. 2020. "Digital Dog Whistles: The New Online Language of Extremism." *International Journal of Security Studies* 2(1): 4.

West, Harry G., and Todd Sanders, ed. 2003. *Transparency and Conspiracy: Ethnographies of Suspicion in the New World Order.* Durham, NC: Duke University Press.

White, B. W. 2007. "La quête du lupemba: rumeurs, réussite et malheur en République démocratique du Congo" [The quest for lupemba: rumors, success and misfortune in the Democratic Republic of Congo]. *Sociologie et sociétés* 39(2): 61–77.

White, Louise. 2000. *Speaking with Vampires: Rumor and History in Colonial Africa.* Berkeley: University of California Press.

Zuboff, Shoshana. 2019. *The Age of Surveillance Capitalism: The Fight for a Human Future at the New Frontier of Power.* New York: PublicAffairs.

CHAPTER 1

Four Ways of Not Saying Something in Digital Kinshasa

Or, On the Substance of Shadow Conversations

Katrien Pype

Posting for Someone Else

This chapter studies cryptopolitics on social media sites such as Facebook, Messenger (Lite and Free, *mode gratuit*),[1] WhatsApp, Instagram, and in lesser fashion the app imo (free video calls and chat). I am concerned with the various layers of hiding and concealing that inform social media practices of Kinois (inhabitants from Kinshasa). On 24 February 2019, Pitshou,[2] an unmarried man in his late twenties, published the following text, written in French, and set in black, bold arial font, against a sober, green background, on his WhatsApp status (a facility of the WhatsApp application, which allows users to post images, photographs, and videos that disappear after twenty-four hours): "If someone shows you that s/he can live without you, then show him/her that you can live without him/her" (my translation from the French).

Contextual information was lacking. There was no caption nor any adjacent posts (as WhatsApp statuses allow, see below) that could help the reader interpret the statement as a communication to an intended receiver. The message raised questions such as: to whom is this addressed? Was something going on in Pitshou's life? Was he disappointed in someone? I knew he was in an unstable relationship with the mother of his daughter and expected a new episode in their on/off relationship. When I called Pitshou, I learned to my surprise that the text did not speak about his personal life, but was embedded in the complex intimate life of one of his male friends, Jeancy.

About two years earlier, Jeancy, like Pitshou also in his late twenties, had migrated temporarily to Brazzaville, the capital city of the neighboring Congo. During his year and a half stay there, he had begun a sexual liaison with a woman in Brazzaville. Upon his return, Jeancy wanted to pick up his previous relationship with Tina, a girl in Kinshasa. As often happens by Kinois standards, he had never formally cut off that link. However, while he was still in Brazzaville, Tina had learned through the grapevine about Jeancy's involvement with this other woman, and she had decided to move on. She had done so quietly, never informing Jeancy about her decision. The latter therefore had every reason to hope he would be able to reconnect quickly upon his return to Kinshasa. Even nine months after Jeancy's homecoming, so Pitshou told me, Tina did not answer Jeancy's calls, leaving him in sorrow and pain.

It so happened then that a few days before posting that message on WhatsApp, Pitshou encountered Tina in a bar in his neighborhood. She was accompanied by another man who she presented to Pitshou as "her fiancé," using the French word, thus announcing that she was in a deep, committed relationship with this man, which may lead to marriage. At least, she wanted to convey such message. The introduction had been a provocation, almost an insult, so Pitshou told me, especially because she knew that Jeancy and Pitshou were close friends, almost like brothers. Presenting the other man to Pitshou as her fiancé was like presenting the man to Jeancy as her fiancé, an action unheard of. After all, even if many men and women in Kinshasa entertain multiple sexual and romantic relationships, dating requires the public performance of monogamy and fidelity.[3] By introducing a man as her fiancé, Pitshou argued, Tina was literally showing that she can live without her former boyfriend. Pitshou had related the information and advice to do the same to Jeancy already in a face to face conversation, but felt the need to remind Jeancy also via other channels, such as the WhatsApp status updates. "That is what good friends do," so Pitshou reminded me in a WhatsApp audiovoice message.

Pitshou's publication on his WhatsApp status was intended to be advice (Lingala, *liteya*, "lesson") directly addressed to his friend. Though, significantly, neither Jeancy's nor Tina's names were mentioned. Pitshou, so he confided laughingly, deliberately played with this ambiguity because some of his siblings and relatives, of whom he considers several as his classificatory fathers, are also his WhatsApp contacts. He did not want to reveal too much information about his friend's intimate life.[4] After all, friends usually know about each other's love life and are expected to protect each other's reputation. Pitshou's laughter betrayed a slyness in his digital dexterity.

The opening anecdote does not speak of an idiosyncrasy of Pitshou nor is obscuring names of addressees in social media communication a gendered practice. As Flavie, a young woman in her early thirties and one of the protagonists of this chapter told me, "every day, at least one of my status updates is addressed to a particular person. Every single day," even though she never mentions a person's name, except for specific congratulations or condolences. Flavie also reads others' status updates and online posts of memes, proverbs, and excerpts of songs and clips as possible locutions about others' unfolding social lives. For most "digital Kinois,"[5] indeed, social media expressions are readily understood as carrying a metonymic relationship with the poster's personal lifeworld.

What emerges from the above is that Pitshou and Flavie, like so many other digital Kinois, play with the said and unsaid, the alluded and implied, the shown and hidden on social media. The described actions belong to a complex set of "idioms of practice," that is, appropriate social uses of technology that have been formed by asking advice and sharing stories with each other about benefits and risks of certain ways of engaging with social media (Gershon 2010: 6).[6]

As will become clear in this chapter, these Kinois idioms of practice, which I describe as *benda bilili na toile*, literally "pulling images on the internet," mirror offline behavior. These are crucial strategies in the negotiating of relationships in Kinshasa in daily life. *Benda bilili* ("pulling the images") is a social dictum that governs social life in the city and with which Kinois are familiar.

In this chapter, I explore the relationships between digital texts (such as the advice Pitshou gave), their cryptic aesthetics, and the social lifeworlds in which these texts find meaning, circulate, and which they maybe even transform. It will become clear that social media usage in Kinshasa is very much embedded in negotiations and calibrations of hiding information, playing with double meanings, and double-crossing. Digital Kinois purposely manipulate the distinction between the surface (the screen, what is said and shown online) and the underneath (the offline, what is meant by what is said). Silencing names of intended receivers of public digital posts is a strategy of protection and is fully embedded within infopolitics (Bernal 2014) governing Kinois sociality. This means that among digital contacts, some are intended receivers of a social media post while others are not but have access to these posts as well because of the simple fact that they are Facebook friends, Instagram followers, or WhatsApp contacts. The presence of one (or more) Receiver-Who-Is-Not-Addressed is significant here, as it adds weight to the seriousness of the message. Receivers-Who-Are-Not-Addressed become invited observers to, in the case of Pitshou and Tina, a conflict in which they do not have any stakes. Yet, suddenly they witness a problem and engage in processes of encoding and decoding messages. They also "pull the images."

To make sense of the ethnographic material, I combine insights from linguistic anthropology, political anthropology, and anthropology of the occult (in particular, divination, witchcraft, and religion). These may seem disparate fields, though most Africanists know that words and communication are intimately entangled with power and spirits. Politics and religion in sub-Saharan Africa thrive on balancing disclosure and concealment, revealing and withdrawing, opening and closing (Ellis and ter Haar 2003; Ferme 2001; Geschiere 1998; Jacobson-Widding 1990; Werbner 2015). Such understandings of the power of the hidden and the occult also feed into Kinois' online actions, for example, posting proverbs, commenting on status updates, or not commenting at all but sending a screen shot to a friend.

This chapter also has a more methodological ambition. As anthropologists, we try to understand how to explore digital materials and especially how to relate these to "offline" experiences and realities. I argue we should not remain "stuck" in the online-offline divide, but try to understand how this divide, difference, or even gap is used, played with, and even mobilized by our interlocutors. To do so, I propose the method of "reconstructing shadow conversations" in line with Judith Irvine's elaboration of "shadow conversations" in Xarxaar insult poetry (1996). This method also bears relevance beyond Kinshasa's ethnography and may inspire a new way of studying digital culture.

In the first part of this chapter, I discern four different categories in cryptic digital communication that beg Kinshasa's social media users for elaborate exegesis and offline hermeneutics: the not yet said, the almost said, the not said, and the loudly said. These are etic categories inspired by discussions with my interlocutors. In the second part, I reconstruct various "shadow conversations" of social media posts published by Flavie. I try to illustrate the thick dialogue between online and offline worlds. In the final part, I situate the method of "shadow conversations" within Congolese ethnography and differentiate between "conversations of the shadow" and "conversations in the shadow." I will draw parallels between social media practices and indigenous notions of personhood and cosmology.

The material for this chapter has been collected online and offline continuously since 2014 when I began researching the dialectics between technology and urban sociality through participant observation in online communication and by interviewing interlocutors about their idioms of practice. I followed people's social media posts, took screen shots, and asked them to narrate stories about their posts. Most of these conversations took place in Kinshasa, in one-on-one conversations.

Since the COVID-19 pandemic (2020), I resorted to informal interviews over private social media platforms. This analysis is limited to posts with social content. Politically and religiously inflected electronic messages and images harbor other forms of cryptic aesthetics (see, among others, Pype 2016b and 2018), and are therefore not included here. Social media posts gossiping about the celebrity scene are not discussed here either. Such electronic communication is often characterized by insults and polemical language.

Four Ways of Not Saying Something

Here, I present four main practices of hiding and concealing. Many more could be discerned, but will not be studied here. My examples draw mainly on interactions with Flavie and Ani, two female interlocutors and mutual friends, both in their mid to late thirties at the time of fieldwork. They disclosed various parts of their personal lives and digital interactions to me. Flavie is a divorced mother of three children (and one deceased child) living in her father's house. Her father resides in eastern Congo and visits irregularly, mainly for medical reasons. Ani is married to the father of her three children. Flavie does not have a job (not even in the informal economy); Ani works for a state office. Her salary comes irregularly, and, if she is paid at all, never exceeds US$150.00. Luckily Flavie does not have to pay any rent. Ani's husband brings home some money, although they rely heavily on financial gifts from Ani's mother who receives a modest sum from a rental house in a nearby city.

Both Ani and Flavie were online almost daily, most often on Facebook Messenger through the Facebook Lite and *mode gratuit* platforms; Ani was less frequently on WhatsApp. Both curated their digital worlds carefully, but did so with varying temporalities and with different social intentions. While Flavie published on her Facebook stories and WhatsApp statuses almost daily, Ani hardly did so, except for the occasional birthday greetings, or some memes. Ani mainly commented on others' publications, and preferred communicating in private contexts, such as the WhatsApp messaging facility and Messenger. Flavie spent a lot of time in digital flirting, trying to find a husband in the Congolese diaspora (Pype 2020). She had three smartphones, all different brands, and each with different kinds of damages: one's screen was broken, but she could still read and watch videos; another one's hardware needed to be kept together with an elastic band; and the third one's sound was faulty. Ani had one smartphone and one dumb phone. Usage of multiple phones is to a large extent dictated by the various telephone companies, who make it expensive to call beyond one's own network. Having SIM cards of various telephone companies is a smart way of economizing on mobile communication. These young women took full advantage of mobile telephony, which is a crucial tool to organize social and economic life in Kinshasa.[7]

The Not Yet Said

I often encountered Flavie with her fingers on the screen of one of her three smartphones, scrolling through social media platforms, and reading various small conversations she was engaged in. She then would reconsider and think about adding a smiley or sending a picture. These reflections are not present in the sentences or the words or the images that she was writing, but they are as much part of the meanings of the published content. While internally Flavie was often conflicted, curious, uncertain, sometimes even worried about her and her children's future, her doubt and anticipation were rarely shown on screen. Flavie's digital persona usually seemed confident in what she wrote and the pictures she posted.

When Flavie's attention was drawn to one of her smartphones, she often smiled when seeing that one of her *djika*'s (Congolese in the diaspora) had answered *bjr* (digitalk for "hello") on her own *bjr* in Messenger. She then sent short text messages, sometimes adding a photograph of herself. Flavie was in these minimal conversations with a wide range of people, mainly men. Even though not exclusively chatting with men abroad, Flavie clearly favored conversations with men in the diaspora. Like many Kinois girls, she desired to marry out. Global hypergamy is an ideal for many girls in Kinshasa (see Pype 2020). At best there would be a question such as "*oza wapi?*" (where are you?) from the other side, which could be answered by some requests from her side (can you give me some money?; are you going to bring me a gift on your next trip to Kinshasa?, etc.).

Such greetings and small questions are phatically thick: they harbor promises. These conversations confirm that there is a relationship, even if minimally entertained. The quality of that relationship is open, undetermined, pregnant with promises, and with possibilities of fulfillment. The "*oza wapi?*" (where are you?) question[8] lifts the relationship to an intimate dimension, one which Flavie eagerly looks for as it is the kind of question that sexual partners in Kinshasa are allowed, even expected, to ask one another. The subtext of the *oza wapi?* question is the writer's assumption that "you are my wife, and I am allowed to be informed about your whereabouts; I should control and surveil you." So, if a contact moves from *bjr* to *oza wapi,* he suggests that he wants to get in a sexual relationship with Flavie, for whom this question is nothing less than a confirmation of the opening of opportunities.

Just before responding on the *oza wapi?* question, Flavie has a lot of agency. She knows very well that the allusion of sexual interest at this point is nothing more than an allusion: it can always be denied afterward. Yet, Flavie has a lot of choice: she can decide whether she will tell the contact where she is. If she does so, she thus confirms that the other man is entitled to know and signals to be keen on a sexual relationship with the contact as well;[9] or, as I observed regularly, Flavie can remain silent, and thus communicate that she is not looking to transform the contact into a sexual partner. Usually, as she told me, she did not respond to a person of whom she suspected it to be a friend of one of her family members or of one of her other love interests.

The Almost Said

While the category of "the not yet said" speaks about digital communication and the cultivation of possibilities of new futures (romantic futures in this case), other forms of cryptic digital communication are more concerned with protecting existing relationships. This is the case for "the almost said."

Again this is illustrated in my interactions with Flavie. After a few days of posting nothing at all on her WhatsApp status, due to lack of money to pay for mobile data, Flavie published a series of two, almost identical pictures. Both showed her wearing white jeans shorts, and a deeply cut black top, drawing attention to her breasts. She had put on an Afrowig, with wild, uncontained long black curly hair. A set of red headphones hanging around her neck was the finishing touch of this picture with which she clearly confirmed her status of a *mwasi mabe*, a bad girl (see Pype 2012: 211–14). In Kinois parlance, "a bad girl" designates girls and young women who play with the appearance of cosmopolitanism, emphasize their sexuality, and project themselves as being fashionable. The pictures were taken from a bird's eye view—clearly photographed by someone else. The background was astonishingly sober. Although unclear to the unfamiliar spectator, she was standing in her bathroom, which only contains a concrete floor and a drain in the left corner.

On both pictures, Flavie was clearly suppressing a smile. The first picture showed her posing, both hands on the hips, and looking straight into the camera. The second one contained her in a slightly different pose: she was pointing her index finger of her left hand toward the camera. This gesture is significant, as in Kinshasa it can be a socially dangerous act. Pointing a finger at someone is harmless when an intimate senior person does so to his or her junior (child/wife). In all other contexts, this gesture is interpreted as a major insult and often provokes physical fights. In this WhatsApp status, Flavie was speaking to an unidentified addressee. A caption below the second picture gave some more information: *attention* (in French, be careful), confirming the provocative nature of the gesture.

I regularly observe similar status updates with written messages or proverbs or sometimes just saying *yo oyebi* (you [to whom this is addressed] know). These kinds of posts, which I call *sala keba* (be careful) publications, are warnings with much ellipsis. The origin, reason, or content of the warning, as well as the addressee are obscured. Nevertheless, *sala keba* texts just like the text with which I opened this chapter are utterly dialogic. Only those who are in the know might understand. Flavie showed a mastery of the codes of respect and protection. Here, the ellipsis of the addressee was a measure of protection because directly addressing and attacking a person, naming the person by name is socially and spiritually risky. Flavie thus averted the risk of becoming the object of revenge or jealousy and becoming embroiled in *kindoki,* sorcerous attacks or witchcraft accusations.

The Not Said/Not to Say

A third category, the "not said/not to say," speaks to practices of self-censorship. I illustrate this with material from Ani, who was scrolling on her smartphone through her husband's Facebook account when I visited her one day in mid-August 2019. A few days earlier, when she had come by my house, she had complained that she felt isolated. Her husband was constantly out of the house, and she felt lonely. Quickly our conversation had turned to the domestic politics of social media. She was worried about her husband's social media behavior.

About a year before, Ani's husband had changed his Facebook password. This had raised suspicion, mainly because it was a breach in their agreement. As so many young married couples do in Kinshasa, they too had promised one another full transparency in their encounters—also online—with others. Ani could not really say or do anything for him to share the new password. She furthermore had noticed that he was posting various photographs about his work trips to Kongo Central and Mbandaka, two areas in the interior of the Democratic Republic of the Congo (DRC). These pictures showed him, an engineer, with some colleagues on various construction sites. Ani found it suspicious that in the previous months he suddenly was more active on his Facebook wall. While before, he posted pictures on their children's birthdays, now she saw that he was informing Facebook contacts about his travels. She did not approve of this though made sure nobody could read her dissatisfaction online. Her digital comments on these pictures flattered her husband. She emphasized how strong and beautiful he looked, and applauded the fact that he was seeing parts of the country she had never been able to go to. Yet, at home, offline, Ani insisted he take these pictures offline (which he did not do), because he was—as she said—"exposing his life."

Flavie agreed with Ani's concerns, and in a private conversation reminded me how important it is to *kobomba ndako na yo*, to "hide your house," meaning not to disclose domestic problems or successes.[10] Hiding and revealing are productive practices in public identities whether they are online or offline. These concerns were aptly described in a textual meme Pitshou posted on his WhatsApp status a few months later (31 May 2019, my translation):[11]

> living hidden means living happily
> Publicness attracts desire
> Desire creates jealousy
> Jealousy facilitates the enemy (smiley)

This reasoning reaffirms how one should not expose too much of one's life because the more one reveals, the more ammunition one gives for jealousy, and one risks attracting others, who might interfere in one's marriage or one's (professional or social) success.[12]

The Too Loudly Said

The final category refers to sentences such as *batika yo* (may they let you alone) or *odondwa* (you are leading/ruling), which despite their shortness, hide much social work. Very often, one sees these phrases as comments on messages and photographs that depict one's success, one's beautiful body, one's trip to another country, one's celebration of a wedding or of a new job. Such phrases are also expressed when thanking a person for a service or gift (without explicitly mentioning the service or the gift). This fourth category, "the too loudly said," is part of flattery. It is as if applause needs to divert attention away from the substance of the celebration.

The *batika yo* utterance speaks to reputation production and social relatedness insofar as it suggests that the content of the image (which the *batika yo* text accompanies) may incur jealousy and could incite spiritual attacks, vulgar critique, and assault on one's reputation. *Odondwa* serves fundamentally as flattery as well. Via the *odondwa* idiom, commenters suggest that the depicted individuals are extremely successful and powerful, and the commenters subordinate themselves in relation to the person in the post. At the same time, the commenters publicly accept this success and thus protect themselves against possible future *kindoki* (witchcraft and sorcery) accusations.

On the Importance of Allusive Language

The previous snapshot of four types of communicative strategies online shows how *toile* (the internet; also the canvas, see below) of social media is a space in which Kinois play with the boundaries between the hidden and the said/shown and thus impact their futures. I discerned two pragmatics that underlie the posts: (a) trying to protect oneself and/or the person depicted in the images (see Ani's feedback on her husband, but also *batika yo* and *sala keba* genres); and (b) trying to provoke someone (as Flavie did with her picture in which she pointed her finger). These messages are very much embedded in a search for urban conviviality. After all, posting elliptic messages on one's digital status is an attempt to arrive at a solution, either for oneself, or for someone with whom one is close, or to maintain a harmonious relationship with the depicted person.

I could have used more standard linguistic nouns to indicate the four forms of speech: ellipsis, allusion, self-censorship, and flattery. I instead want to make an explicit connection with the poetics of divination. My approach to the unsaid and the hidden is very much inspired by Richard Werbner's study of language politics and linguistic texture of divination interactions. In *Divination's Grasp* (2015), Werbner provides us a thoughtful and culturally sensitive understanding of highly allusive and suggestive communication in divinatory interactions. In these sessions, as Werbner (2015: 3) describes, enigmatic words serve reflection, "even as they arouse emotions." The suggestivity of divinatory discourse, another manifestation of "the almost said," is necessary because of an inadequacy of language to get at the occult, at the real.

There is a significant analogy in the suggestivity of divinatory discourse and with that of Kinois digispeak in the WhatsApp status updates and other digital spaces. The practice of circumventing "the real" by "almost saying," either by not mentioning the addressee, by silencing certain truths, or by using metaphorical language, is prevalent in Kinois' discourses on the *toile* where personal relationships find expression. Pitshou's ultimate goal is, just like in the cryptic divinatory poetics described by Werbner, to push for reflection, not to raise anger, and even to protect others (spirits or social others).[13]

Divinatory practices show that "the world around you is divided, some share truly with you, others secretly spit behind your back and greedily heap your fruits for themselves, not for you. Remember who to eat and share with, and who not to trust" (Werbner 2015: 3). Similar advice or wisdom is shared on social media platforms: a warning that the world is full of antagonism and conflict, but that is how the world goes. There is a social- and future-oriented approach toward concealment in the digital world. Furthermore, suggestive language also speaks to incompleteness, to enhancing possibilities, openness, and opportunity, as "almost said" posts do.

Shadow Conversations

Digital hermeneutics of elliptic electronic communications as described in the previous part of this chapter requires far more information than digital content shows. Even if emojis, icons, images and captions are used, these publications are fragments, snapshots of moments in a person's unfolding social life. Kinois know very well that digital conversations are always partial. In order to get a better grasp of the unsaid on Kinshasa's *toile*, I propose we study "shadow conversations."[14] I want to illustrate this with a longer ethnographic elaboration of digital communication by Flavie during one of the rare occasions on which Flavie showed herself in distress and anger on her WhatsApp statuses. The material will show that people like Flavie carefully curate their digital person, even if it appears in the fleeting space of status updates and stories. After all, these online spaces are very much public spaces where people meet with friends and joking partners but also with those they are in a hierarchical or even rivalrous relationship with.

Flavie and Samourai

From mid-April 2020, Flavie had been posting WhatsApp statuses showing despair and asking for God's help. Even though emotions were expressed loudly and clearly, the context was nebulous. In WhatsApp phone calls, Flavie gave me more information: her youngest daughter could not walk anymore, hardly spoke, and was losing weight by the day. Flavie urgently needed money to visit doctors, get X-rays done, and buy the medicine the doctors were going to prescribe. During that period, Flavie was in a difficult romantic relationship with Samourai, a Kinois man in his early thirties and a few years younger than she was. It was full COVID-19 time, and a few weeks after the distressing digital posts, Flavie's daughter was diagnosed with tuberculosis, and urgently needed US$400.00 to pay for the doctor's bills and the required medicine. Via phone calls, SMS messaging, and online texts, Flavie had contacted almost everybody that she thought she could reach out to for financial assistance and was carefully monitoring who responded and who did not. To her dissatisfaction, Samourai told her he was short of money and could not help Flavie. In the ensuing days, he never called to inquire about Flavie's daughter. "Radio silence," so Flavie told me with a mixture of anger, regret, and astonishment.

On 30 April, Flavie posted on her WhatsApp status a sequence of mixed media: the first part contained the words *bonne chance* (good luck), written in French in white font against a sky-blue background. A heart emoji was placed underneath the text. After a few seconds, the WhatsApp status moved to two short clips of the Congolese duet *tshobo,* sung by the Congolese rumba musicians Fally Ipupa and MJ 30. Flavie had selected two excerpts of the song and cut these sequences with an app on her mobile phone. She then uploaded these on her WhatsApp status and added the caption "and this will be the last (time). Your girlfriend!" (*et ça sera la dernière. Tshobo na yo!*) twice, as if to put emphasis on the message. The sequences were carefully chosen: they contained some phrases in which the singers lament their lover's silence. Addressing their lovers, they cry out "I had promised myself I would never let me be hurt again. I would never cry over someone else. But I cannot help myself. I guess it is love."

Fast forward to mid-May. Samourai, who had seen Flavie's WhatsApp status updates, indeed had understood that Flavie's laments, mediated by the song, were inspired by hardship that she endured because of his attitude. He did not react on her posts online but phoned her, and they began talking again. However, their relationship did not really improve or not as quickly enough as Flavie would have liked. So, mid-May, Flavie happily accepted the invitation of an admirer, who proposed a photoshoot at Kinsuka, one of the photogenic places in town, where young (aspiring) couples stroll and engage in romantic flirtation. The week before their date, the suitor paid for a trip to the hair saloon, where she got new hair extensions. This is a common practice among aspiring and actual lovers: the man pays for beauty treatments (hair, nails, skin, clothes, etc.) for his girlfriend. That Sunday, Flavie took a few sets of clothes along to Kinsuka, where they spent the afternoon flirting, eating fish, and taking photographs. On Monday morning, Flavie posted ten pictures on her WhatsApp status and on her Facebook wall. They all elicited flattering comments.

Flavie's social media publications are excellent examples of the double meanings online postings may have. She was confirming her outer person as a beautiful, joyful, and fashionable young girl, wearing long white, braided hair extensions which almost reached her buttocks; the blue suede shoes perfectly matched the fashionable yellow-blue blouse of the popular *ya mado* series. In some other photographs, she was wearing a black and white summer dress. Her poses were well-thought out: in some she was squatting; in others she was lightly turning away thus drawing attention to her behind; in other pictures she was playfully draping herself around picket fences of the old fishing village; and in a few of these photographs, she was just standing upright, confidently gazing into the lens. The pictures had a semi-professional glow; the photographer clearly knew how to use the natural light.

While the photographer would usually ask US$20.00 for these pictures; Flavie did not have to pay. Yet, while the photographer was using his camera to capture Flavie, she was thinking of Samourai. And, on Monday afternoon, she told me in a voice message that she had deliberately posted these pictures on her WhatsApp profiles and Facebook walls to get Samourai jealous. "I want to show him that I am happy without him; I want to make him jealous. He will see my posts, and by tonight he will have called me with a series of questions: who took these pictures? When did that happen? How do you know the photographer? Who paid for the shoot? etc. etc."[15]

On the surface, these photographs may just be an expression of Flavie as a young, mobile woman; yet underneath these pictures lay emotions of play (with the photographer) and provocation (toward Samourai). Any of her Facebook and WhatsApp contacts commenting on how *canon* (killing) she looked, were feeding Samourai's jealousy, so Flavie assumed. "Oh yes, he will watch my status; he always does. And if for one reason or the other he cannot, I am sure his friends will show the pictures and the comments to him," Flavie argued confidently. For Flavie, the comments made by her Facebook contacts were amplifying the provocation and play that were inscribed yet hidden in the digital publications. Ultimately, Flavie did not expect Samourai to comment or respond online at all nor did she want that. She had other expectations: she wanted him to take action, that is, to re-start their conversation and come to a solution.

The above description contextualizes a series of digitally published expressions. I have situated these publications in a set of discourse histories. The telephone conversations that preceded Flavie's posts, as well as the interactions that she was aspiring too, are all part of "shadow conversations" without which the meanings of the "good luck" post, the music clips, and the uploaded photographs are difficult to grasp.

I am inspired by Irvine's notion of "shadow conversations" coined in her analysis of the Senegalese Xarxaar insult genre (Irvine 1996). In

Xarxaar, insults are told during rituals, such as weddings, and very often voiced by socially appropriate intermediaries, such as griots. Insults are composed in the days preceding the wedding while women gather to prepare food, clothes, and other stuff. During these activities, gossip, inside information, excitement, frustration, and other emotions are shared. The conversations of the preceding days, feeding insults expressed in the ritual moment of the wedding party, are what Irvine calls "shadow conversations." These are moments of social interaction to which the larger public of the wedding does not have access. I argue that similar conversations are going on in social media updates and other posts. A wide range of "other" (not always electronically mediated) discussions and interactions form the background of digital posts, and inspire the publication of other posts. Even when invisible online, these are very much part of chains of discourse and social action that one can observe online.

The proposed method of reconstructing shadow conversations of the digital sphere is complementary to Jennifer Deger's (2016) study of "thick photography." In an inspiring article on "digital labor" that Yolngu interlocutors carry out on digital photographs, for example, inserting flickering animation, writing captions, adding filters, and more. Deger draws attention to practices of intense bodily engagement with screens of smartphones and with the digitally represented. Practices of handling devices and working on digital content are full of meaning, affect, and purpose.

In my focus on "shadow conversations," I am not undermining the spectral labor that people like Flavie carry out on their status updates and social media platforms: after all, people curate a large body of texts, various kinds of images included, in their phone and tablet galleries and on social media platforms; social media users need to choose wisely from their digital archive; and select aptly the image or the part of a song that speaks most to their situation. Yet, the notion of "shadow conversations" is mainly oriented on the discursive for three reasons. First, it tries to capture various "discourse histories" that came before and after the status updates and other online communication. Second, many status updates, memes, and digital texts of Kinois contain a strong discursive component: they are composed of proverbs, lyrics, slogans, congratulations, and warnings. Finally, as Flavie reminded me: the goal of her WhatsApp statuses is to start the conversation, so that dialogue can begin and a solution can be found. These "shadow conversations" thus are part of the "thickness" of the status updates; through and by attending to shadow conversations, we are able to understand how digital content is woven into the social fabric; how online media gain social significance and performativity; and how social media users like Flavie work toward new futures. What is shown on the *toile* (digital screen) are snapshots, almost like bullets, targeted at someone, yet it requires a skilled eye to understand who the target is and why. The ethnographer thus has the same task as the hermeneutical practices Kinois digital contacts engage in: they all know that there are many implicit dialogues at play, and like the participants in the Xarxaar wedding festivities, they all "projectively construct," these "as part of the pragmatic reasoning by which they interpret an utterance and understand its significance" (Irvine 1996: 140).

Digital Persona

The metaphor of "shadow conversations" in the description of a method to study digital content anthropologically, gains a deeper meaning in Congolese ethnography, because of its connection with west Congolese notions of personhood in which "the shadow" references a "vulnerable self" (Jacobson-Widding 1990: 31). Here, we arrive at a second interpretation of the "shadow" in the "shadow conversations": Flavie was exposing her vulnerability on WhatsApp status updates.

During fieldwork in the 1980s in western Congo, Swedish anthropologist Anita Jacobson-Widding observed a "clear-cut opposition between an 'inner man' and an individual 'outer man,' yet emotional experiences of selfhood are expressed in ambiguous metaphors, which are not appropriate topics for public discourse" (Jacobson-Widding 1990: 31). Two elements of this quotation are relevant to think about how Kinois manage digital persons and interactions: first: there is a difference between an "inner man" and an "outer man." The outer man is the moral person; while the inner person refers to the emotional and interactional experience of personhood, in particular in connection with individual agency (1990: 34). Second, emotions were not suited for public conversations. To make sense of this distribution of the outer and inner person over different forms of discursive interaction, Jacobson-Widding drew on Paul Ricoeur's distinction between "text," expressed by the moral person, and "talk," where the self finds expression. Whereas the former contains a kind of fixity and can appeal to a certain universality; "talk" is fleeting, it is difficult to fixate the meaning, and has a more informal character.

The idea of protecting the inner person, that is, one's emotional life, resonates strongly when we look into the semantic field of the "shadow." A Lingala dictionary translates the "shadow" as *elili*, which can mean (1) (animated or non-animated) image, photograph, shadow, portrait, symbol; or (2) invisible material body, in contrast to the visible material body (*nzoto*).[16] Portraits and shadows are related to one's invisible material body. The latter, one's soul, contains vitality, fertility, strength, success, and health. This invisible body dwells in the invisible space. Protecting that invisible body happens first and foremost by protecting shadows, photographs, and one's emotional life. The relevance of this distinction between one's visible and invisible person can be illustrated with a fieldwork anecdote from one of my earlier research projects in Kinshasa. When I was studying media engagements of elderly Kinois, one of my interlocutors showed me with much reluctance an X-ray picture of his thorax. His younger wife, who trusted me, wanted me to have evidence of his affliction. Only after a few visits, when his wife started talking about the X-ray again, he took it out of the cabinet, while telling me that I was the first person (besides his wife and doctor) who saw this. He was afraid of sorcerers (*bandoki*), who could take advantage of the information that the X-ray contained: the X-ray showed his weak spot, and others could use his illness to kill him spiritually.

The anecdote may help us to think about the risk of visibility in the digital world. Very much like the meeting in the living room, social media platforms are spaces in which Kinois calibrate inner and outer aspects of their lives. As they are careful not to give easy access to their "inner person," or their shadow, or the X-ray, people will act similarly online.

Probably not surprisingly then, Jacobson-Widding noted how people would be "fairly secretive about their notions of the shadow" (1990: 40), because it had a highly sensitive nature. Informal discourse in intimate circumstances was the only way Jacobson-Widding's interlocutors talked about their shadow, photographs, and personal names (1990: 40). These had to be cherished and protected, so Jacobson-Widding learned (1990: 46). People lowered their voices, searched for words, sometimes showed signs of embarrassment or got excited and expressed personal fears and glanced around to see if anyone was listening. There was an "air of secrecy" around people's conversations about their inner person. This secrecy, so Jacobson-Widding infers, was the outcome of fears of loss of vitality and health, loss of control over oneself, and loss of one's power of initiative, potency, and agency. She added that "[c]ertain aspects of personhood may be omitted if the interlocutors have a hierarchical relationship, or if the interview situation has a formal or public character. The missing information may be delivered in a quite different kind of social context" (1990: 33).

Taking cues from Jacobson-Widding's ethnography, we can argue that various platforms on social media provide room for "different kinds of social contexts" and allow for new shadows to be cast. First of all, different apps and different technical possibilities of these apps allow for a further differentiation between the "inner" and the "outer" person and between one's emotions and one's public persona. Flavie chose to show her despair on the WhatsApp status, not on her Facebook wall. And she conversed about it with me, in private conversations, online and offline, not on public social media fora. Second, the digital allows for new platforms on which one's visible, yet immaterial, self circulates and is exposed to other's opinions, intentions, and projects.

Shadow conversations allow us entry into the realm of the inner person, that subjectivity full of vitality, health, initiative, agency, and potency. The distinction between an "outer" and "inner man" does not only pertain to digital and their shadow conversations, as I elaborated upon above. It also draws our attention to the fleeting character of the WhatsApp status updates, and Facebook stories in which the above conversations are published. None of these digital spaces have a permanent character, in contrast to Facebook walls or WhatsApp and Messenger conversations. Rather, stories and status updates only last for a maximum of twenty-four hours. It is no coincidence that Flavie and Pitshou choose these social media platforms, fleeting by design, to publish their advice, warnings, and laments. The impermanence of these spaces of the social media platforms communicates to the contacts that these messages have an intimate relevance, and should be read as such. Social media thus allow people to express elusivity and fragility through shadow conversations as in and around the WhatsApp status updates, the Facebook stories, and Instagram stories. The fleeting, temporal character of these online spaces fits the intimacy of emotions, fears, uncertainties, and desires.

Such reflections on the distribution about personal information over various social media channels is in character with various challenges I experienced when carrying out research on personal social media worlds in Kinshasa. Usually, people shy away from giving much information about ongoing hardship. I often had to wait sometimes until a crisis had ended before getting information. I have become familiar with vague answers, and unanswered questions about contextual information regarding certain memes and photographs posted on social media platforms. So, very often, when I see a *sala keba* post, and I ask for more information, I am told that these are just general comments. Or, I get responses such as: "I liked the proverb; it contains a lot of wisdom"; "This is my favorite part of the song"; or "I was just fooling around on the net." In such instances, I do not press, even though third parties might have already given me background information, helping me to reconstruct the context or parts of it. The refusal to give further information is significant, as it shows that most posters actually do not want the majority of the receivers to recontextualize the message. These refusals are part of the *kipe ya yo* sociality, (mind your own business) (see Pype 2016b: 243–44). Very often, weeks or even months afterward, I get updates and background information, usually after the conflict or crisis has been resolved. This conscious playing with disclosure and concealment and the temporalization of these practices of publication and explanation are common strategies, fully embedded in Kinois' management of their inner person and social life.

Online Pragmatics—"Pulling the Images"

Elsewhere, I described how Flavie used magical powders before making digital phone calls with (potential) lovers (Pype 2020). These phone calls were full of promise, sweetness, and erotic longing, while also expressing hardship, suffering, and lack. Flavie played with these men's feelings, trying to get attention, money, or material gain. Of course, she could not phrase her intentions directly: she had to mask these, cover these up in flattery and seduction. Therefore, Flavie often sent *des photos sexy* (seductive images). Her addressees, of course, knew that Flavie was playing, as much as they were playing themselves.[17] Both parties engaged in seductive appearances, *impressionisme* or *aspè* as it is called in Kinshasa, though they all knew that the surface hides uncomfortable truths such as the other's unavailability or need for financial assistance. Yet, sometimes it is better to ignore these worlds beneath the (screen) surface.

In Kinois parlance, the skills of reading into people's words, gestures, or actions are not unique for digital interaction. Part of quotidian urban smartness is the skill to *benda bilili* (to pull the images). The major assumption is that reality is not what one is seeing, but rather what is hidden. To *benda bilili* means to understand that the visible is very much a smoke screen and that one needs to be able to see through and beyond it. The visible is literally blurring and misguiding vision. There is an epistemological dimension to this. It is commonly accepted in Kinshasa that one can never fully know what is real nor what is in other people's hearts and minds (Pype 2015); people deliberately play with appearances and suggestion.[18] All of this entails that people perceive of the "canvas," the digital screen, as merely another screen that blurs and obscures "the real." With the *benda bilili* trope, the "shadow" gains a third meaning here: the "shadow" references the invisible, very often, although not limited to spiritual, invisible worlds.

So, even if posts in the social media platforms display a deliberate aesthetics of ambiguity, allusion, and disguise, the described management of the undisclosed and the hidden in the digital is not new; the exegesis of digital communication is fully in line with nondigital strategies to find meaning and value in signs, indexes, and symbols.

Marianne Ferme's observations about the cultural order of dissimulation in Sierra Leone perfectly describe Kinois' *benda bilili* dictum: "the visible world (as it appears for instance, in ritual, political, and domestic appropriations of public space) is activated by forces concealed beneath the surface of discourse, objects, and social relations" (2001: 2). All of this entails a disposition of constant alertness toward a potential disruption of the deceptive order of ordinary appearances. "What appears on the surface as a generous action toward friends, family, and strangers, may suddenly change into a violent encounter with the enemy," so Ferme (2001: 2) wrote about life in Sierra Leone where histories of slavery and war destabilized social life. In such a precarious social universe, friends may turn into enemies in cases where someone is accused of *kindoki* (witchcraft and sorcery). Relations are unstable, and people are constantly searching for signs to understand how others are positioned toward themselves. In Kinshasa, a context of postcolonial violence enacted by the former Mobutu regime (1966–1997), civil war (1996–1997), and more than three decades of economic crisis, have rendered social relations very fragile. Therefore, Kinois advise each other and outsiders, like myself, to distrust others, as "we do not know what is in people's hearts" (*toyebi motema ya batu te*).[19]

While Ferme illustrated this necessity of protecting one's private and emotional life with various kinds of (material and immaterial) masks, this comparison can be extended for the digital world: the online world is a similar representational space where digital alter egos serve as masks; the digital screen becomes one additional surface that conceals, and through which people can be fooled, but also can protect the inner person.

It is thus unsurprising that Kinois hermeneutics of digital posts have a very pragmatic orientation: one tries to reconstruct intentions and emotions. The digital depth does not necessarily orient toward an epistemological, cosmological world full of spirits. Rather, the shadow conversations and the hidden world of the online *toile* are very much of "this world," embedded in material affairs and personal projects.

These observations help us to further our reflections on the ontology of the virtual world (Mbembe 2016; Newell and Pype 2021). In the study of social media communication, it is most probably no coincidence that

Kinois speak about *la toile* not as a spider web (which would be the most conventional translation in this context), but as a canvas, a screen. The *toile* provides a platform for metonymic relations. When understanding the *toile* as a canvas, a (conscious or unconscious) link is made with paintings. Paintings present individual presentations or emplacements of the visual world. This positioning is the outcome of agency and intentionality. A similar make-up or composition happens with online posts. Digital aesthetics draw on concealment (as Flavie did not show or mention the day out with the flirtatious photographer) and on make-up (Flavie literally prepared her day out by spending time in the hair salon and selecting various outfits). The *toile* is thus not necessarily an access point into a hidden, ontological space, but it is first and foremost materially and aesthetically connected to the experiential world. The internet, social media included, provides an artificial, purposeful space that performs new realities in close relationship to the lived material world.

The connection with paintings seems even more fruitful for my focus on "shadow conversations" when considering the social relevance of popular paintings of Congolese colonial and early postcolonial times. Popular paintings were, just like the cryptic digital posts now are, fully embedded in a chain of discursive practices. Both Johannes Fabian (1998: 52) and Bogumil Jewsiewicki (2003) argued that the social purpose of Congolese popular paintings was not so much aesthetic pleasure, but rather pragmatically establishing a discursive realm in which colonial and postcolonial traumas could be expressed. The paintings served as conversation openers. The popular paintings and digital posts thus share the goal of opening up a discursive sphere. As mentioned above, Flavie hoped that Samourai would start talking to her again. The visual (and its specific arrangements of themes and protagonists) on paintings and on the digital canvas serves equally to facilitate conversations, spark debate, and trigger responses.

On the Necessity of Reconstructing Shadow Conversations

Given that online communication is very much embedded in a pragmatics of everyday life, especially the management of social relationships, and that encoding and decoding are practices familiar to many, the main argument of this chapter was that, if we want to grasp the social bearings of online communication such as WhatsApp status updates, Facebook stories, and Instagram publications, we need to acknowledge and analyze the online exegesis and hermeneutics along local communicative practices. The material about the four ways of not saying something shows how as ethnographers, we need to combine online and offline research. Only then can we fully grasp that cryptic digital communication in Kinshasa is purposive, embedded in relationships, and speaks to vulnerability, emotions, and more importantly, to personal (aspired) futures.

Following points can be made regarding cryptopolitics online based on the ethnography. First, in contrast to *palabre*, the speech genre that aims at resolving conflict, digital status updates and stories are never conflict resolving in themselves. Moreover, they *should* not be the endpoint. Just like Flavie's texts messages to Samourai were supposed not to be the final utterance. They are embedded in a chain of discourses: they have discourse histories. The interpretative labor that the "talk" of WhatsApp status updates, memes, and digital story telling seem to beg for requires social skill. One needs to know if and how to react. Appropriate forms of reacting are consoling and giving advice. If one does not feel concerned, the best way of reacting is telling the WhatsApp contact "to pray to God," "to stay determined," or some random advice about not trusting others.

Second, the chapter has brought together two types of "shadow conversations." The first type of shadow conversations are those conversations in the background of digital media posts: those that lead up to a post and those that are expected to be generated by reactions on a post. The second type of shadow conversations relates to the particular status of the fleeting WhatsApp statuses, Facebook stories, and other more temporal, public posts. In these online temporary frames, Kinois social media users dare to express vulnerability or dare to enter into more provocative language. These relate to people's "shadows," their inner person, which are usually not expressed in public talk.

Third, this double status of "shadow conversations" points to methodological issues. It draws attention to users' navigations of social media and their deliberations about affordances of particular platforms and technical modalities. Kinois users fragment emotions, subjectivities, and aspirations, break these up and distribute them over different platforms and modalities. It is to these varying ways of "distributing the digital person" that we need to be attentive. Social media are literally plural and polymorphic; very much like identities and subjectivities are emerging, varied, and multiple. Users deploy various possibilities of the digital skillfully, while they simultaneously dialogue with offline social expectations and codes. We need to study these multifarious interactions.

Fourth, the digital publications under scrutiny here reveal something about Kinois sociality and the positionality of the individual therein. Ultimately, reconstructed shadow histories teach us that social relationships in Kinshasa are unstable, delicate, and fragile. People constantly try to protect their personhood by trying to figure out who their allies are, on whom they can and cannot rely. By managing their digital persona, they are caring for their "shadow", ànd their connectivity to social others.

Finally, while Irvine was more concerned with the sender's role (addressee, sponsor, ghost writer, and so on), here I was more concerned with the receiver's role. The receiver of many social media posts is plural: some are "addressees," while others are not, yet they are also receivers. A text or utterance can be made in the public domain (such as a WhatsApp status update) but is only meaningful to an individual or a small group of people.[20] Nevertheless, as the ethnography has shown, the presence of this receiver-who-is-not-the-addressee is socially significant for the social media user: on the one hand, posting cryptic messages can be a way of soliciting help (you never know who will come up with a solution); on the other hand, it can also be a way of warding other people off—"I have too many problems now, don't bother me with something else"—and at the same time it can also be intended to show people "I'm strong, even in moments of hardship, I am resilient." One finds here striking parallels with other research on the aesthetics of popular culture in sub-Saharan Africa. Karin Barber (2007) noted how the audience is treated as internally differentiated, with its own foci or centers of attention, which performers acknowledge and address. In the WhatsApp *sala keba* texts, the same is going on: images and texts are deeply meaningful to certain people, those who feel addressed, but only contain superficial meaning to other (WhatsApp) contacts.

Katrien Pype (associate professor at KU Leuven, Belgium) is a cultural anthropologist, mainly interested in media, popular culture, and technology. She has written about the production of television serials, television news programs, TV dance shows, and long-distance communication, all in the context of contemporary Kinshasa. Her work is published in edited books, and in journals such as *Africa, Ethnos, Journal of the Royal Anthropological Institute, Journal of Modern African Studies, Journal of African Media Studies,* and others. Her monograph *The Making of the Pentecostal Melodrama: Religion, Media, and Gender in Kinshasa* was published with Berghahn Books (2012). Pype also co-edited, with Jaco Hoffman, *Aging in Sub-Saharan Africa: Spaces and Practices of Care* (Policy Press, 2016).

Notes

Field research was generously funded by the FWO Odysseus budget (G.A005.14N). I wish to thank Charlie Mbavumoya, Constantin Mboliaka, and Triphe Kialungila for assisting me in this research. I greatly acknowledge many conversations with the Kongo, Lukesa, Mbungu Six, and Muyeye families. I presented this material at the ECAS 2019 conference (Edinburgh), at the MediaLab of Sciences Po (November 2021), at the Textures du Pouvoir en Afrique workshop (SciencesPo, Paris, May 2022), and at the Symposium "The Art and Science of Visual Research" (University of Antwerp, October 2022). Organizers and participants of these events provided valuable feedback, as well as Sasha Newell and Richard Werbner, whose comments on a draft have been important.

1. Facebook *mode gratuit* came with smartphones and SIM cards purchased with Congolese telecom, through which users could have minimal access to Facebook without consuming any mobile data. It was suspended in late May 2022. Facebook Lite is a similar app, with some more functions (though no gifs, polls, or live functions), but which consumed some mobile data. Since August 2020, the app is not available in the Play store or on IOS anymore, and thus is not updated but remains functional. Both were part of Facebook's "Free Basics" initiative, which started in 2016. Both were very popular in Kinshasa during fieldwork.
2. All names in this chapter are pseudonyms.
3. Informal polygamy and polyandry are common in Kinshasa. For girls, this phenomenon is called *chic-choc-chèque*, indicating the various "services" that the lovers cater to (cloths, sex, money). Girls should not inform the men about their rivals, otherwise they risk losing that connection. See Pype (2012: 232–90) for a discussion of how Christian churches advocate against urban informal polygamy and polyandry in Kinshasa.
4. (Classificatory) sons and fathers keep details of their friendships, their romantic lives and even much of their economic activities hidden from one another. Friends from the same gender, on the other hand, usually are well-informed about each other's intimate lifeworlds, because these are often literally involved, going from having a hand in the establishing of a romantic relationship through mediating quarrels and disputes and taking revenge on behalf of the friend after a romantic relationship has ended badly for the friend. Friends also protect each other's public reputation, especially because speaking about someone as being affected by another's actions risks weakening the reputation of a "strong man" (*moto makasi*), a masculine ideal in Kinshasa (Pype 2007).
5. With "digital Kinois," I indicate people who identify as "Kinois", by writing in Lingala or KiKinois, and dialoguing with others about Kinois life, in the digital sphere, even though they may be residing elsewhere in DRC or abroad.
6. See Aubrey Graham (2019) for a detailed discussion of how media ideologies may contradict one another when an image is interpreted by audiences familiar with other media ideologies. The image in this case is a digital photograph of rebel violence in eastern Congo posted by a German journalist on her Twitter account, which went viral (2019: 267).
7. See Pype (2021) about the importance of mobile phones and social media in the lifeworlds of Kinshasa's inhabitants; and Pype (2017) for a discussion

of "smartness" in Kinshasa. Tanzanu (2012) describes similar dynamics in Cameroon; Schneidermann (forthcoming) explores "intimate infopolitics" of girls and women in a Capetonian township.

8. There is an accidental overlap with US conventional digispeak "where you at?", which may indicate how inquiring about someone's location serves as a general greeting or a general quizzing about someone's well-being. The Kinois context is different, as the "*oza wapi?*" question is a conversation opener among (aspiring) lovers. In other conversations, it is not polite to ask someone where she or he is as it would mean that the person asking the question assumes a kind of entitlement to know about the other's whereabouts. Kinois sociality is very much concerned with "mind your own business" (*kipe ya yo,* Pype 2016b)—except in the intimate relationship of (aspiring) sexual partners. Though, there is a gendered distribution here: men are expected to ask their female lovers this question, not vice versa.
9. Even if Flavie lies about her exact whereabouts, she confirms to the contact that he is entitled to check in on her.
10. In other contexts, like South Africa, it has been documented that hiding one's private space online is an effective strategy against potential burglary.
11. vivre caché c'est vivre heureux
    La publicité attire la convoitise
    La convoitise cree la jalousie
    La jalousie faconne l'ennemi (smiley).
12. These observations should caution us to read visual representations of lifestyles not always as a reflection of what people actually experience. Furthermore, scholars have shown how photography sometimes stages one as a "desired other" (Beherend 2002), this also occurs on Facebook, e.g., Claudia Böhme's (2019) research among Sudanese refugees' digital self-representations shows how people sometimes stage themselves as living their dream (as a fashion designer, a successful carpenter) as means of prefiguration or active future-making.
13. On divination in the Kinshasa region, see among others Devisch (2012, 2018).
14. Obviously, "Digital Kinshasa" is also a space of trolling and exchanging hate speech. However, these are usually expressed in conversations with unknown digital others, and are often connected to posts about politics, public figures, or global events. In this chapter, I focus on micropolitics of social media communication insofar as the posts relate to people's intimate lives.
15. The photographer remained a friend with whom Flavie had regular encounters, although he understood pretty quickly that their relationship would not transform into a love relationship. From time to time, he helps her financially, as friends do.
16. Newell (2012: 259–60) has observed a similar distinction between the physical outer and spiritual inner body.
17. In Pype (2020), I argue that Flavie was "playful" and thus trying to change her reality, though many of her "digital husbands" were merely "playing".
18. These practices of playing with suggestion and appearance have also been analyzed in other urban African societies. See Newell (2012) on bluffing in Abidjan; Luisa Lombard (2016) on practices of camouflage in the Central African Republic; and Archambault (2017) on the economy of pretense in Inhambane (Mozambique).

19. See Benjamin Rubbers (2009) for a discussion of this generalized feeling of distrust in the Congolese Katanga region.
20. Similar to the layers of meaning in evangelizing television serials (see Pype 2012: 164). The serials' producers expect that born-again Christians, other Christians, and "pagans" all relate differently to the broadcast images and sounds.

References

Archambault, Julie-Soleil. 2017. *Mobile Secrets: Youth, Intimacy, and the Politics of Pretense in Mozambique.* Chicago: Chicago University Press.

Barber, Karin. 2007. *The Anthropology of Texts, Persons, and Publics: Oral and Written Cultures in Africa and Beyond.* Cambridge: Cambridge University Press.

Beherend, Heike. 2002. "'I Am Like a Movie Star in My Street'. Photographic self-creation in postcolonial Kenya." In *Postcolonial Subjectivities in Africa,* ed. Richard Werbner, 44–62. London: Zed Books.

Bernal, Victoria. 2014. *Nation as Network: Diaspora, Cyberspace, and Citizenship.* Chicago: Chicago University Press.

Böhme, Claudia. 2019. "The Illusion of Being a Free Spirit—Mobile Phones and Social Media in Transit Places of Migration with the Example of the Kakuma Refugee Camp in Kenya." *Stichproben: Wiener Zeitschrift für kritische Afrikastudien* 19(36): 51–74.

Deger, Jennifer. 2016. "Thick Photography." *Journal of Material Culture* 21(1): 111–32.

Devisch, René. 2012. "Of Divinatory Connaissance in South-Saharan Africa: The Bodiliness of Perception, Inter-subjectivity and Inter-world resonance." *Anthropology & Medicine* 19(1): 107–18.

———. 2018. "La divination et ses sources primordiales en milieu yakaphone" [Divination and its primordial sources in the Yakaphone environment]. *Anthropologie et sociétés* 42(2–3): 247–69.

Ellis, Stephen, and Gerrie ter Haar, 2003. *Worlds of Power: Religious Thoughts and Political Practice in Africa.* London: Hurst & Company.

Fabian, Johannes. 1998. *Moments of Freedom: Anthropology and Popular Culture.* Charlottesville: University of Virginia Press.

Ferme, Marianne. C. 2001. *The Underneath of Things: Violence, History, and the Everyday in Sierra Leone.* California: University of California Press.

Gershon, Ilana. 2010. *The Break-Up 2.0.* Ithaca, NY: Cornell University Press.

Geschiere, Peter. 1998. *The Modernity of Witchcraft: Politics and the Occult in Postcolonial Africa.* Charlottesville: University of Virginia Press.

Graham, Aubrey P. 2019. "Hostile Visual Encounters: Fighting to Control Photographic Meaning in the DRC's Digital Age." *Africa: Journal of the International Africa Institute* 89(2): 266–85.

Irvine, Judith. 1996. "Shadow Conversations: The Indeterminacy of Participant Roles." In *Natural Histories of Discourse,* ed. Michael Silverstein and Greg Urban, 131–59. Chicago: University of Chicago Press.

Jacobson-Widding, A. 1990. "The shadow as an expression of individuality in Congolese conceptions of personhood." In *Personhood and agency: the experience of self and other in African cultures,* eds. Michael Jackson and Ivan Karp, 31–58. Uppsala: Acta Universitatis Upsaliensis.

Jewsiewicki, Bogumil. 2003. "Une société urbaine "moderne" et ses representations: la peinture Populaire à Kinshasa (Congo) (1960-2000)." *Le Mouvement Social* 3(204): 121-148.

Lombard, Luisa. 2016. "Camouflage: The Hunting Origins of Worlding in Central Africa." *Journal of Contemporary African Studies* 34(1): 147–64.

Mbembe, Achille. 2016. "Knowledge Futures and the State of the Humanities." Abiola Lecture, delivered at the Annual Meetings of the African Studies Association, Washington, DC, 1–3 December.

Miller, Daniel, Elisabetta Costa, Nell Haynes, Tom McDonald, Razvan Nicolescu, Jolynna Sinanan, Juliano Spyer, Shriram Venkatraman, and Xinyung Wang. 2016. *How the World Changed Social Media.* London: UCL Press.

Newell, Sasha. 2012. *The Modernity Bluff: Crime, Consumption, and Citizenship in Côte d'Ivoire.* Chicago: Chicago University Press.

Newell, Sasha, and Katrien Pype, 2021. "Decolonizing the Virtual: Future Knowledges and the Extrahuman in Africa." *African Studies Review* (Special issue—Forum on the Abiola Lecture 2016) 64 (1): 5–22.

Pype, Katrien. 2007. "Fighting Boys, Strong Men and Gorillas: Notes on the Imagination of Masculinities in Kinshasa." *Africa: Journal of the International African Institute* 77(2): 250–71.

———. 2012. *The Making of the Pentecostal Melodrama: Religion, Media, & Gender in Kinshasa.* New York: Berghahn Books.

———. 2015. "The Heart of Man. Pentecostal Emotive Style in and beyond Kinshasa's Media World." In *New Media and Religious Transformations in Africa,* eds. R. Hackett and B. Soares, 116-136. Bloomington: Indiana University Press.

———. 2016a. "Blackberry Girls and Jesus's Brides: Pentecostal-Charismatic Christianity and the (Im-)Moralization of Urban Femininities in Contemporary Kinshasa." *Journal of Religion in Africa* 46(4): 390–416.

———. 2016b. "On Interference and Hotspots: Ethnographic Explorations of Rural-Urban Connectivity in and around Kinshasa's Phonie Cabins." *Mededelingen der Zittingen van de Koninklijke Academie voor Overzeese Wetenschappen* 62(2): 229–60.

———. 2017. "Smartness from Below: Variations on Technology and Creativity in Contemporary Kinshasa." In *What do Science, Technology, and Innovation Mean from Africa?,* ed. Clapperton Mavhunga, 97-115. Cambridge, MA: MIT Press.

———. 2018. "The Devil is in the Rumba Text. Commenting on Digital Depth." In *Palgrave Handbook for Media and Communication Research in Africa,* ed. Bruce Mutsvairo, 245-262. Houndmills: Palgrave.

———. 2020. "*Bolingo ya Face*: Digital Marriages, Playfulness and the Search for Change in Kinshasa." In *New Media Practices in a Changing Africa,* ed. Jo Helle-Valle and Ardis Storm-Mathisen, 93–124. Oxford: Berghahn Books.

———. 2021. "(NOT) IN SYNC—Digital Time and Forms of (Dis-)Connecting: Ethnographic Notes from Kinshasa (DR Congo)." *Media, Culture & Society* special issue on "Media and Time" (ed. S. Milhej, E. Keightly, and Peter Yeandle) 43(7): 1197–212.

Rubbers, Benjamin. 2009. "'We, the Congolese, We Cannot Trust Each Other': Trust, Norms and Relations among Traders in Katanga, Democratic Republic of Congo." *The British Journal of Sociology* 60(3): 623–42.

Schneidermann, Nanna. Forthcoming 2023. "The Intimate Infopolitics of Township Sociality in Cape Town: Mobile Phones, Mothers and Respectability." In *Anthropological Quarterly* 96(4).

Tanzanu, Primus. M. 2012. *Being Available and Reachable: New Media and Cameroonian Transnational Sociality*. Mankon, Cameroon: Langaa Research & Publishing.
Werbner, Richard. 2015. *Divination's Grasp: African Encounters with the Almost Said*. Bloomington: Indiana University Press.

CHAPTER 2

Social Media and Sounding Out in the Cryptopolitical Landscape of the Burundian Conflict

Simon Turner

After decades of an oppressive one-party system and more than a decade-long ethnic conflict, Burundi saw a veritable blossoming of free and vibrant media in the first decade of the twentieth century. Independent radio stations emerged, supported by international NGOs that—with the experiences of the wars in Yugoslavia and the genocide in Rwanda in the 1990s—saw information as central to conflict escalation and de-escalation. In other words, the international community supported independent media as an integrated part of the peacebuilding exercise (Frère 2009), and Burundi was in many respects a model of international peacebuilding (Street, Smith and Mollet 2007). However, in 2015 the country once again experienced widespread violence, a massive outflux of refugees, and the closure of independent radio stations. Most journalists as well as civil rights activists went underground or fled the country while others were attacked or arrested. Overnight, the critical, vibrant radio stations were silenced and instead Burundians inside and outside the country made use of Twitter, WhatsApp, and other digital platforms in order to understand what was going on in their country (Falisse and Nkengurutse 2019; Frère 2017). In this chapter, I explore the relationship between the renewed violence and the media, and I do so by exploring the widespread idea that politics in Burundi always has a hidden agenda, an unseen truth beneath the surface—what we might call cryptopolitics. I argue that (social) media users simultaneously want to uncover cryptopolitics while also being constitutive of such speculative politics of secrecy and conspiracy. I further explore how cryptopolitics is affected by and plays into violent crises.

In my previous research on Burundi from the late 1990s and early 2000s, I found that ideas of secrecy and hiding true intentions have been prominent in Burundians' understanding of politics (Turner 2007b).

Through rumors and conspiracy theories, Burundians—from peasants to professors—tried to unveil the secret machinations of power and find the ulterior motives and grand schemes of politics; what Mbembé calls the underbelly of politics (Mbembé 2001) and what we in this volume term cryptopolitics.

How do Burundians deal with cryptopolitics and the art of revealing and concealing in a situation of crisis—and how do digital media play into this? While tweets, WhatsApp messages, and Facebook updates try to uncover and reveal the true workings of cryptopolitics—whether the secret violence committed by the state or rebel plots—they may also get caught up in a new set of deception politics. Furthermore, Burundian actors try to control and conceal their emotions while sounding out the emotions of others. Social media draw national cryptopolitics into the intimate and affective spheres of family, kin and neighbors, interpellating them and making them relate to these emotionally challenging issues, forcing them to play along with the game of veiling and unveiling.

In the following, I try to unpack the notions of secrets and lies that are so pervasive in Burundian society and relate this to issues of trust and mistrust, arguing that sociality may also be constituted through mistrust. I then explore the history of cryptopolitics in Burundi based on my own ethnographic engagement with the country for more than two decades. I explore how the media landscape has changed in this time period and how this has affected the shape and position of cryptopolitics in Burundi and its diaspora.

Cryptopolitics and the Power of Concealment in Burundi

While I previously have perceived of cryptopolitics as a product of conspiracy theories that are ultimately about making sense of a chaotic world (Feldman 1995; Turner 2007a), I shift focus here to understanding cryptopolitics as a means of conducting politics itself. In other words, those in power also rely on cryptopolitics: on secret plans, hidden scripts, and ulterior motives. Following historian Aidan Russell (2019a, 2019b) and anthropologist Ethel Albert (1964), I argue that, in Burundi, politics is always seen to be a game of manipulating the truth and to rule is to have control over the word. Similarly, it is seen as extremely unwise to simply reveal your intentions as that would leave you open to attacks by your enemy. Not telling everything is not simply a cynical game of sovereignty, however. It can also be a means to help neighbors get along despite great antagonisms and memories of violence—as has been shown in for instance Bert Ingelaere's work on post-genocide Rwanda (2009b).

As mentioned in the introduction to this book, duplicity is not always linked to manipulation but can also be a sign of discretion. I found this in neighboring Rwanda in 2011, where I noticed that nobody used the word "genocide" (*yenoside* in Kinyarwanda) but simply talked about "the troubles" or perhaps "the war." When I inquired about this, I was told that it was out of courtesy to the other people present, as one never knew which side they had been on during the genocide nor how they perceived the events.

Andrea Grant (2015) found that the insecurity of the state seeped like metastases into the everyday lives of Rwandans in what she called "quiet insecurity" where everyone was on guard in subtle manners. The political and the private are in other words entangled, forcing ordinary citizens to be attentive to cryptopolitics in all aspects of life. Although there are clear differences in the ways that the Rwandan and the Burundian states have dealt with conflict, genocide, and ethnicity, I would argue that the cryptopolitics of national politics also "metastases" into the everyday lives of Burundians. In my recent fieldwork in Kigali in 2016, I talked to a young Burundian woman (I call her Josephine), who had fled to neighboring Rwanda during the 2015 crisis. The following year she traveled clandestinely to Burundi to collect some documents and attend a family wedding. When she met a young man from her neighborhood and he asked where she lived and what she did for a living, she only told him part of the truth. Although she assumed that he is an informer, she could not know for sure, so she tried to avoid telling him the whole truth. However, she could not reject him either, because that would give away her suspicion about him being an informer and consequently reveal that she probably had not told him the whole truth. So, she ended up giving him her phone number with a polite smile, "but my heart was beating" she explained to me afterward. In other words, everyone acknowledges the art of deceit, and what is at play is to be able to hide "just enough" and reveal "just enough"—of both one's own intentions and the intentions of the other. The art of deception requires skills and is emotionally demanding.

When talking to Burundians about politics, the question of secrets and lies always emerges (Turner 2005). Burundians from all walks of life would tell me that the problem with politicians is that they hide their true intentions and tell lies to the outside world in order to stay in power. I met Jean-Pierre (fictive name) at a café in Brussels in May 2005. He was very active in various newly established Tutsi groups online because he was afraid that the whole peace process was a hoax and kept repeating that he feared for the safety of the Tutsi. His greatest concern was not the Hutu now entering political positions but the previous Tutsi president Buyoya who in Jean-Pierre's eyes had blood on his hands and who had cut a deal with the Hutu génocidaires to avoid persecution for his own war crimes (Turner 2007b). On the other side of the ethnic and political divide, I talked to Louis at a Burundian wedding in Copenhagen in 2006. He was a middle-aged Hutu who used to be an ambassador but at the time of our conversation was unemployed and lived in a housing estate outside Copenhagen, and he explained that he did not trust the transition either. The Hutu politicians in the transition government were simply lured in by the titles and the houses and per diems, he claimed. During my latest fieldwork among urban, middle-class Tutsi, exiled in Rwanda, their greatest concern was the ways in which the Burundian government pretended that everything was fine in the country while secretly abducting and killing people, leaving their bodies in communal graves.

A Culture of Lies?

The concepts of secrecy and concealment go further than to politics, and Burundians often lament their own *culture du mensonge* (culture of lying) as something that permeates society in general. In fact, they would often warn me as a researcher that my results would be biased as nobody would tell me the truth. One Burundian, living in Belgium, told me that it is important in Burundian politics and society to not tell everything. You must keep some things *dans la poche* (in your pocket), he explained, or else it might be used against you. In other words, you put yourself in a weaker bargaining position if you lay all your cards on the table. "It is somehow related to witchcraft," he continued. The reference to witchcraft—he used the French term *sorcellerie*—was surprising to me, as Burundians rarely talk about witchcraft. But the comparison makes sense: your adversary needs something from you (hair, nails, blood, excrements, intimate possessions) in order to cast a spell on you or exploit you in other ways (White 2019).[1] Likewise, in politics, your adversary needs something from you in order to harm you. In the following I elaborate on this idea of needing to hide information—not in order to harm or deceive others but to protect oneself.

The concept of a culture of lies often has an ethnic/class twist to it, depending on with whom I was talking. The educated Hutu and Tutsi whom I met in the diaspora in Belgium and Denmark as well as the Tutsi in Rwanda and Burundi would not cast this in ethnic terms and instead claimed that it is a cultural trait of the Barundi as such. Meanwhile, the Hutu refugees in camps in Tanzania or living precariously on the outskirts of Nairobi would talk openly about the differences between Hutu and Tutsi. Mostly, the Hutu refugees dismissed the "ethnic body maps" that were recounted to Liisa Malkki in Mishamo in the 1980s (Malkki 1995: 79–80) as a means to tell the difference between Hutu and Tutsi and explained instead that the differences lie in the behavior of the Tutsi. The Hutu get angry and then forget, they would explain, while the Tutsi can hide their feelings and do not forget. The Hutu are gullible while the Tutsi can carry a grudge and then hit back much later. This explained, to them, the reason why the Tutsi had been able to subjugate and dominate the Hutu when they arrived in the Great Lakes region centuries ago. It was their cunning deceit that allowed them to conquer the gullible Hutu (see also Malkki 1995: chapter 2; Turner 2010: chapter 7). The Tutsi minority, in these narratives, told by the Hutu refugees, used cryptopolitics to manipulate and rule the Hutu majority. Withholding truth and hiding emotions were central to their political power, according to the Hutu narratives. In other words, to wield this kind of power is to control emotions such as anger and fear and use them strategically instead. Feelings of anger, revenge, and rage are best kept hidden, they claim. I will explore the issue of controlling emotions in more detail later in the chapter.

When I asked about the conflict between Hutu and Tutsi, Hutu refugees would claim that they—as children and as Hutu—had been naïve and "blind" to the conflict, while the Tutsi children whom they had trusted as friends had known all the time. What exactly they had known remains unclear. It was only at critical events in history of widescale, open violence—like the selective genocide in 1972 and the ethnic violence in 1993—that the Tutsi would show their true intentions and the Hutu would "open their eyes" (Turner 2007a: 133). During my latest fieldwork among urban, middle-class Tutsi who had fled to the capital of neighboring Rwanda, I heard a slightly different version of this narrative about the gullible (Hutu) peasants. When asked whether they feared a genocide, they answered that the peasants had been easily manipulated by Hutu politicians in the past to believe that the Tutsi were their enemies. However, at present, the peasants in Burundi are too intelligent and can see through the politicians' games. In other words, the ethnic and class stereotypes proscribe that Hutu/peasants[2] are gullible, easily manipulated, and hot-headed. However, these stereotypes are not set in stone and Burundians believe that history can teach them to behave differently. The Hutu are allegedly more "intelligent" now, with intelligence meaning the ability to "sound out" the ulterior motives of cynical politicians and navigate the cryptopolitical landscape of deceit and manipulation. The Hutu refugees in the camp similarly believed that their position had changed with history. The violence of 1972 and 1993 "opened their eyes," making them more "intelligent." In their own words, intelligence is strongly connected to being able to see—see through the web of lies of the Tutsi and see their true intentions. And although intelligence and lack thereof are assumed to be linked to ethnicity and class, the poor Hutu peasants can also become "intelligent" once the Tutsi secrets have been revealed.

The Aesthetics and Power of Speech

Based on fieldwork in the 1950s, Ethel M. Albert explored the role of speech and how it "is explicitly recognized as an important instrument of social life" (Albert 1964: 35). While the article certainly reflects the time it was written in, with its understanding of "cultures" as units, her findings might help us understand the relationship between concealment and power in Burundi. She shows how rhetoric, eloquence, and aesthetics are central to the command of speech and explains how this is linked to a very elaborate social hierarchy based on gender, age, ethnicity, and class. Highborn boys are trained, she argues, from the age of ten in the art of speech.[3] "Training includes mastery of a suitable, elegant vocabulary, of tone of voice and its modulation, of graceful gestures with hand and spear, of general posture and appropriate bodily displacements" (Albert 1964: 37). It is important not to get agitated, raise your voice, or display emotions. Women are trained to be quiet and timid. Meanwhile, peasants may speak in clumsy sentences, their voices too loud, their gestures wild, and their emotions freely displayed (1964: 38). The similarities between her analysis and that of the Hutu refugees I met in the camp in Tanzania are striking. They also claimed that the Hutu are loud and carry their emotions on the outside while the Tutsi know how to hide their emotions and intentions. We see here, how cryptopolitics—the art of concealing and revealing—is not simply about concealing and revealing information but also emotions. It is important to hide fear and anger if one is to be in control.

Albert links these conceptualizations of speech to local "cultural conceptions of truth, falsehood, and fiction" (1964: 44). What is important for the Burundians, she argues, is not whether a statement is objectively true or false but whether the argument is beautiful and whether it therefore is able to bring something good to its designers. "The key concept for appreciating the norms and values associated the uses of language is *ubgenge*,[4] 'successful cleverness.' *Ubgenge* chiefly applies to intellectual-verbal management of significant life situations" (1964: 44).

It is cleverness that uses emotions and beautiful rhetoric to achieve its goals. Political skills are therefore about being able to manipulate convincingly and elegantly. The art of political language is meant to speak to emotions and aesthetics through controlling and hiding emotions and manipulating facts.

Taking his cues from Ethel Albert and from the Burundian Catholic priest and philosopher André Makarazi, Aidan Russell (2019b) distinguishes between understanding the truth in Burundi at three levels. First, in philosophical terms, the distinction between truth and falsehood is similar to what we know from Western Enlightenment; there is an absolute truth. Second, in social terms, the truth can be powerful and potentially dangerous. It is therefore unwise to always tell the truth, as it can hurt you and others. Third, in political terms, "the words of an authority defined what functioned as true in public" (Russell 2019b: 22). For our purposes, we are concerned with the social and political aspects, and I will argue that the neat distinction between them makes little sense in practice.

Russell has warned against the myth of the *culture du mensonge* (2019b: 33). It is a culturally essentialist way of characterizing a whole people, and it reinforces racist stereotypes about the deceitful native.[5] However, the myth still exists among many Burundians as a kind of autoethnography and local theory, helping them make sense of politics, power, and social hierarchy in the Great Lakes region. Furthermore, a consciousness of how to reveal certain truths and hide others is still prevalent in the region today (Ingelaere 2009a; Nee and Uvin 2010; Russell 2019a). In their study of the (lack of a) truth and reconciliation process in Burundi, Ann Nee and Peter Uvin found that the vast majority of Burundians prefer to leave the past in silence. They argue that this approach to the past can be related to a general lack of trust in society, due perhaps to decades of violence and their "profound vulnerability" (2010: 173). This vulnerability means that it is important to maintain relations with people whom you do not trust. "Burundians protect themselves by nurturing relations, by compromising, by maintaining a poker face of acceptance under all conditions" (Nee and Uvin 2010: 173). Important here is not only to hide information but also emotions. A truth and reconciliation commission might bring truths to the fore that can jeopardize the volatile social relations between people.

Nee and Uvin further observe that Burundians themselves attribute this lack of trust to culture, describing themselves as masters of dissimulation and refer to proverbs such as "[t]he one who doesn't lie has no food for his children" (2010: 174). Local intellectuals in Burundi—and in particular in Rwanda where similar debates take place but in a different manner due to the political situation of the country—would tell me that there is no such tradition of concealing the truth; the mistrust is due to the genocidal violence. Their analysis is similar to that of Nee and Uvin. In everyday conversations, however, Burundians would constantly make references to the way they would never say things straightforwardly. Like when I was commended for my way of posing questions during interviews because they were not blunt like other Europeans—sometimes making my interlocutors laugh, smack their tongues, and snap their fingers if I posed a "trick question" about a sensitive issue: "you are like [a] Burundian!" While the Hutu would sometimes call this a Tutsi trait, both Hutu and Tutsi would claim that it was a Burundian—and Rwandan—trait.

The Sociality of Mistrust

While secrecy, suspicion, and a culture of lies may seem to challenge and be at odds with sociality, several authors have shown how social relations can be maintained through suspicion and mistrust. In his study of how Burundians managed to co-habit after more than a decade of civil war, Peter Uvin (2009) found that Burundians had a deep-seated mistrust of one another. In a reversal of Putnamian ideas of social capital, he further suggests that this suspicion was the driver behind social relationships in Burundi, as it only makes sense to "keep your enemies close" so as to avoid betrayal. I saw these relationships all the time. My research assistant in Kigali in 2015 and 2016, a young Burundian woman who had fled to Rwanda in 2015, was telling me one day about some land that her family owned outside Bujumbura where they lived. She loved to visit the farm, she claimed, but she would only visit during the daytime because she feared that the neighbors and the farm laborers would kill her if she stayed the night. They were envious of her family's wealth, she explained. Only her old grandmother stayed at the farm all the time. Her family did not confront the neighbors or go to the police. They would even have parties with the neighbors and laborers whom they assumed wanted them dead. In his thought-provoking work on mistrust in the Atlas Mountains, Matthew Carey warns us not to see mistrust as simply lack of trust and therefore infer that societies with low levels of trust are some kind of a "chaotic Hobbesian world of solitude, anomie, and pitiless mutual predation" (Carey 2017: 12). The proximity or familiarity of neighbors does not guarantee knowability or certainty, he argues. "(O)ther people are, in some sense, unknowable per se . . . their personality cannot be identified or used as a basis for prediction" (Carey

2017: 16). And yet, they manage to create sociality, he argues. We might say that neighbors are constantly sounding each other out, trying to know the unknowable. In my earlier work, I have similarly argued that the mutual suspicion and the perception that everyone is hiding their true intentions create a kind of tense sociality where everyone is playing hide and seek—with the added complication that everyone is hiding and seeking at the same time. Elegant rhetoric and the use of silences and euphemisms are central in this sociality, where truths are kept hidden "in the pocket"; whether they be about facts, about intentions, or about emotions. In the case of my research assistant, the fact was her family's wealth, the intentions were—perhaps—to kill her family, and the emotions were her fear. All of these were hidden away in order to continue an edgy, nervous co-habitation.[6]

These constant attempts to conceal one's true emotions and true intentions while also sounding out the intentions of others, create a world where nothing is what it seems and below the surface that can be seen and heard is another world that controls our world. In his study on marginalized urban poor in Guinea Bissau and among Bissauean migrants in Portugal, Henrik Vigh argues that a "nervous sociality" is created while they are constantly probing and scanning social life, looking for hidden intentions and negative potentials (Vigh 2018). Achille Mbembé invokes the idea of every "thing" having a "double" (Mbembé 2001) and argues that in Africa "everything almost always conceals something else" (2001: 148) and this something else—the invisible that lies within the visible—is just as important in determining the fate of things. In other words, in this "African" cosmology that he proposes, it is just as important to understand the invisible underbelly of things as to understand their visible surface. Mariane Ferme (2001) elaborates on the importance "the underneath of things" and the role of secrecy during and after violent conflict. She claims that the violence has created a "hermeneutic of suspicion" (Ferme 2001: 7) where people never trust the surface value of things and instead dig for deeper meanings "underneath." She calls this "deep knowledge" of past violence, often lodged in mundane material objects and places. While there is a danger in her interpretation to render this knowledge more true or authentic than other knowledge, I find her idea that violence creates this "hermeneutics of suspicion" very helpful in understanding the widespread suspicion and secrecy in Burundi. Harry West and Todd Sanders (2003) argue that conspiracy theories are the product of modern enlightenment ideals about politics, truth, and transparency. The idea that a transparent "surface" permits us to look inside to the more "real" workings of power, strengthens the suspicion that power operates behind a "facade" (West and Sanders 2003: 16).

Conspiracy theories seek to shed light in dark spaces, but they are also content with opaqueness leaving some aspects undecided (West and Sanders 2003). Taking this argument further, Kathleen Stewart (2017) argues that conspiracy theories are mimetic of the internet. "The Internet was made for conspiracy theory; it *is* a conspiracy: one thing leads to another, always another link leading you deeper into no thing and no place, floating through the self-dividing and transmogrifying sites" (in Vine and Carey 2017: 56).

In sum, the profound sense of mistrust creates a sense that nothing and nobody is fully knowable. This leads to a constant search for underlying truths—often in the shape of rumors and conspiracy theories (Turner 2007a)—and the internet and social media seem the perfect place for these. In everyday interactions, Burundians find a means of sociality where everyone is "on their toes" concealing and revealing just enough to get along. In the realm of politics, power of the word is crucial, and the word of the ruler is the truth, Russell (2019b: 22) argues. However, Burundians operate with layers of truth, allowing them to act as if the word of the ruler were the only truth while simultaneously sounding out[7] their adversaries in order to ascertain their hidden intentions and be prepared for alternative actions.

Conflict and Conspiracy in Burundi

Burundi gained independence from Belgium in 1962 and has since experienced ethnic violence, authoritarian rule, and civil war. From shortly after independence from Belgium until 1993 the country had been ruled by army officers in charge of a one-party authoritarian state (Chrétien 2003; Lemarchand 1996). They kept power tightly in the hands of Tutsi from the Bururi region in the south of the country while banning mention of ethnicity, because it was allegedly a false identity introduced by the colonialists to divide and rule the country. Under pressure from the international community, then President Pierre Buyoya introduced reforms in the early 1990s leading to the election of the country's first democratically elected president—a moderate Hutu from the opposition. He was, however, killed by Tutsi officers, triggering widespread ethnic violence and a civil war that lasted almost ten years, costing an estimated 300,000 lives. The Arusha Peace Accords—signed in the year 2000 and leveraged through by Nelson Mandela—provided a road map for a sophisticated power sharing deal that sought to serve the needs of all groups (Lemarchand 2007). It was not until 2003, however, that the largest rebel group, CNDD-FDD (Conseil National Pour la

Défense de la Démocratie—Forces pour la Défense de la Démocratie), signed a peace agreement and put down arms. In 2005, elections were held, bringing CNDD-FDD to power and their leader Pierre Nkurunziza to the presidency.

When I did fieldwork for over a year in a refugee camp for Burundian Hutu refugees in Tanzania in the late 1990s, they were deeply concerned with—and engaged in—the war in their home country. Central to their concerns was what they perceived to be the manipulation of "the truth" by "the Tutsi," and they were adamant that the truth about the oppression of the Hutu come out to the outside world (Turner 2002, 2005). They would often ask me to tell their story to "the big nations" because they were convinced that the Tutsi regime in Burundi was feeding the "big nations" with lies. Once the outside world knew the truth, they would help the Hutu, according to the refugees in the camp (Turner 2004). The struggle, as they perceived it, was not just to be carried out with guns in the forests of northern Burundi but was equally a battle of words—lies and secrets. And the audience was Burundians and the international community.

In 2003–6, I did fieldwork among the Burundian diaspora in Denmark and Belgium. This was during the period of transition when the peace process was still fragile, and while some Burundians in Denmark and Belgium chose to return to Burundi to get their share in the peace deal, others remained skeptical of the process, claiming that it was all a trick by the Tutsi to co-opt the naïve Hutu. The diaspora had always seen it as its prime goal and raison d'être to combat what they saw as the misinformation that the state propaganda machine was churning out to the Burundian public and to the international community. Burundian Hutu in exile in Belgium, France, Germany, and Denmark were eagerly gathering information about the wrongdoings of the government and publishing it online on websites like ARIB[8] and AG News (Africa Generation News).[9] Central to their strategy was an understanding that the Burundian government was deeply engaged in cryptopolitics and one should never take the statements of the Burundian government at face value. There were always hidden scripts and conspiracies to be unearthed and uncovered, they claimed. They claimed that they had better access to the truth outside the country than those living inside Burundi (Turner 2006). With the peace process and the transition to democratic rule including the development of vibrant media in the early 2000s, the diaspora gradually lost its raison d'être as political watchdogs. However, many Burundians in the diaspora claimed that the peacebuilding process and transition to democracy with its complicated system of ethnic quotas in the political system, the judiciary, and the army were simply a veneer to cover up the real power of the Tutsi. This was, in other words, a much more dangerous kind of cryptopolitics than the more brutish oppression of the old regime (Turner 2007a, 2008a, 2008b, 2009). They were warning against taking the peace process at face value and sounding out negative potentialities (Vigh 2018).

The peace lasted, and the media became famous in the region with dedicated journalists contributing to a lively debate (Frère 2009). By 2005, "the Burundian media sector had become a model of pluralism and journalistic professionalism" (Frère 2017: 4). However, the new regime, headed by the popular ex-rebel leader and born-again Christian, Pierre Nkurunziza, turned increasingly autocratic, limiting the freedom of expression in several ways—most notably with the media law in 2013 (Frère 2016). The state crackdown on journalists was met by vocal protests from local independent media and civil society organizations. The case of the imprisoned Bob Rugurika became iconic for this struggle.[10] He was arrested in January 2015 after his radio station (RPA, Radio Publique Africaine) broadcast a confession implying government involvement in the murder of three Italian nuns in 2014. After massive popular protests and pressure from independent media, he was released a month later.

In early 2015, tensions ran high, as speculations circulated that the sitting president would decide to run for a third term in the presidential elections later that year—despite the move being considered unconstitutional. In April, President Nkurunziza announced his decision to run for the presidential elections and people took to the streets in Bujumbura and other cities to demonstrate against a decision that they considered unconstitutional and against the spirit of the Arusha Peace Accords. The crisis escalated from day one, as the police clashed violently with protesters—and with excessive force (see Van Acker 2015). The youth wing of the ruling party, the Imbonerakure, in collaboration with the secret service threatened, beat, and abducted individuals from the so-called *quartiers contestataires* (the parts of Bujumbura where the protests took place). The local radio stations played a central role in the period leading up to the demonstrations, as did the idea of cryptopolitics. In the words of Antoine,[11] a middle-aged, man who had held a high position in an international organization in Burundi and who I met in Kigali in 2015 and in 2016, whereto he had fled in 2015: "Before the president announced his intention to run for the presidential elections, everyone was asking themselves what would happen. The media and civil society were posing the question of whether or not he would run for a third term" (my translation). Rumors began circulating, and people began discussing whether this was actually in contradiction with the Arusha Accords. "With the discussions about the Arusha Accords and the constitution and the radio and TV programs, we realized that this would not be easy." In other words, the radio and TV stations were seen as crucial for uncovering the true, malign intentions of the president. Even before he officially announced his intention to run for a third term, journalists, activists, and other public figures were trying to predict whether he might have such intentions on radio. They were sounding out the president's intentions, even before he had made any announcement, and were speculating about the possible outcomes and consequences. Sounding out can be future-oriented and anticipatory.[12] While there was much anxiety, according to Antoine, about the possible unconstitutional move by the president, it was also a time of great engagement by civil society and the media, debating the constitution and criticizing the potential decision of the president. There was, on the one hand, the fear of cryptopolitics, while on the other hand, there was hope that the present "openness" in the public sphere could reveal these hidden agendas and hence diffuse them. The mere fact that they were debating these issues in the media and that various actors, from the Catholic Church to human rights organizations, were criticizing such a decision was a sign in Antoine's mind that common people could influence the outcome of politics.

When the president finally announced his decision to run for a third term and people took to the streets, the demonstrations were intensely covered by the local media and spread on social media as well. Pictures of colorful crowds of urban youth, chanting on the streets of Bujumbura also quickly made their way to international media (mostly in the Francophone world, as usual).[13]

The months up to the president's announcement had been marked by speculation. Speculation can be seen as a means to explore possible futures and theorize about motives, hidden agendas, and possible causalities behind events. The speculations in Burundi in early 2015 brought the assumed hidden aspects of cryptopolitics into the daylight of public debate. But the debate was still uncertain and speculative, as the president might or might not decide to run for a third term. The speculations carried with them both anxiety and hope, and cryptopolitics remained cryptic. Once the president actually made his announcement to run for a third term, the speculations ceased to be speculations, as Nkurunziza revealed his intentions. The result was that many Burundians saw no choice but to go to the streets and openly air their anger and frustration. It was a moment where the hidden side of cryptopolitics was revealed on both sides. My interlocutors like to talk about the conflict always being there, but sometimes it is closed and other times it is open. Now it was open. And yet the struggle to define the truth and unveil the other's deceptions continued.

My latest fieldwork in 2015 and 2016 has been in the capital of neighboring Rwanda, the destination of twenty thousand fleeing Burundian refugees in 2015. These were mostly middle-class, urban Tutsi who had felt targeted by the regime in the wake of the 2015 violence, either because they lived in the areas of the capital city, Bujumbura, where the anti-third term demonstrations had taken place or because they were journalists, human rights activists, or members of opposition parties. They were experiencing a very different media landscape than the refugees I had met more than a decade earlier. Rather than a small group of political entrepreneurs controlling the information from exile, information was moving much faster in all directions via social media on mobile phones inside the country and abroad (Turner and Berckmoes 2020).

Unearthing the Secrets of Power

Meanwhile, the government seemed unprepared for the media war. In May 2015, the police looted and burned the premises of several independent radio stations, and most journalists went into hiding or fled abroad. By July 2015 more than eighty Burundian journalists had left the country, most of them settling in Rwanda (Frère 2017).

With the destruction of the independent broadcasting sector in Burundi (Frère 2016), Burundians inside the country and abroad turned to social media for communication on the crisis. The government attempted clumsily to block the use of Twitter and WhatsApp but people simply dodged the system with other VPNs (Vircoulon 2016). Social media were used to maintain contact with people in other locations, to share information about dangers in particular areas, as well as to speculate about developments in the political domain (Vircoulon 2016).

Burundians have experienced a large growth in use of and access to social media. In 2000, 0.1 percent of the population were internet users. This figure rose to 1.1 percent in 2011 and 5.5 percent in 2017.[14] Similarly, the number of mobile phone subscriptions rose from 64,000 in Burundi in 2003 to 5.92 million in 2017.[15] In December 2017, there were 450,000 registered Facebook subscribers in Burundi.[16] Furthermore, news that is received via social media may be shared with many more people (Paviotti 2019: 353). For Burundians in the diaspora, this rise in the use of mobile phones and internet users inside the country meant that connections with family and friends could be re-established and intensified, as Facebook, WhatsApp, and Viber, among others, enabled cheap, direct communication.[17] I have been fortunate to have followed the use of online platforms among Burundians in exile from the beginning of the twenty-first century and hence see the changes.[18] It can be argued that the increased reliance on social media marked the beginning of a new era where information was no longer in the hands of an elite, as it was at the beginning of the twenty-first century, because most Burundians inside and outside Burundi had access to the internet and a phone with a camera (Frère 2016). However, as Jean-Benoît Falisse and Hugues Nkengurutse (2019) argue, despite the supposed flattening and two-way nature of the social media, they remain dominated by a small group of "influencers." This is especially the case for Twitter accounts where most tweets are in English or French rather than Kirundi or Swahili (2019: 182), indicating that the intended audience is international (Dimitrakopoulou and Boukala 2018: 132). Furthermore, there are profiles on Twitter that have tens of thousands of followers making them more of a one-way media than a platform of equal exchange as we see with WhatsApp and Facebook.

It is important to keep in mind that only few Burundians use Twitter and that much of the social media sharing happens on an everyday basis when friends and families share news and views. This news can be personal, like when your sister sends you a WhatsApp message that her son is in prison and can you please help by sending money for a bribe or by calling your childhood friend who is now the local head of police. It can also be news that is shared like gossip.

Politicians, journalists, and other professionals still play a role, yet they have to play it differently. For instance, some journalists in exile in Rwanda were able to create alternative media outlets with radio programs such as *Inzamba* and *Humura Burundi*, which are disseminated through social media networks and supported by European donors. Other journalists became activists who started to share their views on blogs, following different professional rules than they would have as journalists. Similarly, journalists in Burundi are struggling to carry out their profession in the radio and newspaper outlets that remain or have been newly established (Frère 2017).

SOS Médias Burundi is an example of this. In the "about" section of its Facebook page, SOS Médias Burundi writes (in French):

> On 13 and 14 May 2015, during a failed coup, radio studios were attacked, looted, and burned down. Journalists and facilitators were chased away from their workplaces. Threatened, some chose to flee the country whereas others hid to escape violence. A few [journalists] continued

> to work by offering coverage of the events on Facebook, Twitter, and Soundcloud. This social network is called "SOS Médias Burundi" (SOS MBDI). This initiative is the work of journalists, civil society actors in Bujumbura and the diaspora and friends of Burundi.[19]

With 57,000 Facebook followers and 54,300 Twitter followers as of December 2020, SOS Médias Burundi has worked to provide an alternative news source for Burundians. From July 2016 to August 2017, SOS Médias Burundi's Twitter @SOSMediasBDI had been mentioned 33,580 times, reaching over 6.1 million accounts.

In the years after the 2015 crisis, SOS Médias Burundi posted frequently, often several times a day. Some posts contain graphic content, with Burundians covered in blood and bruises. They also post links to lengthier articles as well as short announcements with only the details of what happened and to whom. Their Facebook page is filled with arrest announcements, often concluding with "no excuse for the arrest was given."

According to the founder of SOS Médias Burundi, it is paramount that they verify their news with old-school news principles. "What you'll get at SOS: no propaganda, no rumors, no support of opposition or government. We do our job."[20] This is reflected in the very factual posts where there are no long speculations or analyses; simply photos, names, and dates. Their aim is to bear witness to the activities that the regime tries to hide.

Meanwhile, individual activists are also very active online and attract massive numbers of followers. Teddy Mazina is an example. He started as a photographer and later became an activist, documenting what he saw in Burundi. This forced him to flee to Europe when the threats from the regime became too intense. He decided to set up a Twitter headquarters in a one-bedroom flat in an occupied building where he and a friend have twelve-hour shifts—but they both use his name in the tweets.[21] As of December 2020, he has more than 14,000 followers on Facebook and 54,000 on Twitter.

Every time he learns of an arrest or a disappearance from his network of informants in Burundi, he posts names, dates, places and preferably photos—tagging various international presidents and UN officials. He is in effect acting as a witness, giving testimony and making sure that those who have the power to act, "see" what is going on. By tagging important international actors, he is forcing them to "see" and to witness the injustices that he unveils. Teddy Mazina and SOS Médias Burundi claim that the Burundian government is breaching basic human rights and committing injustices against the Burundian population, and that the authorities are doing their best to cover their tracks. The primary task for these journalist/activists is therefore to document these crimes and bring them to light. By doing so, they claim that they can combat the cryptopolitics of the regime. For this to work, however, they also need an audience: hence the tagging of important "others." The journalists in exile and others sharing information on social media are trying to unearth and uncover the secret, hidden, dark sides of the regime—the sides that the president and his advisors prefer not to be seen. The basic message is that you should not believe what President Pierre Nkurunziza and his advisor, Willy Nyamitwe, are saying because they are hiding their true misdeeds. Therefore, much of the information being shared on Twitter, WhatsApp, and other platforms is about documenting—bringing into the light—and revealing cryptopolitics. By revealing this to important international actors—hence the tagging of these—his intention is to unveil the deceit of the regime and hence delegitimize it.

Social media may also be used at a very different level for the same purpose. An example is Reverien whom I met in Kigali in 2016. His story is long and painful, and I am not doing it justice by shortening it here, but it illustrates how hiding and revealing were central to his strategy of survival when avoiding the secret service. At one point he was arrested by unknown men, beaten, given an injection that made him sleep, and taken to a dark house in the forests. When he woke up, he realized that he still had his phone on him and quickly sent messages to two contacts via WhatsApp, immediately deleting the messages again. His friend shared this information on Reverien's Facebook profile and within hours the message had "become hot" as he expressed it. In the meantime, he was beaten, interrogated, and left in the dark room, and he could hear his abductors discuss his execution. Then he heard his abductors receiving phone calls and discussing heatedly what to do. Finally, they gave him another injection, and next thing he knows, he woke up on the side of the road in Bujumbura. His life was saved because he was able to witness the secret violence of the regime and tell the world about it via social media. If they had killed him, they would have proven him right in his accusations. Cryptopolitics plays two ways, however. On the one hand, the state is vulnerable to the kind of revelation that Reverien made possible with his WhatsApp message. On the other hand, its strength depends on people "knowing" that it is capable of committing such secret violence. The violence of the state—its cryptopolitics—must remain a "public secret" (Taussig 1999).

At the beginning of the first decade of the twenty-first century, the Burundian opposition—often in the diaspora—were also busy unearthing the hidden truths of the regime. However, they did so through long-winding conspiratorial analyses of Burundi's history, unveiling diabolic conspiracies that involved the Vatican, France, Belgium, and regional leaders. In the words of Kathleen Stewart, quoted in the beginning of this chapter, "the internet was made for conspiracy theory . . . one thing leads to another" (Stewart in Vine and Carey 2017: 56). On these websites, links were made—both literally through the use of hyperlinks that took the reader deeper into myriad connections, often going in circles, and figuratively, as signs, words, phrases and actions were read as omens and inserted into speculations about large plans to exterminate the Hutu/Tutsi (Turner 2008a). I have also heard these conspiracy theories told by Burundian individuals in Tanzania, Kenya, Belgium, and Denmark. However, when transmitted orally they retain a sense of being ephemeral and temporary. The links that are made are tentative rather than absolute, allowing them to change. The websites of Burundi-sites.com and others made them somehow "stick" and become more real.

The strategy of Teddy Mazina and SOS Médias Burundi is very different. They also want to unearth the secret, hidden truths of the regime and subvert its narrative. But rather than analyze possible causes and speculate on connections, they simply bring facts to the table: photos of maimed bodies, names, documents, and dates. These appear as indisputable facts that cannot be denied or explained away. They demand a response from their viewers whether they are international human rights organizations, the African Union, or members of the Burundian government. Mazina makes this link even more clear by tagging the actors that in his mind should witness his posts.

In sum, I claim that the internet sites of the beginning of the twenty-first century were run by a handful of individuals, often based in Belgium, Denmark, or Switzerland, who interpreted events in Burundi and presented ideologically shaped narratives that were mostly consumed by those with the same understanding of the situation. By contrast, the recent events in Burundi are shared "undigested." Those who share them make a point out of not interpreting them and feeding them into a narrative but rather letting them "speak for themselves," only adding facts such as time, date, place, photographic evidence, and names, leaving it up to the viewer to make sense of them. My point is that they become "real" in the process and that they interpellate the viewer. They cannot be ignored and demand some kind of (re-)action.

While this is an efficient means of revealing cryptopolitics because it proves the flaws of the regime's narrative, it is also an emotionally challenging strategy for those who witness. I encountered several Burundians in Kigali who had a hard time receiving pictures of maimed bodies because they felt that they should do something while they also felt that they were unable to make a difference. In some cases, they attempted to avoid the constant flow of information coming from Burundi in order to protect themselves. We have called them "reticent diasporas" (Turner and Berckmoes 2020), and they show why simply uncovering the truth is not always a desirable option. Living in and with cryptopolitics is a balancing act between veiling and unveiling. Just as deception can be both treacherous and cautious, unearthing deception can be both empowering and hurtful.

Ubgenge and Social Media

With the new importance of social media, information has become instant, multidirectional, and a site for conflicting parties to clash and mobilize people for their cause. On the one hand, opposition groups, activists, and journalists—inside and, in particular, outside the country—are doing their best to discredit the regime by revealing all its clandestine deeds. On the other hand, the regime in place is striking back via the same media, trying to delegitimize the opposition. The president's advisor, Willy Nyamitwe, has been actively defending the regime and undermining the opposition on Twitter. Nyamitwe has, as of 14 December 2020, over 113,400 followers and has tweeted 41,400 times. In the year from 8 May 2016 to 6 June 2017, @willynyamitwe was mentioned 141,400 times. He often enters online discussions and challenges his opponents on Twitter, and he openly threatens journalists, accusing them of being traitors who spread rumors about the president (Dimitrakopoulou and Boukala 2018: 140).

In November 2016, the International Federation of Human Rights (FIDH) launched a Twitter campaign with the hashtag #StopThisMovie. It linked to what resembled a trailer for a fictive movie called *Genocide in Burundi: The Only Movie You Don't Want to See* with scenes of terrified children running along red earth paths accompanied by ominous music. Shortly afterward, Willy Nyamitwe launched a countercampaign, using the hashtag #ThisIsMyGenocide. Andrea Purdeková argues that such campaigns are about playing on anticipation and fear of an imminent danger of genocide, drawing on a register of memories from Rwanda and Burundi (2019). We may see this as an example of the ways both sides are accusing the other of concealing the truth. At a deeper level, we see how they are able to draw on a number of anxieties about possible futures, based on memories of past violence.

Where SOS Médias Burundi and Teddy Mazina use social media to expose the hidden cryptopolitics of the regime by posting what appear to be irreducible truths—bodies, names, documents—#StopThisMovie uses a radically different strategy to warn against the hidden truths of the regime. It provides no details whatsoever and instead hints through its aesthetics at memories of previous mass violence, stoking anticipations of potentially catastrophic futures. As Purdeková notes, the movie clip "mirrors" the genocide in Rwanda in 1994, ignoring the fact that this took place in another country and in another political context. Through this mirroring, it also points toward possible future disasters, creating what Purdeková calls a sense of imminence. There is a sense that this is a country on the brink (Purdeková 2019). The hashtag #StopThisMovie works to mobilize emotions of fear and anxiety, linking them to memories of past violence. This is a very different strategy to the ones of SOS Médias Burundi and Teddy Mazina who stick to "facts." It sounds out the hidden truths of the regime through emotions and memories, claiming that there are undercurrents that have links to the violence of 1993.

Nyamitwe's response was to simply post small videoclips of people dancing, having fun on speedboats on the lake and other quotidian, happy forms of being together. Below these videoclips he added the hashtag #ThisIsMyGenocide, insinuating that the FIDH had no clue about the reality on the ground in Burundi. In general, the government response has been to portray Burundi as a country that is peaceful where life goes on as usual. Along with these posts are direct or indirect accusations that the idea of violence and crisis is made up by Europeans and by Burundians in the diaspora and has nothing to do with reality on the ground. It is worth noting that almost half of the accounts using the hashtag #StopThisMovie were based in France with less than 7 percent based in Burundi, while 67 percent of the users of #ThisIsMyGenocide were based in Burundi.

In sum, attempts to uncover the hidden "underneath" of the Burundian regime, and to reveal the truth about its intentions, have taken place on the internet for decades. However, it seems that there has been a shift away from elaborate conspiracy theories to a focus on unearthing and documenting the "brutal facts" of the regime, calling on the viewer to witness the hidden, violent side of the regime. When FIDH tried to make a more speculative account, appealing to fears and anticipation, it might have backfired, at least inside the country when the presidential spokesperson launched a counter campaign. This campaign was however, delegitimized by some of the important Twitter activists when they once again linked it to concrete names and bodies, thereby trying to subvert the government claim that everything is business as usual.

Trying to Remain Invisible to the Eye of the State

In situations of open violence, the underneath spills over into the visible world of words and actions. Violence is committed against bodies, which leaves marks and traces that cannot be denied. My interlocutors almost preferred these moments where "true intentions" saw the light of day over the long periods where conflict was hidden, and intentions were secret. This was the case of the selective genocide in 1972 and the ethnic violence in 1993. In the case of the 2015 crisis, violence also emerged but the regime still tried to hide it. I was told that the militia and the secret service would arrive in the *quartiers contestataires* at night in cars without numberplates and with no headlights. People were abducted and taken to secret facilities for torture and interrogation, their bodies dumped in communal graves or in ditches across the city.

Nobody knows who is in danger of being arrested, beaten or killed. But people are busy making theories about this. Basically, it is claimed that young people—in particular men but also women—are targeted, because they were most active in the demonstrations. People from the *quartiers contestataires* are also targeted, they claim. Finally, individuals who are journalists, human rights activists, or members of opposition parties are targeted. The Burundian refugees with whom I talked in Kigali had to navigate in relation to these assumed patterns of regime violence. This meant that they had to make themselves invisible or unrecognizable to the authorities and the militias as they navigated their way through and out of the city, playing a game of hide and seek in quite literal terms. Young people would not take the direct bus from Bujumbura to Kigali—a trip of roughly four hours—but take several buses, sometimes even via Congo, often taking days. Jean-Paul is a young man I met in Kigali in 2015. He had lived in Mutakure, which is one of the problematic parts of Bujumbura, and when he left on his own, he took a bus to Kivu in DRC (Democratic Republic of the Congo) and from there to Rwanda. As the bus was leaving Bujumbura, he was stopped at a roadblock and ordered to leave the bus because they could see in his papers that he was from Mutakure. Fortunately, other passengers intervened, and he was able to stay on board. One strategy to avoid being spotted was to get an ID from another part of the country. Another strategy was to get a passport, because it does not list one's address. The problem with passports, they claim, is that you get a stamp each time you cross the border. Reverien, whom we met earlier and who was abducted and almost killed, had previously had problems at roadblocks because he had many stamps in his passport and had to explain that this was due to his work at the airport. This was partly true, although he no longer worked at the airport and had fled to Kigali with his wife and children.

Not only identity papers but also bodies give away truths about individuals. Truths that they might prefer to hide from the regime. Because Mutakure and other *quartiers contestataires* are historically Tutsi neighborhoods, the police may suspect anyone who looks "Tutsi" of being from these areas and hence a rebel. And while many Tutsi and Hutu look alike, some individuals have classic Tutsi looks that can play against them in these tense situations of trying to hide from the authorities. The militia, manning the roadblocks use these visual signs—the ID card and phenotypes—in their attempts to sound out who is an enemy of the state and who can be allowed to pass.

Another way for the police to identify the true identity and intentions of those they suspect of being "rebels" is to control people's mobile phones to see whether the owner follows known critical figures or organizations—such as Teddy Mazina and SOS Médias Burundi. As a counter strategy, people would erase their WhatsApp accounts and remove their contacts from their phones before traveling outside the capital. One Burundian man in Kigali told me that it was better to install fake WhatsApp and Twitter accounts where they follow uncontentious stories or pro-government personalities. This man displays great skills in the art of veiling and unveiling his intentions.

The skills of sounding out and the emotional management involved often took more subtle forms and could seep into relationships between neighbors as well. We saw this in the case of Josephine's childhood friend and neighbor who asked her where she lived and how she made a living. And we saw it when my research assistant would visit her family farm but not stay the night.

In the game of cryptopolitics in the African Great Lakes, it is not just the state—or other political actors—trying to hide their true intentions and activists and ordinary citizens trying to uncover these intentions. The authorities are similarly trying to unveil the true identity of its citizens who are doing their best to hide their identities—or rather, they are trying to hide certain aspects and paint another picture of themselves. A picture that might not bring danger upon them.

Conclusions

The ability to control and conceal information, intentions, and emotions gives access to political power, according to common understanding in Burundi. The result is that politics is never taken at face value and that whatever is stated always has an underneath. Therefore, politics in Burundi is about trying to second-guess what people "really mean" and what the ulterior motives are of this or that statement or action. I have used the concept "sounding out" to capture the subtle ways actors try to unveil the intentions of others without revealing their own intentions in the process.

Sounding out and the art of concealment are not just concerned with facts. They are equally about emotions. It is important to hide one's emotions in order to achieve one's goals. While this may put someone in a superior position, it may also be used by the dominated, as when Josephine hides her fear and repulsion and gives the young man, who has the power to put her in prison, her phone number. However, hiding the truth can also be a means to protect the emotions of both parties, as when family members do not tell their kin about the difficulties that they are in. Often people avoid talking about certain historical events if they do not know what side their interlocutors were on during a particular event. Finally, the game of cryptopolitics—of sounding out—can create emotional strain, leading some people to simply avoid the field altogether, like when they stop using WhatsApp and Twitter.

Against this hidden, secret violence, activists and journalists attempt to make the victims visible by bringing pictures of their maimed bodies, ID cards with names and photos and the date of their disappearance. All this is meant to bear witness to the violence of the regime and make visible its cryptopolitics—its hidden underneath.

When I explored how the conflict played out in cyberspace almost twenty years ago, the diasporas in Europe and North America—at first Hutu but increasingly also Tutsi—were busy on various websites fighting a war of words. They would create and reproduce grand conspiracies about Hima empires and Hutu genocidal ideologies, involving the Vatican, Belgium, France, and most regional leaders. They would bear witness to the various types of violence that the people of Burundi had experienced, and they would immerse these accounts into large schemes. While some of these sites still exist and continue to create grand conspiracy theories,[22] much of the activity on today's social media is about documenting the violence with pictures and names. Perhaps it is the instantaneous and multidirectional character of social media that promotes such fast, short updates. In terms of unearthing the "truth" about the power in place, it finds its legitimacy not in lengthy exposés of possible conspiratorial links but in the authenticity of bodies and names as facts that cannot be brushed away and denied. They demand answers of the onlooker, creating emotional strain at times. They do not go away and cannot be solved by excuses. In one sense they follow the art of cryptopolitics because they sound out the other while keeping their own intentions opaque. In other senses, they transgress the rules of cryptopolitics because they so bluntly state the facts.

Social media are a means to unveil the cryptopolitics of the regime. But they are also dangerous, because the regime may use these networks to unveil the unveiling. In the game of hide and seek that has always characterized politics in Burundi, digital media are a strong means to try to destabilize both the sovereign and the subject—revealing true identities that are best kept hidden. Therefore, both the sovereign and the subject are desperately trying to cover their tracks or even better to create new, fake identities.

Simon Turner is a professor of social anthropology at Lund University.

Notes

1. A number of scholars argued in the late 1990s that such witchcraft rumors can be linked to neoliberal exploitation and what the Comaroffs call the "casino economy" in Africa (Comaroff and Comaroff 1999; Geschiere 1997; White 2000).
2. Hutu would most often use the ethnic terms while Tutsi would prefer to talk about peasants. Often "peasants" (or "poor people," "uneducated people") was used a euphemism for Hutu. This speaks to a large political tension that dates back to the time of independence at least. Very shortly and crudely put: On the one side, the Hutu used their ethnic identity to claim emancipation from centuries of feudal rule by the Tutsi. On the other side, the Tutsi argued that ethnicity was invented by the Belgians in order to divide and rule the country and claimed national unity to combat colonial rule.
3. Speech translates as *imvuga*, from the verb *kuvuga* (to speak, to discuss, and to claim). The art of speech, as we shall see below is often related to the term *ubgenge/ubwenge.*
4. *Ubgenge* (sometimes written as *ubwenge*) is translated as wisdom, knowledge, sense, intelligence, and consciousness. The concept has been the subject of various scholarly and political debates. In his most recent book, Rene Lemarchand calls it "a sort of street-smart knack to tell lies and get away with it" (Lemarchand 2021: 129). Pierre Erny claims that *ubgenge* "désigne l'intelligence, la ruse, la débrouillardise, le fait d'être malin" (refers to intelligence, cunning, resourcefulness and being smart) (Erny 2003).

5. I might add that along with the colonial stereotype of the deceitful Tutsi native, there is a corresponding colonial stereotype, namely, the happy-go-lucky native. In this case it is the hard-working, honest but gullible Hutu.
6. There are many parallels to the world of witchcraft and witchcraft accusations, so nicely explored by Peter Geschiere among others. He shows how witchcraft emerges in the uncertainty of the most intimate relations. The fear of betrayal among kin is larger than any betrayal. While I rarely came across witchcraft in Burundi, the vulnerable sociality of mistrust and the risk of accusations are similar (Geschiere 1997).
7. To sound out: "to try to find out the opinions of someone by asking questions." This very much explains what is going on. "Sound out." *Merriam-Webster.com Dictionary*. Retrieved 14 January 2023 from https://www.merriam-webster.com/dictionary/sound%20out.
8. ARIB. "Kaz-Bienvenue." Retrieved 14 January 2023 from www.arib.info.
9. AG News (Africa Generation News). "Recent News." Retrieved 14 January 2023 from www.burundi-agnews.org. The site was created in 1994 and was formerly called www.burundi-sites.com.
10. BBC News. 2015. "Burundians Celebrate as Journalist Bob Rugurika Freed." BBC News, 19 February. Retrieved 14 January 2023 from https://www.bbc.com/news/world-africa-31535621.
11. Not his real name.
12. For a discussion on anticipation and anxiety around the recent crisis, see Turner (2020).
13. They were more aesthetically pleasing than the ragtag rebel groups of Hutu peasants in the hills in the 1990s. While such rebel groups also have a certain exotic appeal, they are not likely to attract the sympathy of Western viewers to the same degree as middle-class Tutsi youth in jeans and clean T-shirts, waving banners with creative slogans.
14. Internet World Stats. 2017. "Burundi." *Internet World Stats.* Retrieved 14 January 2023 from https://internetworldstats.com/af/bi.htm.
15. ITU Statistics. "Statistics: Individuals Using the Internet." ITUWRC. Retrieved 14 January 2023 from https://www.itu.int/en/ITU-D/Statistics/Pages/stat/default.aspx.
16. Internet World Stats, "Burundi."
17. Elsewhere I have explored the emotional strain of being constantly online and in touch with the conflict while in exile (Berckmoes and Turner 2021; Turner and Berckmoes 2020).
18. For a fascinating study of such developments in Eritrea, see (Bernal 2014).
19. https://www.facebook.com/pg/sosmediasburundi/about/?ref=page_internal
20. Quoted from Julia Steers. 2016. "How Burundi's Activist Journalists Fill a News Void Using Facebook and Whatsapp." *Quartz*, 23 February. Retrieved 14 January 2023 from qz.com/622660/how-burundis-activist-journalists-fill-a-news-void-using-facebook-and-whatsapp/
21. Ibid.
22. See, for instance, AGnews (burundi-agnews.org). This organization also existed at the beginning of the twenty-first century and continues to disseminate very ethnicized theories about international plots against the president and the Hutu people.

References

Albert, Ethel M. 1964. "'Rhetoric,' 'Logic,' and 'Poetics' in Burundi: Culture Patterning of Speech Behavior." *American Anthropologist* 66(6): 35–54.

Berckmoes, Lidewyde, and Simon Turner. 2021. "Pursuing Futures Through Children: Crisis, Social Reproduction, and Transformation in Burundi's Transnational Families." *Migration Studies* 9(3): 1399–417. https://doi.org/10.1093/migration/mnab004.

Bernal, Victoria. 2014. *Nation as Network: Diaspora, Cyberspace, and Citizenship.* Chicago: The University of Chicago Press.

Carey, Matthew. 2017. *Mistrust.* Chicago: HAU Books.

Chrétien, J.-P. 2003. *The Great Lakes of Africa: Two Thousand Years of History.* New York: Zone Books.

Comaroff, Jean, and John Comaroff. 1999. "Occult Economies and the Violence of Abstraction: Notes from the South African Postcolony." *American Ethnologist* (26): 279–303.

Dimitrakopoulou, Dimitra, and Salomi Boukala. 2018. "Exploring Democracy and Violence in Burundi: A Multi-Methodical Analysis of Hegemonic Discourses on Twitter." *Media, War & Conflict* 11(1): 125–48. https://doi.org/10.1177/1750635217727311

Erny, Pierre. 2003. "*Ubgenge*: Intelligence et ruse à la manière rwanda et rundi" [*Ubgenge*: Intelligence and cunning in the Rwandan and Rundi way]. *Cahiers de sociologie* économique *et culturelle* 40: 73–86.

Falisse, Jean-Benoît, and Hugues Nkengurutse. 2019. "From FM Radio Stations to Internet 2.0 Overnight: Information, Participation and Social Media in Post-Failed Coup Burundi." In *Social Media and Politics in Africa,* ed. M. Dwyer and T. Molony, 173–95. London: Zed Books.

Feldman, Allen. 1995. "Ethnographic States of Emergency." In *Fieldwork under Fire,* ed. Carolyn Nordstrom and Antonius Robben and, 224–52. Berkeley: University of California Press.

Ferme, Mariane C. 2001. *The Underneath of Things, Violence, History, and the Everyday in Sierra Leone.* Berkeley: University of California Press.

Frère, Marie-Soleil. 2009. "After the Hate Media: Regulation in the DRC, Burundi and Rwanda. *Global Media and Communication* 5(3): 327–52. https://doi.org/10.1177/1742766509348675.

———. 2016. "Silencing the Voice of the Voiceless: The Destruction of the Independent Broadcasting Sector in Burundi." *African Journalism Studies* 37(1): 137–46. https://doi.org/10.1080/23743670.2015.1092455.

———. 2017. "'I wish I could be the journalist I was, but I currently cannot': Experiencing the impossibility of journalism in Burundi." *Media, War & Conflict 10*(1): 3–24. https://doi.org/10.1177/1750635217698334.

Geschiere, P. 1997. *The Modernity of Witchcraft: Politics and the Occult in Postcolonial Africa: Sorcellerie et politique en Afrique— la viande des autres.* Charlottesville: University Press of Virginia.

Grant, Andrea M. 2015. "Quiet Insecurity and Quiet Agency in Post-Genocide Rwanda." *Etnofoor* 27(2): 15–36. http://www.jstor.org/stable/43656017.

Ingelaere, Bert. 2009a. "'Does the Truth Pass Across the Fire without Burning?' Locating the Short Circuit in Rwanda's Gacaca Courts." *Journal of Modern African Studies* 47(4): 507–28. https://doi.org/10.1017/s0022278x0999005x

———. 2009b. “Living the Transition: Inside Rwanda’s Conflict Cycle at the Grassroots.” *Journal of Eastern African Studies* 3(3): 438–63. https://doi.org/10.1080/17531050903273735.

Lemarchand, Rene. 1996. *Burundi: Ethnic Conflict and Genocide.* Washington, DC: Woodrow Wilson Center Press.

———. 2007. “Consociationalism and Power Sharing in Africa: Rwanda, Burundi, and the Democratic Republic of the Congo.” *African Affairs* 106(422): 1–20.

Malkki, Liisa H. 1995. *Purity and Exile: Violence, Memory, and National Cosmology among Hutu Refugees in Tanzania.* Chicago: University of Chicago Press.

Mbembé, J. Achille. 2001. *On the Postcolony.* Berkeley: University of California Press.

Nee, Ann, and Peter Uvin. 2010. “Silence and Dialogue: Burundians’ Alternatives to Transitional Justice.” In *Localizing Transitional Justice: interventions and priorities after mass violence,* ed. R. Shaw and L. Waldorf, 157–183. Stanford, CA: Stanford University Press.

Paviotti, Antea. 2019. “Ethnic memory and interactions in periods of crisis: An analysis of Burundi’s Twittersphere” In *Conjonctures de l’Afrique Centrale,* eds S. Geenen, A. N. Bisoko and A. Ansoms, 351-375. Paris: L’Harmattan.

Purdeková, Andrea. 2019. “StopThisMovie and the Pitfalls of Mass Atrocity Prevention: Framing of Violence and Anticipation of Escalation in Burundi’s Crisis (2015–2017).” *Genocide Studies and Prevention* 13(2): 22–37. https://doi.org/10.5038/1911-9933.13.2.1700.

Russell, Aidan. 2019a. “Euphemism, Censorship, and the Vocabularies of Silence in Burundi.” In *Truth, Silence and Violence in Emerging States,* ed. A. Russell, 63–87. London: Routledge.

———. 2019b. *Politics and Violence in Burundi: The Language of Truth in an Emerging State.* Cambridge: Cambridge University Press.

Street, Annie, Jennifer Smith, and Howard Mollet. 2007. *Consolidating the peace? Views from Sierra Leone and Burundi on the United Nations Peacebuilding Commission,* ActionAid, CAFOD and CARE International. Retrieved on 5 February 2023 from https://gsdrc.org/document-library/consolidating-the-peace-views-from-sierra-leone-and-burundi-on-the-united-nations-peacebuilding-commission-2/

Taussig, Michael. 1999. *Defacement: Public Secrecy and the Labor of the Negative.* Stanford: Stanford University Press.

Turner, Simon. 2002. “Dans l’œil du cyclone: Les réfugiés, l’aide et la communauté internationale en Tanzanie” [In the eye of the storm: Refugees, aid and the international community in Tanzania]. *Politique Africaine* (85): 29–45.

———. 2004. “Under the Gaze of the ‘Big Nations’: Refugees, Rumours and the International Community in Tanzania.” *African Affairs* 103(411): 227–47.

———. 2005. “‘The Tutsi Are Afraid We Will Discover Their Secrets’: On Secrecy and Sovereign Power in Burundi.” *Social Identities* 11(1): 37–55.

———. 2006. “Inside-Outside: Political Transformation in Burundi and its Diaspora.” In AMID Working Paper Series.

———. 2007a. “Corruption, Conspiracy and the Power of Concealment in Burundi’s Political Landscape.” In *Corruption and the Secret of Law: A Legal Anthropological Perspective,* ed. Monique Nuijtens and Gerhard Anders, 125–42. London: Ashgate.

———. 2007b. “The Precarious Position of Politics in Popular Imagination: The Burundian Case.” *Journal of Eastern African Studies* 1(1): 93–107.

———. 2008a. “Cyberwars of Words: Expressing the Unspeakable in Burundi’s Diaspora.” *Journal of Ethnic and Migration Studies* 34(7): 1161–80.

———. 2008b. "The Waxing and Waning of the Political Field in Burundi and its Diaspora." *Ethnic and Racial Studies 31*(4): 742–765. http://dx.doi.org/10.1080/01419870701784505

———. 2009. "Betraying Trust and the Elusive Nature of Ethnicity in Burundi." In *Traitors: Suspicion, Intimacy and the Ethics of State-Building*, ed. Tobias Kelly and Sharika Thiranagama, 110–26. Philadelphia: University of Pennsylvania Press.

———. 2010. *Politics of Innocence: Hutu Identity, Conflict and Camp Life.* Oxford and New York: Berghahn Books.

———. 2020. "Hope against hope: changing emotions in the Burundian crisis." In *The Journal of the Royal Anthropological Institute* 26(4): 715-732.

Turner, Simon, and Lidewyde Berckmoes. 2020. "Reticent Digital Diasporas in Times of Crisis: The Shifting Emotion Work of the Burundian Diaspora." *African Diaspora* 12(1–2): 38–63. https://doi.org/10.1163/18725465-01201001.

Uvin, Peter. 2009. *Life after Violence: A People's Story of Burundi.* New York: Zed Books.

Vigh, Henrik. 2018. "Lives Opposed: Perceptivity and Tacticality in Conflict and Crime." *Social Anthropology* 26(4): 487–501. https://doi.org/10.1111/1469-8676.12545

Vine, Michael, and Matthew Carey. 2017. "Mimesis and Conspiracy: Bureaucracy, New Media and the Infrastructural Forms of Doubt." *Cambridge Anthropology* 35(2): 47–64. http://dx.doi.org/10.3167/cja.2017.350205

Vircoulon, Thierry. 2016. "Burundi turns to WhatsApp as political turmoil brings media blackout". The Guardian. Retrieved 5 February 2023 from https://www.theguardian.com/global-development/2016/jun/14/burundi-turns-to-whatsapp-as-political-turmoil-brings-media-blackout.

West, Harry G., and Todd Sanders. 2003. *Transparency and Conspiracy: Ethnographies of Suspicion in the New World Order.* Durham, NC: Duke University Press.

White, Luise. 1993. "Cars Out of Place: Vampires, Technology, and Labor in East and Central Africa." *Representations* 43: 27–50. https://doi.org/10.2307/2928731.

———. 2000. *Speaking with Vampires: Rumor and History in Colonial Africa.* Berkeley: University of California Press.

CHAPTER 3

Digital (Dis)order, Twitter Hashtags, and the Performance of Politics in Kenya

George Ogola

Social media platforms such as WhatsApp, Facebook, Snapchat, and Twitter have gradually become indispensable platforms for everyday communication. In Kenya, precisely because of their relative ubiquity, they are increasingly facilitating new everyday practices and slowly assuming significant cultural and political agency (Ogola 2019). It is perhaps germane to note that in Kenya, the production and circulation of information have generally been attended by various economies of control, often part of a much broader strategy by successive governments to "husband" or protect power. The control of information and its enabling infrastructures have been particularly pertinent in the manufacturing of political legitimacy, usually lacking for the most part. We may draw on Victoria Bernal's (2014) notion of "infopolitics" to explain this regime of information management but more importantly, how this is subsequently resisted through various digital political performances by the public. I refer here particularly to the emerging digital practices largely defined by their ambiguity, "techniques of evasion" (Bayart 1993), and their use of what James Scott (1990) describes as "hidden transcripts," in their engagement with the state.

This chapter examines how Kenya's online community, commonly referred to as #KOT (Kenyans on Twitter), instrumentalize digital performances to facilitate the creation of new spaces and aesthetics of political practice. The formative part of the chapter briefly explores Kenya's tightly controlled information regime as one of the state's apparatuses for political domination. It then looks at how the growth of Kenya's digital infrastructure and the emergent online digital practices, which manifest as a form of "disorder," are subverting these controls. In the latter part of the chapter, I focus specifically on the micro-blogging site Twitter and how Kenya's digital community #KOT are using it to create new spaces and ways of performing cryptopolitics. It is a practice that extends a familiar popular tradition of "concealment and evasion," shaped in part by the country's history of political suppression.

Infopolitics and Kenya's Digital Transformation

Infopolitics has been a dominant feature of Kenya's postcolonial history. Successive governments have either directly or through proxies, maintained influence or control of the dominant public communication platforms such as the mainstream media (Ogola 2016). By way of illustration, one could point to the case of Kenya's public broadcaster, the Kenya Broadcasting Corporation (KBC), which has, since the country's independence in 1964, operated primarily as a state broadcaster, faithfully beholden to the interests of the governing political party. Although by law a public broadcaster, KBC long reneged on this role. Successive administrations have also maintained their grip on the private media sector by deliberately undermining the spirit of media liberalism by operating a licensing regime that often only benefits those with whom they can transact political business. Several media owners are, therefore, one way or another, part of the dominant ruling class hence facilitate government media influence. In the few cases where this is not possible, the government has resorted to withholding state advertising to media organizations deemed too critical. This is significant because the state remains the single largest source of advertising revenue in Kenya (Ogola 2019).

It is within this context of state control that we should locate the rapid proliferation, adoption, and the resulting significance of new digital media practices in Kenya over the last ten years. It is arguable that social media has disrupted some of the older economies of information control. Social media has incubated a different information regime partly unencumbered by the older forms of control, thereby providing, however nominal, multiple opportunities for the growth of a new, even potentially transformative aesthetics of political practice.

I make this point about the disruptive role of social media while acknowledging that these platforms are simultaneously enabling new forms of control. We need to recognize that social media are part of a broader national and international economic and political infrastructure primed to advance provincial corporate interests (Srinivasan, Diepeveen, and Karekwaivanane 2016). These interests invariably mean that exclusions do occur. One may of course recall Michel Foucault's (1982) cautionary note about the dialectical relationship between new media technologies and the participatory practices these technologies enable. To borrow the words of Lilie Chouliaraki (2010: 227), Foucault characterized this relationship as a dual economy of freedom and constraint hence the concepts "democratization of technology" and the "technologization of democracy." In the latter, he pointed out that technologies have their inherent economies of control, enabling the reproduction of the existing power asymmetries they apparently seek to destabilize. Indeed, one cannot ignore the structural and material conditions that limit popular participation on social media platforms. Popular participation is undermined by limitations of access, affordability, and digital literacy.

It is equally important to note that research on the impact of digital/social media platforms in Sub-Saharan Africa have been relatively instrumental in approach. With few exceptions, social media has largely been assigned a singular role—facilitation of progressive politics in Africa. Tim Markham (2014) observes that many scholars thus expect social media to "birth" revolutions, for example, when such "expectations" are not realized, social media are rendered lacking meaningful political agency (see Fenton and Barresi 2011). I want to argue that while it is true that social media use in Kenya has changed the way Kenyans communicate and organize politically and socially, this is not something that necessarily inheres in the technology. Instead, I argue that the significance and popularity of social media platforms in the country is because they have been able to successfully acculturate and reconfigure older forms and traditions of social and political communication and practices to interpret and intervene in the present. In a study on how an administrative chief in Nakuru, a town in Kenya, used Twitter rather than the traditional *baraza* (local open-air meetings organized and presided over by local chiefs primarily to promote government policies) to engage locals in his administrative unit, Dan Omanga, for example, argues that social media in this case "expanded both the spatial and temporal aspects of the *baraza*" (2015: 1), transforming it into a new deliberative space. The chief used Twitter to address his constituents, respond to their questions, and to discuss government policies. It is therefore analytically profitable to pay more attention to these processes of reconfigurations of old communicative practices. Indeed, as Patrick Chabal and Jean-Pascal Daloz (2010) note, to understand change, we should always focus on the continuities and historicity of what is changing.

Social media's (political) significance in Kenya therefore lies not in their capacity or potential to facilitate mass political movements or force structural institutional changes. Instead, it is in their transformative character as sites of the everyday, capturing the quotidian, both serious and the mundane, revealing daily existential anxieties, organizing publics around ordinary issues, and providing spaces for direct engagement with the state and its agents by reconfiguring and reconstituting older forms of political expressions and practices. The grand narratives about revolutions or such monumental disruptive impact renders invisible the contexts and complex textures of technological appropriations. These processes are best understood within the realm of the everyday. It is in the everyday practices—in cryptopolitics, in the rumor, the multiple registers, euphemisms, even "fake news," that lay the "hidden transcripts," described by Scott as "the anger and reciprocal aggression denied by the presence of domination" (1990: 16).

The absence of well-formed singular social or political ideas or projects in these spaces, the disorder that so often appears to deny social media platforms coherent agency is precisely the politics of social media. In fact, I argue that the agency of these platforms lay in their users' creative instrumentalization of disorder as political practice. It is difficult to police a narrative that appears so dispersed, fragmented, and confusing.

Instrumentalization of Disorder as Political Practice

The instrumentalization of disorder as political practice is a concept I tease out from Chabal and Daloz's (2010) notion of "disorder as political instrument." I use it as a conceptual tool in discussing how social media users in Kenya are instrumentalizing disorder politically online. "Disorder as political instrument" refers to "the process by which political actors in Africa seek to maximise their returns on the state of confusion, uncertainty, and sometimes even chaos, which characterises most African polities" (2010: 150). Yet Chabal and Daloz remind us that the notion of disorder here does not index dysfunction or "a state of dereliction" (2010: 150). It is, in fact, merely a different order, one that features a number of key characteristics. First, they argue that it is "a reflection of the fuzziness of what constitutes the primary and secondary registers informing politics." Second, "it makes explicit the observation that political action operates rationally, but largely in the realm of the informal, uncodified and unpoliced," and third, "in a world of disorder there is a premium both on the vertical and personalized infra-institutional relations through which the business of politics can be conducted and on access to the means of maximizing the returns which the domestication of such disorder requires" (2010: 150). Theodore Trefon (2004) develops a similar idea in his attempt to retheorize African urbanism by looking at the case of Congo's Kinshasa. He shows how through everyday practices, unregulated, messy, and yet creatively novel local residents are able to cope with the difficult conditions created by Kinshasa's dysfunctional municipal authority. To understand how users instrumentalize disorder as political practice then is to engage with both the infra-institutional uses to which these platforms are put as well as their institutional appropriation by the state and its agents. I will however focus largely on the infra-institutional practices.

My discussion primarily focuses on the political. But my reading of the political is of course broad. In reading the political, I borrow from Natalie Fenton and Veronica Barresi (2011) who argue that our conception of the political should go beyond the narrow confines of politics or of formal institutions (my addition) to simultaneously include the personal, gendered, and the cultural, routinely visible in everyday practices. I argue that social media is generative of individual and individualized political subjectivities and that this is crucial in understanding the politicality of citizens' usage of the platform. Secondly, à la Chabal and Daloz (2010), Achille Mbembe (2001), Karin Barber (1997), and many others, I argue that the political in Africa cannot be limited to the realm of formal institutions and processes. It is conceptually useful to adopt Chabal and Daloz's conception of the political in Africa as functionally fluid, where "boundaries are notoriously porous" and where politics "is not functionally differentiated, or separated from the socio-cultural considerations which govern everyday life," where "[t]here is a constant and dynamic interpenetration of the different spheres of human experiences: from the political to the religious" (2010: 1). The relevance of this interpretation lies in the fact that while the apparently mundane dominate conversations on social media in Kenya, it is also the case that citizens engage the political from a variety of non-political ways. In addition, as Chabal and Daloz observe, there is "a multiplicity of registers according to which individuals participate politically" (2010: 152). Therefore, they note that it is "both judicious and legitimate to switch from one register to another without undue concern for the political contradictions which such behaviours might appear to induce" because "this lack of distinction between various registers is utilized as a resource by those political actors able to do so" (2010: 152). The aim here however is certainly not to "overlook the continued relevance of the professional, institutional and deliberative aspects of politics" (Markham 2014: 92) or to advocate for what Fenton and Barresi (2011) refer to as "a deinstitutionalisation of politics." The case made here is for the relevance of horizontal informal political practices as facilitated by and through social media to be recognized as important political performances and interventions.

The Digital Context in Kenya

The ubiquity of the mobile phone in Kenya, the existence of a largely youthful population, and the relative freedom provided by platforms such as Twitter, Facebook, WhatsApp, Instagram, Telegram, and Snapchat, have made them hugely popular communication tools in the country. Nearly 75 percent of Kenya's population is below the age of thirty-five, which is an estimated 35.7 million according to the country's 2019 population census[1]. The youth (18–34 years old) constitute 29 percent of the population[2] (KNBS 2019). Nearly 80 percent of this group are active social media users[3]. Only 28 percent of young Kenyans reportedly read newspapers regularly with social media increasingly becoming their platform of choice for news and other forms of information. Meanwhile, two out of three young Kenyans now either own a mobile device or have access to one[4].

It is similarly important to note that internet penetration and use in Kenya are significantly higher than the continent's average. According to recent statistics from the Communications Authority of Kenya (CAK), 43 million Kenyans now have access to the internet, mainly through mobile phones. Internet penetration is estimated at nearly 85 percent (CAK 2019). Meanwhile, a study by SIMELab found that more than 8.3 million Kenyans are active on social media with the most used platforms being WhatsApp (89 percent), Facebook (81.7 percent), and Twitter (34 percent) (Wamuyu 2020). Twitter is dominantly used as a platform for civic and political debate in Kenya (Wamuyu 2020), making it especially relevant for this discussion. This political bent has been the subject of various research projects on social media use in the country (see Tully and Ekdale 2015; Ndlela 2014; Ogola 2018; Portland Communications 2016). In this chapter, I am interested in two intersecting "political" issues: the emergence of new as well as the simultaneous reconfiguration of old political practices through Twitter, and much more broadly, the nature of those political practices via the same platform.

Kenyan Twitter users are reputedly among the most active in Africa, coming fourth after Egypt, Nigeria, and South Africa (Portland Communications 2016). As noted earlier, the Kenyan Twitter publics congregate under an amorphous yet easily identifiable group called Kenyans on Twitter, usually referred to as KOT and identified through a common hashtag #KOT. Twitter users use this hashtag when discussing topics where Kenya is their primary reference to index the subject and to encourage participation among KOT. This group is "loud" and oftentimes narratively "unruly" as they discuss issues of shared interest. George Karikwaivanane (2019) identifies a similar characteristic in

Baba Jukwa, a Facebook account that facilitated heated political discussions in the run-up to the 2013 Zimbabwean elections. He describes these publics as characterized by their "heteroglossic qualities, their use of multiple registers, reasoned arguments, diatribe, religiosity and the use of carnivalesque as a mode of expression (2019: 57). He observes that Baba Jukwa "stubbornly denied ZANU-PF's efforts to discipline public debate, a stance which was underscored by the slogan *Tapanduka Zvamuchese* (we have rebelled completely), which was chanted by participants of the debates on the page" (2019: 57).

But as observed earlier, the material and structural realities that both enable and constrain the use of digital media are such that in practice, particular exclusions can occur even in the use of apparently "open and inclusive" platforms such as Twitter. Variable access to the internet, uneven digital literacies, and other economies of use structurally privilege particular voices online just as they do offline. Accordingly, most conversations on KOT timelines are generally scaled up or popularized by a few well-known bloggers, activists, politicians, celebrities, journalists, and mainstream news organizations (Ogola 2019). These individuals and organizations have also become almost by default "primary definers" of what trends on Twitter and seem to have significant impact on which stories go viral and therefore which are picked up, for example, by the mainstream press. This re-ordering of the online space into hierarchies of participation does, of course, have implications for Twitter's claims of horizontal participation.

Yet it is precisely because of this hierarchization of the platform that KOT have adopted alternative discursive political practices and narrative strategies that open up conversations to as broad a public as possible and to encourage participation. Similar to Baba Jukwa, the archive of knowledge, truth, and ways of expression is wildly elastic. Users have the freedom to use various registers, circulate rumors, invoke religion, and prosecute and pass judgments on the state and its agents. There is a conscious appropriation of familiar "ways of speech" and knowing, a preponderance of narrative intertextuality, and the use of popular cultural forms such as satire and humor as strategic "techniques of evasion" (Bayart 1993; See also Street 1997). These strategies creatively adopt and reframe Twitter's standard vernaculars such as hashtags and memes as to make them much more open to political inflections and popular appropriations thus facilitating broad participation. I discuss some of these practices below.

Researching Twitter, of course, presents significant methodological challenges (Bruns and Burgess 2013). Although now a site of increasing scholarly interest, there is no single approach in social media research that has been widely adopted. Twitter datasets are notoriously large, requiring a big financial investment in appropriate analytics software. Other challenges include "the self-selecting nature of social media users, inequalities in access to social media platforms and data, the difficulty of obtaining meaning from heterogeneous data of variable quality and provenance, and a dependence on observing and interpreting what is 'out there' in a way that differs from traditional sampling approaches" (Taylor and Pagliari 2017: 3). This discussion is however more conceptual than empirical and focuses primarily on a close reading of Twitter hashtags as a way of understanding the instrumentalization of disorder as a form of political practice. The hashtags are purposely selected from 2016 to 2020. I focus only on hashtags that trended in Kenya during this period and only those whose focus was primarily political.

Hashtags and the Politics of the Everyday

Subversion through popular cultural forms has traditionally been a defining characteristic of oppositional cultures in Kenya. From popular music to visual art to theater productions, sites of dissent have long existed outside the formal institutional structures. The subversion of the state and its policies particularly through the creative use of humor has been one of the most distinctive features of Kenya's political cultures and the subject of many scholarly works (see Ligaga 2012; Ogola 2010). Kenya's post-independence governments have historically invented a particular majesty of the state, enforced both symbolically through mythologies (Ogola 2010) and through violence. To puncture this majesty, citizens have in the same way invented ways of unraveling this majesty, fundamentally through cryptopolitics, where, for example, humor becomes a powerful stick with which to undress and beat the state. To borrow and paraphrase the words of the Ugandan writer John Ruganda, in Kenya the truth has always been told laughingly (Ruganda 1992: 20). These are traditions that have now been reconstituted and appropriated by KOT in their political instrumentalization of Twitter hashtags.

Hashtags provide several communicative possibilities ranging from facilitating user interactivity, organizing publics around specific issues or debates, to framing debates. In technical terms, hashtags are metadata tags used to index particular topics to make them discoverable by users hence facilitating their virality. On KOT, hashtags commonly draw from the "disorder" that characterizes everyday life. For illustration, I want to use one popular hashtag *#BoraUhai*, arguably one the most famous hashtags that have been used on social media in Kenya for a few years now, but which continues to retain its discursive relevance and agency. I examine the *#BoraUhai* hashtag to demonstrate how Twitter is used as a discursive space for the instrumentalization of conversational "disorder" and how this discursivity informs its politicality.

Bora Uhai is a Kiswahili phrase meaning "so long as there is life" or "as long as life prevails." Although it has a much older history in popular lore, its appropriation in everyday (online) speech can be traced to the relatively recent impact of the gambling industry in Kenya. The phrase was commonly used by punters whenever they lost their money while gambling. Punters used the phrase to wish away their losses, exclaiming that such material loss was incomparable to the gift of life. The appropriation of this phrase online however has seen it invested with a broad range of meanings, both literal and metaphorical, its power and popularity lying precisely in its ambiguity. It is a term that refuses definitional capture and its constructed meanings are as varied as its uses. It is creatively used online to anchor narratives on national politics and to reflect on individual anxieties in equal measure, its narrative possibilities are endless.

The looseness of the discursive boundaries of *#BoraUhai* is typical of such everyday phrases adopted as hashtags on the Kenyan twittersphere. They create a strategic disorder that is conducive to the disruption of hierarchies in online conversations and help in challenging various presumed norms of order. On her Twitter account, @Niwachera, for example, writes, "the Slogan [*bora uhai*] consoles Kenyans emptiness . . . . The trending of this 'Bora Uhai' slogan depicts an underlying serious, psychological problem in Kenyan society! It means a good number have given up on their dreams . . . All they value is being alive to see a day at a time." The phrase here is layered in meaning. It can be interpreted literally but also as a direct indictment of the poor state of the nation and the sense of desperation that has engulfed many Kenyans.

This flexibility in interpretation enables users to adopt the hashtag in anchoring and facilitating multiple discussions; from the expression of individual and collective angst and apparent despair to using it as a shorthand for various narratives of political protestations. These features make it particularly difficult to police. This is an example of how narrative that seems to be in disorder is instrumentalized especially politically. It congregates people around particular issues and creates important pockets of indiscipline. Thus, for example, retweeting a tweet from the Liberian President George Weah following his announcement that tuition fees would be free for all students at the University of Liberia and all other public universities in Liberia, @sonkokelem tweeted: "Some people are lucky to have working leaders in the world, *sisi tu ni borauhai* [trans: for us it is as long as life prevails] #nawekila-wakati [trans: may He [God] be with you all the time]."

Note here that the country's leader is not named but is in fact pointedly inferred by his very absence from the tweet. The subject of the criticism is obvious and particularly coming at a time when a number of university students were struggling to raise university fees or get loans from the state. Such direct comparisons would not have been made in straight news stories in the local media. Twitter users exploit an important strategic narrative style; the use of silences, a notable feature of conversations on KOT. These are what Scott (1990) describes as "strategies of resistance" and what Bayart calls "techniques of evasion and pretence" (1993: 254).

#BoraUhai primarily manifests as a hashtag but functionally does much more. As a hashtag it is used to refuse narrative closure. This is because it is not specific to the discussion of a particular subject or topic. Instead, it is open to appropriation by users to discuss multiple issues, indexing them to congregate publics around such discussions. It is further used to link apparently unrelated stories in a manner that encourages intertextuality. For example, a story about Liberia is used to critique the state in Kenya. Drawing upon experiences and examples from the international circuit both dramatize the criticism and more importantly, lends it legitimacy. In addition, this constructed ambiguity, the fact that the subject of the criticism is not named, protects users from possible state reprisal.

In another example, @dotmusya commenting on the controversial 2018 Finance Bill, a piece of legislation that led to an increase in fuel taxes in the country, writes; "Not much surprised by the turn of events, after all, the loans have to be paid, budget funded and corruption money factored too. #KOT tighten your belts, we will know the real meaning of the phrase *#borauhai* #2018FinanceBill#TaxVoteKe."

This is an open rebuke of the government and the observation that corruption is now endemic, even budgeted for. The writer worries about the level of fiscal indiscipline and hence raises concerns about the inevitable impact of these practices on the lives of Kenyans. The *#borauhai* hashtag in this instance also provides further scope for the discussion with the addition of two other hashtags #2018FinanceBill and #TaxVoteKe. Other users following or participating in these two hashtags are invited to this particular discussion through the *#borauhai* hashtag, broadening the "imagined" public and widening participation.

Following the passing of this bill, Okiya Omatata, a well-known Kenyan political activist, now a member of parliament, who has taken the government to court numerous times, often to the chagrin of the state, Parliament, and the Kenya Law Society went to court. A Kenyan human rights activist based in the United States quickly organized an online fundraiser for Omtata to help him pursue the case. Using the hashtag #OmtataNiWetu, Kenyans were asked to send their contributions to a mobile money number (M-Pesa) included in the hashtag. Hundreds of thousands of Kenyan shillings were raised. @Mwachondahuey thus wrote; "I hope anthropologists are documenting Kenyans in #OmtataNiWetu conversations this #OmtataFriday. The apologists, the naysayers, the #BoraUhai specialists, the #SioUshawiNiMaobi crew, the apologists for the thieves stealing our future. The clueless #UhuRuto and crew." The hashtag #UhuRuto is a contraction of Uhuru and Ruto, the surnames of then Kenya's president and his deputy, now president The textual hybridity in the tweet appears complicated yet is quite easily accessible to Kenyans. Here @Mwachondahuey is expressing the power of Kenya's online community to mobilize not only discursively around national issues such as the 2018 Finance Bill but also to pool together financial resources to fight unfair government policy.

Other notable protest hashtags illustrative of these political practices include #Wanjikuamechoka trans: Wanjiku is tired) and #Punda-mechoka (trans: the donkey is tired often used interchangeably. Wanjiku is a female Kikuyu name (Kenya's most populous ethnic community). The name was however invested with subversive political meaning in the 1990s. During the agitation for constitutional change in Kenya in the 1990s, then President Daniel Moi dismissed the calls for change and popular participation in the constitutional process saying: "Wanjiku haelewi mambo ya constitution. Katiba haitaongezi sufuria ya ugali kwa jikoni ya Wanjiku" (trans: Wanjiku does not understand these things about the constitution. The constitution will not add a pot of ugali to Wanjiku's kitchen). In what was a subversive rebuke to the president, Kenyans began referring to the common wo/man as Wanjiku and around her are now conversations and debates that generally speak against the government. The hashtag #Wanjikuamechoka thus indexes the cries of the common citizen standing up against the tyranny of the state. The hashtag is used to expose and criticize government failings and mobilize common citizens to speak up against government oppression in its various manifestations. For example, @brian_kavuwa writes: "It's no longer important, even if we vote or not, the elites will steal. The best thing for Kenyans is total abstinence toward actual voting. The elites can marshal their relatives to vote for them #wanjikuamechoka." The author of this tweet despairs at the failure of representative politics in Kenya. In another condemnation of the failure of representative politics in the country, @DuniaNiDuara writes, "@StateHouseKenya we are waiting for the Bunge [trans: Parliament] to be dissolved asap. God has a way of saving His people if they repent. He has heard Wanjiku prayers #WanjikuAmechoka thank you." @Classic105Kenya provides similar criticism, writing: "I guess it's a wake-up call to Kenyans that we should not vote for someone coz they are popular or they come from ur tribe. Each and every corrupt individual should go. #Wanjikuamechoka."

Meanwhile, protesting against the tax burden on ordinary Kenyans, @kelvin_ngondi writes: "The debt burden on Wanjiku will soon become unbearable, we cannot continue with the trend of borrowing money to enrich a few corrupt people while the majority remain unemployed and lack the basic needs #WanjikuAmechoka."In support, @koosano writes, "I am tired of paying taxes that then get stolen #WanjikuAmechoka."

As noted above, the hashtag #Wanjikuamechoka is commonly used interchangeably with #Pundaamechoka. Ordinary Kenyans here are metaphorically compared to a donkey, historically the beast of burden. @MukamiWaEmbu writes: "We must #ReduceParliament to have (1) At most 100 MPs, (2) Reduce Constituencies to 100, (3) Scrap off (sic) Women Rep post, (reduce women representatives posts) (4) Reduce Counties to 25, (5) Elect 25 Governors, (6) Elect 50 Senators (2 from each County), (7) Reduce Wards to at most 500. #WageBillFromHell #PundaAmechoka." Meanwhile, @Mutugian_K calls for a revolution against the government, writing: "The only #KenyansForKenya we need is taking to the streets with the Mother of All Demos and show the reality of #JubileeTumechoka and #PundaAmechoka." A similar call is made by @ClariseLizarazu who writes: "When I imagine Uhuru being in power for another 14 years I'm frightened and shaken to the bone #DespotsMustFall #PundaAmechoka."

Criticizing a government housing scheme to which many Kenyans were compelled to contribute to @VitalGideon complains: "A govt that wants to build affordable houses in Kenya using our salaries but can't build enough classes since 1963 #PundaAmechoka."

The collective fury in these hashtags is palpable. The hashtags provide possibilities for engagement with many topics at different levels. But what is perhaps most notable is the fact that they give citizens narrative agency, helping them develop and shape the narrative beyond the closely monitored parameters of such discussions in traditional public communication platforms such as mainstream media.

Twitter Hashtags and Political Performance

We may further draw on Robert Entman's (2004) work on "framing" to understand how hashtags are employed politically by Kenyan Twitter users. For Entman, communication practices are essentially framing exercises. I want to argue that to engage the political, hashtags are increasingly framed performatively by Kenyan users. Two narrative styles are usually adopted. Users frame certain hashtags to emphasize or validate a commonly agreed position (emphasis frames) or deploy a framing strategy that destabilizes a contested position or narrative, what is normally referred to as equivalence frames. Entman argues that "emphasis frames" are "messages constructed in such a way as to help people make a judgement" (Entman 2004: 20), normally encoded in the message. Hashtags framed in this way typically direct the contours and boundaries of a discussion by focusing on the development and validation of a singular narrative or supporting a preferred argument. The scope for the contestation of such a position is minimal. On #KOT, hashtags employing this "emphasis frame" typically focus on the symbols and examples of state failure. The targets of censure are usually state institutions or its sanctioned practices, and the political and economic elite. These hashtags have a pre-determined agenda, emphasized through the affirmation of a statement around which the hashtag is constructed. For illustration we can cite the hashtags discussed above #Pundaamechoka or #Wanjikuamechoka. Another illustrative example is #lipakamatender (trans: pay promptly like a [government] tender), a hashtag that was created during a crippling doctors' strike in Kenya in 2016. The hashtag was framed in support of Kenya's striking doctors. The hashtag mobilized public opinion to force the government to pay doctors their dues. Beneficiaries of government tenders, often individuals with connections to government bureaucrats tend to be paid promptly and generously. The hashtag makes that contradiction quite apparent. Other examples include #systemyamajambazi, #mtuwetunonesense, and similar. In the case of #systemyamajambazi, local slang that loosely means a "system of thieves," there was an implied invitation of users to focus on the predatory nature of the Kenyan state. Through examples, publics convened around the hashtag were not expected to contest the validity of the declaration but rather to provide evidence to confirm that the system is indeed one that thrives on predation. Contributions to the hashtag included the following examples: @isaiahmusindi writes, "#SystemYaMajambazi MPs Cut SRC [Salaries Remuneration Commission] Budget After it Blocked Their 250,000 monthly house allowance."

Commenting on the huge wealth disparities in the country, @KenyanHorn writes: "Jubilee folks contributed billions within two hours to fund its campaign. Why don't they come together now and contribute to help starving Turkana Residents? *Ama wanangoja* [trans: or they are waiting for] 2022 [election year]? #SystemYaMajambazi."

Meanwhile @ColloSalasya criticized government leaders for normalizing a culture of cheating in the country. This was in response to allegations of cheating in the national O-Level examinations of the Kenya Certificate of Secondary Education (KCSE). She thus writes, "If Waiguru and the likes of Mailu [Waiguru and Mailu were former cabinet secretaries] stole NYS and Health money but govt tells us they didn't, yet Kenyans know. These students are only copying their leaders. Kenyan leaders are rotten. What do u expect kids to do if not emulating that #systemyamajambazi #KCSEExamCheating."

When the government decided to employ Cuban doctors at far better salaries than Kenyan doctors, @jumaf complained: "With Sh 10.5B stolen from NYS [National Youth Service] and Sh 1.7B potentially missing from MoH [Ministry of Health], these two ladies are now moving on to "Health Specialists" from Cuba. And then we will all gasp and be horrified when those scandals land. #UhuruAppointees #SystemYaMajambazi #GangstaRegime." In the examples above, the government, its institutions, and the political class are variously criticized through the hashtag #systemyamajambazi.

Hashtags, Discursive Openness, and Political Indiscipline

While "emphasis"-framed hashtags focus attention on the development and validation of a particular argument, the non-declaratory frames or equivalence frames tend to be open-ended and encourage the discussion of multiple topics. To do so, they are styled to encourage the appropriation of other narrative forms for political engagement most notably humor. These types of hashtags work through much looser discursive boundaries thus allowing for multiple, even contradictory narratives, using disorder that is deliberate, for through such ambiguity, political "indiscipline" is encouraged. Some illustrative examples include hashtags such as #babawhileyouwereaway (trans: father while you were away), #whatwouldmagufulido, #thingsjesusdidnotdie4, and the hashtag discussed above, #borauhai.

The hashtag #babawhileyouwereaway, for example, was created in the aftermath of Kenya's contested 2017 elections. The country's charismatic opposition leader, former Prime Minister Raila Odinga (commonly referred to as *baba*) left the country for a relatively long overseas trip. On his return to the country, taking on a familiar filial trope, Kenyans on Twitter exploited the opportunity to discuss the state of the nation. In Kenya, it is widely agreed that on returning home from work, children often tell their father (*baba*) what happened at home in their absence hence the creation of the hashtag #babawhileyouwere away. Exploiting this trope, the hashtag was used to anchor many political issues to dramatize state failure under President Uhuru Kenyatta. Some illustrative examples include: @Purity_Bisieri writes, "#BabaWhileYouWereAway We were sold to China and 'Ochieng' became 'O Chi Yeng.'" This was a pointed reference to the government's appetite for Chinese loans, whose repayment was being seen as a burden to ordinary people. The ultimate surrender of sovereignty was dramatized in the alleged name change of "Ochieng" to a Chinese-sounding name "O chi Yeng." @InsecurityKE writes, "#Babawhileyouwereaway Kenya police service was ranked the worst in the World." This was in response to a report that indeed ranked the Kenya police service as one of the worst in the world.

Meanwhile, @kmwanzia writes, #Babwhileyouwereaway Zimbabwe reached Canaan before us #railareturns." This tweet was a reference to the ouster of Robert Mugabe in Zimbabwe. During election campaigns, politicians often draw on religious symbols and metaphors to validate their suitability for political posts. Raila had used the metaphor of Moses leading the Israelites from Egypt to Canaan [the Promised Land] to make his case for wanting to be Kenya's president. His "promised land" was a Kenya in which as president he would tackle the many ills and challenges ordinary Kenyans were facing. The Bible in Kenya is at once a spiritual book, a reference text for making sense of the everyday, but also a political text that provides politicians and the public alike a common vocabulary for political engagement. To be sure, Christianity has always occupied a central place in Kenyans' popular imagination. The appropriation of biblical hermeneutics in political debates in the country is thus common. Through these hashtags, such Christian discourse is effectively utilized to generate conversations and provide a familiar archive for political interpretation.

Conclusion

The political instrumentalization of Twitter hashtags in Kenya opens them up to various discursive possibilities. Discussions on Twitter are reputedly chaotic and characterized by narrative disorder, yet through the creative use of hashtags, we see how a new order is created, one in which narrative agency is reconstituted and reconfigured by users. We see a near elimination of traditional hierarchies of political order both concerning who gets to define and speak politically and also what constitutes the political. Mainstream media have strict gatekeeping processes that help sustain particular orders in conversations. Who speaks and what is said is determined by a set of structural and professional rules, which more often than not privilege the dominant economic and political voices in society. Within the context of Kenya in which the visible and invisible tools of control ensure the pre-eminence of the state in defining and setting the parameters of political discourse, social media has become notably disruptive. It is therefore eminently arguable that social media has provided new possibilities for Kenya's political practices especially as far as communication is concerned. Even as we take note of its material and discursive limitations, we cannot ignore the uses to which platforms such as Twitter have been put by users. Indeed, these limitations have made users narratively much more inventive.

This discussion has attempted to demonstrate how Kenyans on Twitter, well aware, for example, of the hierarchies that have emerged on the platform, have developed less vertical narrative strategies and discursive practices that are much more inclusive. These employ familiar everyday idioms to expand publics, encourage participation and anchor various narratives by way of either legitimizing commonly agreed positions or disrupting those that are contested.

It is important however that we look at the use of social media platforms such as Twitter in Kenya as part of a historical evolution of Kenya's political practices. Users have stylized the platform to capture present realities and challenges and exploited its affordances while appropriating and reconfiguring older forms of political practices. This discussion further demonstrates the need to reflect on the dominant even teleological analytical paradigms used to study politics in Africa that elevate the significance of formal political institutions and processes. The case I make here is that the loci of political practices and ultimately of power in Kenya, as in many parts of Africa, is much more dispersed than we often acknowledge. Sites such as social media and the practices they facilitate can no longer be ignored or Othered.

George Ogola is Professor of Media Industries in the Department of Cultural, Media and Visual Studies, University of Nottingham. He has published widely on African journalism/media and popular culture. His research broadly focuses on the intersection between technology, the media, and politics. He is interested in the impact of digital technologies on journalistic and organizational media practices, and on processes of governance and political accountability in Africa. He has also worked extensively on the interface between African popular culture and popular media, examining Africa's cultural economy as a site and means through which to understand questions of power and its performance in the postcolony.

Notes

1. See full census reports at www.knbs.or.ke/. The Kenya Bureau of Statistics conducts population census every 10 years.
2. See full census reports at www.knbs.or.ke/.
3. See www.ca.go.ke/. The Kenya Communications Authority is the regulatory body for the communications sector in the country.
4. See www.ca.go.ke/.

References

Barber, Karin. 1997. *Readings in African Popular Culture.* London: The International African Institute.

Bayart, Francois. 1993. *The State in Africa: The Politics of the Belly.* London: Longman.

Bernal, Victoria. 2014. *Nation as Network: Diaspora, Cyberspace, and Citizenship.* Chicago: University of Chicago Press.

Bruns, Alex, and Jean Burgess. 2012. "Researching News Discussion on Twitter: New Methodologies". *Journalism Studies (13):801-814.*

Chabal, Patrick, and Jean-Pascal Daloz. 2010. *Africa Works: Disorder as Political Instrument.* London: James Currey.

Chouliarak, Lilie. 2010. "Self-Mediation: New Media and Citizenship." *Critical Discourse Studies* 7(4): 227–32.

Entman, Robert. 2004. *Projections of Power: Framing News, Public Opinion and US Foreign Policy.* Chicago: University of Chicago.

Fenton, Natalie, and Veronica Barresi. 2011. "Alternative Media and Social Networking Sites: The Politics of Individuation and Political Participation." *The Communication Review* 14: 179–96.

Foucault, Michel. 1982. "The Subject and Power." *Critical Inquiry* 8(4): 777–95.

Karekwaivanane, George. 2019. "'Tapanduka Zvamuchese': Facebook, 'Unruly Publics', and Zimbabwean Politics." *Journal of Eastern African Studies* 13(1): 54–71.

Ligaga, Dinah. 2012. "Virtual Expressions: Alternative Online Spaces and the Staging of Kenyan Popular Cultures." *Research in African Literatures* 43(4): 1–16.

Markham, Tim. 2014. "Social Media, Protest Cultures and Political Subjectivities of the Arab Spring." *Media, Culture & Society* 36(1): 89–104.

Mbembe, Achille. 2001. *On the Postcolony.* Berkeley: University of California Press.

Ndlela, Martin. 2015. "Social Media and Elections in Kenya." In *The Routledge Companion to Social Media and Politics,* ed. Axel Bruns, Gunn Enli, Eli Skogerbø, Anders Olof Larsson, and Christian Christensen, 460–71. Abingdon: Routledge.

Ogola, George. 2010. "'If You Rattle a Snake, Be Prepared to Be Bitten': Popular Culture, Politics and the Kenyan News Media." In *Popular Media, Democracy and Development in Africa,* ed. Wasserman Herman, 173–200. London: Routledge.

———. 2016. "The Political Economy of the Media in Kenya: From Kenyatta's Nation-Building Press to Kibaki's Local-Language FM Radio." *Africa Today* 57(3): 77–95.

———. 2019. "#Whatwouldmagufulido? Kenya's Digital 'Practices' and 'Individuation' as a (Non)Political Act." *Journal of Eastern African Studies* 13(1): 124–39.

Omanga, Dan. 2015. "'Chieftaincy' in the Social Media Space: Community Policing in a Twitter Convened Baraza." *Stability: International Journal of Security & Development* 4(1): 1–16.

Portland Communications. 2016. "How Africa Tweets." Retrieved 5 October 2022 from http://portland-communications.com/publications/how-africa-tweets-2016/.

Ruganda, John. 1992. *Telling the Truth Laughingly: The Politics of Francis Imbuga.* Nairobi: Heinemann.

Scott, James. 1990. *Domination and the Arts of Resistance: Hidden Transcripts.* New Haven, CT: Yale University Press.

Street, John. 1997. *Politics and Popular Culture.* Cambridge: Polity Press.

Taylor, Joanna, and Claudia Pagliari. 2017. "Mining Social Media Data: How Are Research Sponsors and Researchers Addressing the Ethical Challenges?" *Research Ethics* 14(2): 1–39.

Trefon, Theodore. 2004. *Reinventing Order in the Congo: How People Respond to State Failure.* London: Zed Books Ltd.

Tully, Melisa, and Brian Ekdale. 2014. "Sites of Playful Engagement: Twitter Hashtags as Spaces of Leisure and Development in Kenya." *Information Technologies and International Development* 10(3): 67–82.

Srinivasan, Sharath, Stephanie Diepeveen, and George Karekwaivanane. 2019. "Rethinking Publics in Africa in a Digital Age." *Journal of Eastern African Studies* 13(1): 2–17.

Wamuyu, Patrick. 2020. *The Kenya Social Media Landscape: Trends and Emerging Narratives, 2020.* Nairobi: SIMELab.

CHAPTER 4

The *Muslim Mali* Video Game

Revisiting the Religious-Security-Postcolonial Nexus in Popular Culture

Marie Deridder and Olivier Servais

In 2013, a video game called *Muslim Mali* appeared on the Internet. The gamer's avatar was a black aircraft whose mission was to fly over the desert and shoot down as many French jets as possible and dodge fire from them before, inevitably, dying. Then, a game-over text would praise the dead player as a martyr to jihad. This game did not make much noise in offline Mali, but did attract widespread online commentary by some Western global media, including mocking commentary. *Muslim Mali* has opened up a discursive digital space containing suspicions, insinuations, rumors, accusations, skeptical interpretations, and conspiracy theories, which offers an original interpretative junction for the understanding of the current armed conflict and power assemblage in postcolonial Mali. Given that these manifestations are characterized by constant processes of encoding and decoding messages and meanings in negotiations of power relations, they are typical expressions of cryptopolitics (see Bernal, Pype, and Rodima-Taylor in the introduction to this book). Online controversies centered on how to decrypt and interpret the video game, its narrative, and its gameplay, and took place in a number of forums, ranging from those involving reportage by US journalists to a blog posted on a forum for gamers and its online comments. *Muslim Mali* was set in a real-world geopolitical hotspot and seems to have been a virtual response to Operation Serval, the French intervention against jihadist groups on the Malian battlefield, which had begun earlier in 2013. *Muslim Mali* was, thus, synchronically virtualizing the conflict in Mali and participating in the constitution of its sociopolitical interpretations. Those interpretations were, and remain, embedded in various local, regional, and global power assemblages that interrogate racism, imperialism, and colonial legacy.

In this chapter, we explore the original cryptopolitical practices and narratives that frame, through digital media, the interpretative junction offered by *Muslim Mali*. For us, this video game contains multiple layers of encryption within its gameplay, narrative, and computational structure. The same is true of the online controversies it aroused. We argue that both the game and its controversies ambivalently reveal the tensions and emotions embedded in popular culture about the former French colonizer and the West. First, this video game has digital cryptopolitics of its own, deeply inscribed in its computational structure, the internal coding and algorithms of the game that shape the way players interact with it. By portraying France, Mali's former colonizer, as the invader, *Muslim Mali* shifts perspectives on world politics and subverts the dominant narrative of the Malian war by blurring moral lines within the postcolonial and conflict-affected setting. Then, we address the cryptopolitics involved in the way racism and imperialism are embedded and naturalized in the US reportage on this video game. US media reporting, which was relayed by global media, echoed the racial stereotypes and representations encrypted in the Global War on Terror's narrative. In doing so, global media contributed to multiple layers of encryption that obscure diverse and complex sociohistorical settings, hide various interests and agendas, and silence local subjectivities. The controversies surrounding this video game opened a digital space for explicit political commentaries and contestations around the Malian conflict, albeit through the mobilization of conspiracy theories involving the former colonizing power. We approach conspiracy theories not to confirm or disprove them but to consider them seriously as sets of representations having a powerful impact on the way people come to their basic assumptions about global politics and through which they express a strong critique of perceived oppressive sociopolitical structures, entangled with unseen powers and remote global hierarchies. These conspiracy theories should be viewed, first, as attempts to unmask racist and imperialist cryptopolitics. These representations echo and amplify discourse we have encountered in postcolonial conversations on Malian streets, discourse visible in (for example) demonstrations in the country's capital, Bamako, which demanded the withdrawal of French forces from the country.[1]

The first section of this chapter provides an overview of scholarship on video games in popular culture, and their entanglement with global politics. Video games such as *Muslim Mali*, like the digital space their controversies have opened up, are part of the broader category of social media. The second section outlines the use of military video games for propaganda and political activism in times of armed conflict and war, which often depicts the "enemy" with negative and degrading stereotypes. The third section contextualizes the Malian armed conflict and the role played in it by France. To explore the digital cryptopolitics of the game, our fourth section turns to public statements some US journalists made about *Muslim Mali*, statements that reproduced racist and imperialist cryptopolitics online. Our final section examines how these media-decontextualized statements, and the game's digital cryptopolitics, were discussed and contested on a gamers' website, where some commenters, like others offline, used conspiracies theories to recall the complexity of the current Malian conflict and its sociohistorical roots in French colonialism.

This chapter is inspired by Katrien Pype's method of "commenting on digital depth" (2018: 247). This is a methodological approach that captures the various layers of meaning encrypted in digital space by analyzing "any virtual text uploaded or posted by either researcher, research participants, or others" (Pype 2018: 248). While this methodological approach may be "fragmentary in its analysis," it corresponds well to the ephemerality of some digital texts, and is, therefore, Pype argues, "the only legitimate ethnographic form" with which to make discursive renditions of the digital space's opacity (2018: 248). Knowledge, experiences, and intertextualities all inform ways of interpreting and commenting on digital texts: digital texts are read and decrypted in interrelation with other texts (Weldes and Rowley 2015). Our commentaries in this chapter are, therefore, equally informed by our own interrelated readings of these digital texts, combined with our knowledge and experiences of the social dynamics we are studying (Pype 2018: 249).

Therefore, this chapter explores the virtual and intertextual networks of digital texts that have been produced at the junction of the *Muslim Mali* video game. Digital texts dating from 2013 and collected on the internet provide this chapter's basis: a YouTube video clip about the game, reports by several journalists, a blog posted by journalist Evan Narcisse on *Kotaku* (a website for gamers), and its commenters' posts. The digital world allows for additional hiding and anonymization, which can create difficulties for the ethnographer. Commenters on the *Kotaku* website employ numerous pseudonyms: the anonymity this provides makes it hard to accurately situate commenters' positionalities. However, their comments resonate with discussions Marie Deridder has had with her Malian interlocutors in the small northern town of Youwarou (Deridder 2012, 2013, 2019, 2021) and in Bamako[2] (Deridder, Laurent, and Konseiga 2021; Deridder and Pelckmans 2020; Deridder, Pelckmans, and Ward 2020).

Video Games at the Crossroad of Popular Culture and World Politics

Since the 1990s, there has been an increasing acknowledgment of the importance of popular culture for world politics[3] (Robinson 2015: 453). Video games, we argue here, are part of this phenomenon, and should be studied by considering this crucial aspect to understand the crypto-politics that video games embody through their technological opacity. As Kyle Grayson (2013: 380) has argued, "a popular artifact may reveal key dynamics underpinning contemporary politics that might not normally register popularly if expressed through the formal conventions of academic or political argumentation, even if it is complicit in reproducing them. The artifacts of popular culture offer an additional capacity to engage in political argument on terms and in a language that is more familiar to a given audience." In a transversal way, our case study corresponds to Iver Neumann and Daniel Nexon's fourfold typology of popular culture (2006: 10), which understands it, in globalized settings, as elements of global political processes or as motivated by political events; as empirical data allowing key insights into dominant norms, ideas, values, and representations about ongoing political process; as a mirror, a medium that brings us to reflect on our own assumptions about world politics; and as constitutive of politics and interacting with other representations of political life. Jutta Weldes and Christina Rowley (2015) stress a point vital to our discussion: that, while being constitutive of politics, popular culture is constructed intertextually. Its meanings depend on its texts being read in relation to the narrative and visual elements of others: world politics and popular culture are often read in interrelation with one another. Through a layer of fictional representations, popular culture intersects thus with the study of world politics. Not only does it represent elements of sociopolitical life, but it also plays a crucial role in discursively constituting that life.

The study of popular culture can help move the understanding of world politics beyond the narratives, statements, and analyses of political elites. Popular culture is especially significant because people are immersed in its discourses in their daily lives (Weldes and Rowley 2015). For many of them, it provides diffuse knowledge they can use to grasp political issues, shape their moralities, and produce and transform their identities (Neumann and Nexon 2006: 6, 18). It is by use of popular culture that "effective analogies and narratives are constructed and altered" (2006: 6). Popular culture, therefore, has a powerful impact on the way audiences come to their assumptions about the world (2006: 19).

Artifacts used to study popular culture have ranged from books, comics, novels, and painting to sport, music, songs, dance, films, theaters, TV programs, and merchandise produced for popular consumption. Video games, which are considered commercial products rather than cultural achievements, have been neglected (Seiffert and Nothhaft 2015: 256). The study of video games has suffered from its perception as a trivial and meaningless activity, a form of computer-mediated escapism for immature youth. Video games have not been seen as a persuasive and expressive medium able at the same time to inform, entertain, distract, express, persuade, and shape public opinion (Bogost 2006a; Seiffert and Nothhaft 2015). Video games, however, have one major peculiarity other artifacts of popular culture lack: their interactivity. This offers players interactive content, narratives, and virtual spaces to explore and is what creates what Ian Bogost (2006a) calls the "procedural rhetoric" of video games, which we consider a central part of their digital cryptopolitics. Video games embody and encrypt representations, ideologies, and norms in their computational structure (their internal coding and algorithmic patterns). Depending on their narratives, they may also theorize and produce knowledge about (and, at the same time, "gamify") historical and political events.

When experiencing the interactive narratives, rules, and encrypted theoretical knowledge of video games and the emotions they provoke, players are able to form novel judgments and expectations, which they can communicate to others. Even if, as Bogost (2006a) argues, video games are not explicitly persuasive, their informational content and the affordances and limitations of their particular gameplay still shape players' experiences and the meanings they derive from them. Gamers can then more or less consciously transpose those experiences and meanings to their offline world in a performative (and more or less critical) way. Miron Lakomy (2019) argues that, compared to video games, no other online or offline medium has the same potential to engage players through enjoyment. In striking keys or clicking buttons as they play, players are "syncing physical action with intellectual and visual cues. Repeated play reinforces the connection between thought and action, between intent and implementation" (Brachman 2006: 158). Video games can also allow players to embody political positions and engage in political actions many will never have previously experienced (Bogost 2006a). Therefore, as an interactive entertainment, video games easily allow for both the appropriation and the experimentation of political activism and radical rhetoric (Bogost 2006a). The unique procedural rhetoric of video games thus adds another quality of persuasion: it allows players to experience the meaning of the argument mounted by the game (Seiffert and Nothhaft 2015: 261).

Finally, as we will empirically demonstrate in the latter sections, video games are part of the broader framework of social media. Generally, as Jens Seiffert and Howard Nothhaft (2015) point out, video games and social media are distinguished by their (assumed) different social functions. While social media sites such as Facebook or Twitter are used to share content, information, and engagement with "real" people, video games should be seen as mere entertainment. However, this distinction by social function is less obvious than it seems. It is misleading to one-sidedly emphasize agency, creativity, and sociality on social media, without acknowledging that gamers not only play video games, but also play with, and exchange views with, other gamers (Seiffert and Nothhaft 2015: 256). Video games can thus play a key role in communication and socialization (Perraton, Fusaro, and Bonenfant 2011), and the formation of players' communities of practice.[4] Such communities can have a strong impact on learning, knowing, communicating, socializing, and understanding the way people think about the world (Zagal 2010). Such communities constitute new social spaces in and around video games, allowing communications, exchanges, and interactions. That constitution occurs through the unique social junction offered by video games, with their interactivity and intrinsic intertextuality, and it occurs even in times of armed conflict and war.

Video Games, War on Terror, and Cyberjihad

Military video games, like other artifacts of popular culture, can be used for wartime propaganda and political activism, and the negative and degrading stereotyping of military "enemies." In this context, it is not surprising to see jihadist organizations and their sympathizers using not only the Internet but also video games. The jihadist online presence that results, should not, we argue, be studied mainly through the prism of radicalization. This approach often suffers from normative and Eurocentric biases that contribute to multiple layers of encryption and obscure diverse complex sociohistorical settings, various interests and agendas, as well as silencing local subjectivities.

Jihadist groups are not the only actors who use the internet for these purposes. The US Army, for example, has used military video games like *America's Army*[5] as recruiting tools.[6] Several of these video games[7] portray the United States as an innocent victim of violence continuously threatened by a hostile world, justifying a military response unbound by international norms and law, as argued for by the Bush administration after the 11 September attacks (Robinson 2015).

Military video games tend to employ rhetoric consistent with that deployed by the War on Terror, which reclassifies prohibited acts like torture and extrajudicial killings as unproblematic, even standard, behaviors (Clarke, Rouffaer, and Sénéchaud 2012; Stahl 2006). In video games, war is coded as an object of consumption that effaces the discursive boundary between soldier and citizen (Stahl 2006). This gives birth to what Stahl calls the "virtual citizen-soldier," reflecting the militarization of society and politics. Existing literature[8] on military video games, which depicts conflicts from the Western point of view, suggests that these games portray representations and stereotypes "based on Orientalism, with the Middle East depicted as backward, violent and resistant to civil order" (Robinson 2015: 452). They present US military intervention and the use of force as the only viable option to liberate oppressed populations and restore a sense of legal and moral order, a view rooted in perceptions of US superiority regarding the rest of the world (Robinson 2012). When these video games stage the War on Terror from a Western point of view, they problematically recast complex geopolitical issues as simplistic conflicts demarcated by a Manichean moral divide between "good guys" and "bad guys," and in which there are known winners and known enemies.

The era since 11 September 2001 has coincided with a significant breakthrough by video games into the world of politics and activism, and their introduction of counternarratives to dominant narratives disseminated by the Western entertainment industry. Bogost (2006a, 2006b) notes that video games are increasingly becoming a forum for artistic endeavor and even for sociopolitical expression that allows resistance to perceived oppressions (Servais 2020). Many of these video games take the form of "mods," electronic game modifications that alter existing commercial games to express political opinions and social critiques (Bogost 2006a, 2006b; Robinson 2012).

In the meantime, jihadist organizations and their sympathizers have also oriented to the Internet, drawing the attention of scholars working on terrorism and counterterrorism. This mushrooming literature[9] problematizes "cyberjihad," including video games like *Muslim Mali*, from a global/macro overview and a top-down approach: it focuses on the Internet web forums, websites, social media, and encrypted virtual spaces used by "terrorists" for routine conversations, exchange of tactics, socialization, recruitment, propaganda, the radicalization of web users, information storage, and the dissemination of training material (Torres-Soriano 2014; Younas 2014; Zelin 2013). Anne Stenersen (2008: 216), however, reminds us that this is not unprecedented. If we look at the paramilitary literature and "explosives cookbooks" that have been circulating online for years or at the US right-wing extremist pages that host forums dedicated to weaponry and weapons training, we see that use of the Internet to spread illegal literature or to prepare criminal or terrorist acts is not a new phenomenon.

The focus here is on online mechanisms of radicalization and their role in terrorism and counterterrorism strategies, as well as their general value for political activism. The aim is to investigate the perception of terrorism in the electronic entertainment industry: scholars were at first reluctant to engage with military video games that look at conflict from a non-Western perspective[10] (Lakomy 2019; Robinson 2012). Counterterrorism scholars have been the exception here: they analyze these games through their security lens and are mainly concerned with the potential for radicalization and recruitment that these games bear in their procedural mechanics. Jarret Brachman (2006: 157) underlines that "while players may understand that such games are based on fiction, the act of playing them arguably increases their propensity to accept ideologies that consist of extreme goals"—this turns video games and gaming into a security issue.

This existing literature, however, suffers from a normative bias and proposes disembodied analyses that fail to consider the intertextuality of popular culture, as well as the local settings and micro-realities that frame online and offline contexts and battlefields. In doing so, these analysts contribute to multiple layers of encryption that obscure diverse and complex sociohistorical settings, hide interests and agendas, and silence local subjectivities. Weldes and Rowley (2015) rightly point out that examination of the everyday phenomena of popular culture reveals the centrality of the many "margins, silences and bottom rungs" of world politics, which is the ambition of this chapter. Indeed, interestingly, video games like *Muslim Mali* reverse the usual gaze by adopting a non-Western point of view and allowing their players to fight against the West. Through their procedural mechanics, these video games offer their players an alternative version of historical and political events. By designating the West as the enemy, these video games challenge the dominant, dividing moral line between the "good" Western side and the "bad" non-Western side. Thanks to their intrinsic intertextuality (characteristic of popular culture in general and video games in particular), these games thus contribute to the replaying and reshaping of past political events, imposing on them other significations that demand scholarly investigation. This is the argument that we empirically explore in the following sections of this chapter.

The Beginning of the Offline War in Mali

Until 2012, in West Africa, Mali was a "donor darling" (Bergamaschi 2014; Siméant 2014), a "poster child for electoral democracy in West Africa,"[11] that had successfully completed both an "economic adjustment" and a "democratic transition" (Bertrand 1992, 1999). Presidential, parliamentary, and communal elections occurred regularly, and without bloodshed or violence. The old rebel movements were now confined to the northern part of the country. In the first decade of the 2000s, when Marie Deridder was conducting fieldwork in Mali's Inner Niger Delta, it was difficult to imagine the turmoil that Mali would experience after 2011. Many scholars have stressed the unexpected character and complexity of the historical moment that began that year (Andersson 2019; Hagberg and Körling 2012; Lecocq et al. 2013; Siméant 2014).

Two months before a new presidential election, in March 2012, a mutiny broke out in the Kati military camp, and then grew, quickly, into a coup d'état. While international institutions unanimously condemned the coup, popular reactions to the event were divided. Driven by the rejection of elites and the political class, this coup d'état revealed a growing social unrest coupled with the revival of insurgent claims in northern Mali and the aftershocks of the Gaddafi regime's collapse in Libya in late 2011. The contested presidential management of this "Northern crisis," the arrival from Libya of ex-combatants and returnees,[12] the rise of insurgent claims in the north and then in central Mali, the spread of jihadist groups, suspicions of collusion between the central government in Bamako and drug traffickers active in the Sahelo-Saharan regions, and the displacement of several hundred thousand people all contributed to Mali's instability (Gavelle, Siméant, and Traoré 2013; Gary-Tounkara 2013).

Amplifying the disorganization of the Malian army, the coup d'état of 2012 indirectly contributed to the crisis of the north or Azawad as the rebel MNLA (Mouvement de Libération de l'Azawad) calls the region. One month after the coup, the MNLA unilaterally proclaimed Azawad's independence. Mali was divided in two, bringing the country's territorial integrity into question, and strongly evoking the example of Southern Sudan. Tensions emerged, also, between rival insurgent groups themselves. These events have reactivated clichéd images of chronic crisis and lawlessness, which have made Mali "a zone of insecurity at the epicenter of the global margins of our new world disorder" (Andersson 2019).

In addition to insurgent groups, the presence of active jihadist groups in this zone has led Western media, along with experts in security and geopolitics, to take the line that this crisis is different from previous postcolonial Tuareg rebellions. Henceforth, what was, and is, happening in northern Mali was connected to the globalized fears and threats felt since the attacks of 11 September 2001 in New York City. In 2012, the destruction of Sufi manuscripts and mausoleums in Timbuktu, a UNESCO World Heritage Site, caused scandal and outrage in the West and elicited comparisons with the Taliban's destruction of the Bamiyan Buddhas in Afghanistan in 2001. Western media such as BBC and CNN reported also on how jihadists had imposed sharia, chopped off the hands of presumed thieves, performed floggings, and stoned presumed adulterous couples. Mali was propelled into the fight against global jihadism.

Yet some media and security experts started referring to a new "catchy" angle of analysis for the Malian situation: the issue was to prevent the fall of West Africa, at whose heart Mali stands, into "Afghanization," "Talibanization," "Balkanization," "Somalization" (see, for example, Solomon 2013). The international community and neighboring countries feared the extension of Malian insurgent and jihadist movements outside Malian borders and the consequent explosion of the region. These terrorist threats definitively internationalized the Malian situation, which was translated into a military issue, as part of the American "Global War on Terror" launched by the George W. Bush administration after the 11 September attacks. Northern and central Mali were now included in the "arc of crisis" that united the Saharan and Sahelian regions.

In a questionable manner, experts in security and geopolitics have, for many years now, depicted northern Mali as uncontrolled and uncontrollable (Brachet 2013). Such depictions construct Mali and other sub-Saharan Africa countries around categories like "weak," "fragile," "failed," or "collapsed" that stereotype and hierarchize African states (Gruffydd Jones 2008). Such discourses of "state failure" legitimize intervention by identifying lack, inferiority, and incapacity, thus reconnecting with the colonial legacy of an imperialism that distinguished colonized societies and states from both the imperial powers themselves and each other (Gruffydd Jones 2008: 197–98). In late 2012, with the support of France, the Economic Community of West African States (ECOWAS) deployed the African-led International Support Mission in

Mali (AFISMA).[13] This offensive operation was authorized by the United Nations Security Council's Resolution 2085 (2012).[14]

France was at first reluctant to intervene militarily in Mali. Then, in early 2013, jihadist groups took the small town of Konna along the Niger River—the first step toward Bamako and the last before the military camp at Sévaré. The battle at Konna lasted several days, and the outcome never seemed certain. Then, at the request of the Malian interim government and with the support of the UN Security Council, France deployed its forces, including Gazelle helicopters and Mirage-D fighter-bombers to Konna: after several bombing runs, the French fighter-bombers routed the armed groups. This battle marked the beginning of the French army's intervention in Mali, with the launch of Operation Serval. Supported by air raids, the French military intervention gradually deployed several thousands of soldiers to Mali. The official objectives of the former colonial power were to stop the progress of jihadist groups and to start the long-awaited reconquest of the north. This was to be led by the Malian army and the support of the ECOWAS intervention forces, which consisted of several thousand soldiers from Nigeria, Niger, Burkina Faso, Togo, Senegal, Benin, Guinea, Chad, and Ghana. Mali became a new material and imaginary battlefield of the African continent, where the majority of non-Western victims of conflict are ignored.

France's entry into the Global War on Terror in Mali briefly drew the Western media spotlight. On several occasions, the media broadcasted images of victorious French troops marching through the streets of reclaimed cities in northern Mali and receiving the acclamation of anonymous crowds. The same media relayed the testimonies of relief and gratitude expressed by local populations following their "release from the terrorist threat." At first, it seemed easy for the international military force to take over the three main cities in the north: but then the situation in the north and the center of the country changed and changed adversely. The intervention troops found themselves quickly bogged down in a strategic environment that favored banditry and guerrilla attacks. At the time of writing, armed conflict in Mali remains a serious problem for that country, and the UN peacekeeping mission in Mali is still one of the deadliest in recent years. Over the span of a decade, the northern and central regions of the country have found themselves transformed into "red zones" (Anderson 2019), a kind of nebula where different armed groups are active. Local communities have been confronted with a context of violence, where feelings of abandonment by the Malian state coincide with growing mistrust between individuals and groups (Benjaminsen and Ba 2019; Pelckmans 2015).

The Subversive Digital Cryptopolitics of the *Muslim Mali* Video Game

In 2013, just after the engagement of the French military intervention in Mali, the website Ansar al-Mujahideen Arabic Forum (AMAF)[15] released an online single-player video game titled *Muslim Mali.*[16] In this section, we turn to the video game *Muslim Mali* itself, to its narrative and visual components, and to the scope of the gameplay options available to its players, which are coded and encoded into the game. While publishing content in Arabic, English, and German, the AMAF occupied a prominent place among globally networked pro-jihadist websites (Torres-Soriano 2014: 737). According to the literature on cyberjihad, these kinds of internet forums are one of the most important manifestations of the jihadist presence on the Internet. Scholars remain divided on the nature of the connection between such forums and terrorist organizations. Stenersen (2008: 216) insists that they are the work of "self-radicalized sympathizers," rather than that of formally enrolled members of terrorist organizations. Manuel R. Torres-Soriano (2014: 736) explains that even if these forums claim to be the independent initiatives of unaffiliated sympathizers, they are mostly embedded with such organizations. Their divergent understandings of jihadists' online presence notwithstanding, these authors agree that the Internet provides an interactive environment where people are able to interact in virtual and transnational communities of practice, while also producing content through their discussions and their exchanges about personal experiences.

The video game *Muslim Mali* seemed to feature the aerial combat of the "battle of Konna," which had happened a few months before in Mali. The home page of the video game displayed the Arabic words "Muslim Mali" (*Mālī al-muslima^{tu}*),[17] immediately locating the game geographically, religiously, and politically. Then, the opening message put the gamer into the picture, addressing him in explicitly jihadist terms: "My Muslim brother, fight off the French invasion from Muslim Mali" (*Akhī al-Muslim qum biṣaḍdi al-ghazwi al-faransiyyi ʕan Mālī al-muslima^{ti}*). Simulating an aerial dogfight, *Muslim Mali* contained no humanizing dimension and was not immersive. The player was thus not able to impersonate a "terrorist" but was playing with a plane as an avatar. At its conclusion, a game-over message would appear on the screen praising the dead player as a martyr to jihad and glorifying such martyrdom: "Our congratulations. You were martyred" (*tahānīna laqad ʾstushidta*).

Muslim Mali was a scrolling shooting game designed in 2D. Its aesthetic was quite similar to games such as *Space Invaders,*[18] popular in the

West from the late 1970s to the 1990s, which highlighted the idea of invasion. Shooting games are categorized by their viewpoint and the restrictions they impose on the player's movements. In the case of *Muslim Mali,* the player views the action from above as the screen scrolls downward. The game restricts the player and the enemies to a single screen and makes them move long one single axis of motion. While the aircraft move, the background remains stationary: the planes appear to be flying over a desert area recalling northern Mali. In this game, as in other vertical shooting games, the player is under constant attack and must contend with a large number of enemies descending from the top of the screen at a constantly increasing speed. Here, the enemies are the French aircraft, easily identified by their blue, white, and red French flags. The French jets try to destroy the gamer's plane by firing missiles at it. The player's avatar, an aircraft draped in a black Al-Qaeda flag, tries to shoot down this procession of French jets while dodging their fire. To present French military aircraft as a foreign enemy is an act that pushes players to enact military opposition to French forces. Facing the threat, the player must rely primarily on reaction times to succeed. The score is indicated in English. The number of lives available to the gamer decreases each time he is hit by a French missile. The player's aircraft can take ten hits before destruction, while the French planes do not survive even one. When the player has zero lives remaining, the game ends. A deadly laser is also available if the player presses a black button in the bottom-left corner of the screen: its use destroys both the player's avatar and the French enemies. *Muslim Mali*'s gameplay is based on repetition: the procedural mechanics of the game trap the player in a no-win scenario.

The design of *Muslim Mali* appeared to Western critics as old-fashioned, outdated, or "retro," especially in comparison with the much more elaborate and sophisticated designs exhibited by other experimental propaganda games of Al-Qaeda.[19] However, in a very surprising way, while these Western critics commented on the archaic design of the game, they also highlighted the fact that the game used HTML5, a language used for structuring and presenting content on the Web. Games coded in HTML5 are easy to promote because the language allows cross-platform mobile applications by including features designed with low-powered devices such as smartphones. This means that the designers of the game were not excluding any audience. *Muslim Mali* was available to potential players on both the European and African continents and all over the world.

In a context where the official narratives of the Malian state and the Western international community were presenting the French military intervention as timely and positive, this game inverted the moral contrast between "the good guys" and "the bad guys": the French forces were the invaders and the black Al-Qaeda aircraft represented the resistance. Many scholars have criticized video games that stage the War on Terror for their general strong pro-American bias and promotion of ongoing War on Terror operations (Allen 2011; Galloway 2004; Nieborg 2006, 2010; Schulzke 2013a, 2013b; Shaw 2010). Jihadist activists are thus not the only actors using online games for propaganda purposes. Lakomy reminds us that, in contrast to the perspectives of pro-American video games, "*jihad* in games is frequently portrayed as a regular, military-like activity, usually undertaken in defense of the imperiled Muslim communities and religion. This simple manipulation allows audiences that are generally critical toward Western activities in the Middle East and in Africa to be reached" (2019: 399). This reversed perspective may be inspirational for many members of the games' target audience, as it allows them to unload emotions while visualizing their political aspirations in a virtual environment[20] (Lakomy 2019: 399). This leads us to the question of how audiences have decrypted *Muslim Mali* by performing intertextuality.

US Global Media: Mocking and Stereotyping

If popular culture is constitutive of world politics then its meanings depend on how it is read intertextually, in interrelation to and with other narratives. While cultural artifacts may carry latent meanings and constructions in them, discursive labor is required to realize those meanings (Weldes and Rowley 2015). We have, in fact, seen this in relation to *Muslim Mali* and its own digital cryptopolitics. Popular cultural artifacts are consumed in diverse ways: they create discursive junctions for diverse readings to be articulated or contested. Their consumption, therefore, is inextricably linked to the production and reproduction of meanings through which people comprehend their place in the world (Weldes and Rowley 2015). Viewing popular artifacts through the prism of intertextuality makes the off/online distinction less obvious, especially when we are interested in a video game that virtualizes the offline Malian battlefield. In this section, we thus investigate the public statements made by some US global media about *Muslim Mali*. We must, therefore, unpack the narratives and tropes through which these journalists have constituted meanings, to show how these reportages are embedded into a racist and imperialist cryptopolitics with roots within

US and Western "coloniality of power" (Quijano 2000) embodied into in/security narratives.

Quickly after the release of *Muslim Mali*, US media was quick to criticize the video game in reports that were soon relayed by international online media such as *France 24* or *The World*.[21] International US expert journalists in security issues mocked *Muslim Mali* and described it as an archaic game that was thirty years out of date. For John Hudson[22] of *Foreign Policy*, a US magazine, this game was "primitive."[23] The same goes for the US journalist Michael Peck[24] who wrote an article for the US business magazine *Forbes*, where he openly mocked the game with the headline "Al-Qaeda's Goofy Video Game Provokes Laughter, Not Terror" and who identified "something pathetic" about the game.[25] In his article, he wrote:

> If Osama Bin Laden hadn't been killed by Navy SEALs, he would have died of embarrassment at his group's latest exploit. Al-Qaeda militants in the African nation of Mali are tired of being blasted by French jets. But instead of defeating the French in a real war, they've done the next best thing. They're wiping out the French Air Force in an online video game . . . Despite looting arms when Gaddafi's regime fell in Libya, they can't destroy real French aircraft, so they reassured themselves by shooting down virtual ones. . . . But there is something pathetic about this game, to the point where you wonder if they really believe it is a magical talisman, a poor man's substitute for anti-aircraft weapons that will protect from French Mirage jets, Gazelle helicopters, and laser-guided missiles. . . . Oh, and one more thing. Vive la France!

Such public statements about *Muslim Mali* reflect a liberal conception of in/security issues, one that is underpinned by an evolutionary myth (Rowley and Weldes 2012: 514). This evolutionary myth is constructed on the idea of "security" as a desirable outcome that can be achieved via a coherent and linear process with a beginning, a middle, and an end state. In/security is perceived through the prism of threat, technological advance, and military capabilities. In this liberal conception, technology is the embodiment of modernity, its inevitable progress, and its promise of wealth and peace. These journalists considered *Muslim Mali* to be "primitive" because of its unsophisticated design. While mocking the game, they stressed, also, the military inadequacy of African jihadists before the French forces, despite their access to Libyan arms after Gaddafi's fall.[26] Significantly, Michael Peck referred to *Muslim Mali* as being, for its creators and players, "a magical talisman, a poor man's substitute for anti-aircraft weapons." He thus reaffirmed the implicit unequal binary opposition between witchcraft/tradition and technology/modernity, evoking once again an evolutionary understanding of these issues, one in which some societies are less evolved than others.

These media reports partly reproduced an old and unsettled story of racialized African Otherness, replaying the guiding trope of "us" versus "them," and glossing the "African them" as inferior. They continue to convey and establish in the international media landscape the images of a primitive and backward "Africa" characterized by witchcraft and superstitions (Sanders 2003). This is an Africa that is lagging behind the West but unable to seize the technology at its disposal, in this case following the fall of Gaddafi. If Western media generally portray terrorists as intrinsically evil enemies and monsters undeserving of respect (Schulzke 2013a), they also underline, as in this case, the miserable inferiority of African jihadists unable to destroy the French jets. This must indirectly discourage audiences from playing such a "backward" video game: who would wish to embody inferiority in a game? This implied evolutionary narrative underpinning in/security issues from a Western perspective denies the contemporaneity of African countries and explicitly reaffirms the imagined superiority of the West and the former colonial powers in general, with France, in particular, seen as a savior.

This racist and imperialist cryptopolitics provides the interpretative frame used by these US expert journalists on security issues to discuss the Malian war. As Jacinthe Mazzocchetti (2012) rightly points out, these media narratives actively contribute to the confinement of sub-Saharan people within simplistic and deeply biased representations, reducing complex realities to an irreducible racialized Otherness, or at least to their reified and negatively connoted cultural traits. This Western media engagement with *Muslim Mali* led to the production and reproduction of a particular imagery of "Malians," "Mali," and "Africa" in general, including the idea that "Africa and Africans can be meaningfully discussed in the singular" by Western media (Sanders 2003: 53). Such homogenizing assumptions underpin the idea that "African Islam," "African wars," and "African technological gap" are purportedly meaningful categories quickly articulated through the lens of barbarianism and backwardness. As Todd Sanders underlines (2003: 62), "such images, though novel in their specifics, hardly spring from thin air: they draw on a lengthy Western history of demonized Others, and are refracted through specific contemporary constellations of power." They resonate strongly with certain historical patterns of colonial rule; those whereby humanitarian and developmental terminology played a key ideological role in justifying paternalistic protection based on a monopoly of violence and a permanent breach of local sovereignties (Deridder et al. 2020).

In doing so, these Western media deny the sociohistorical complexity of the Malian situation, the imagined and real roles played by France, and the main issues and concrete consequences of the ongoing deadly conflict. They contribute to multiple layers of encryption that obscure diverse interests and agendas, as well as silencing local subjectivities. Behind the alibi of the fight against terrorism, these criticisms reaffirm imperialist relations that structure on a global scale racial asymmetries between, on the one hand, European countries and the United States and, on the other hand, African countries, in a context where Western hegemony is wavering. This reveals the "infopolitics" (Bernal 2014) of asymmetric power relations that lie concealed behind technologies, discourses, and debates between the former metropolis and its former colony.

The online articles of these Western global media were not open to any comments by the audiences. However, a blog on *Muslim Mali* written by Narcisse Evan on *Kotaku*, a website dedicated to gaming and popular culture, opened the digital floor to audiences seeking to engage with and comment on both the game and its various interpretations.

Counternarratives in the Digital Space of Gaming

While some US media outlets were publishing their articles on *Muslim Mali*, the blogger Evan Narcisse, a forty-year-old writer, journalist, and consultant in video games, comic books, and TV was also publishing a piece on this game (under the headline "Islamic Extremists Made This Video Game"[27]) on the website *Kotak*. This is a website and blog launched in 2004 as part of the Gawker Media network based in New York.[28] A native New Yorker and African American, Evan Narcisse has 1,265 followers on *Kotaku*: in his writing, he seeks, among other things, to understand the intersection of blackness and popular culture and to critique the representation of blackness in video games. He argues that black characters, if not invisibilized, are all too often reduced to outdated and negative stereotypes portraying devastated black lives.[29] In its presentation section, *Kotaku* claims to be "an inclusive site for gamers of any ethnicity, gender or sexual orientation," and presents itself as "a news and opinion site about games and things serious gamers care about."[30] The site is dedicated to gaming and popular culture: it covers new games and offers gaming reviews, blog opinions, interviews, news, tips, and opportunities to debate. Its audience of 5 million readers per month includes both gamers and "people who don't play games but are curious about them."[31]

In his blog, Evan Narcisse described the game without resorting to patronizing superiority: "It's a rudimentary HTML5 browser game where you control an al-Qaeda fighter jet shooting down and dodging fire from French fighter planes. Islamic Mali virtualizes the very real conflict in Mali, where local rebel forces have been fighting jihadi soldiers with help from the French military." He identified the game's creators as "Islamic extremists" and underlined the fact that this game joined "the ranks of other explicitly political titles from other countries" that are "a testament to how fervently their creators want their particular ideologies to permeate every aspect of people's lives." Narcisse also stressed that "while the claim can be made that political mindsets and cultural biases seep into those video games [American video games like *Call of Duty*, *Battlefield*, and *Medal of Honor* series], they're not explicitly made to froth up ideological allegiances." His blog entry received 329 comments, ranking it as one of his most commented-upon publications on *Kotaku*. Within these comments, three main issues deserve attention: propaganda and its racial dimension, jihad and religion, and France's engagement in the Malian offline conflict.

First, regarding the racial issue, a commenter questions the moral classification suggested by Evan Narcisse that implied that *Muslim Mali* would be a more explicit propaganda tool than other Western military video games. This commenter raises the racialized implicit dimension underpinning these Western video games and their hierarchization with *Muslim Mali* (all punctuation and capitalization are as in the original):

> I fail to see how this is worse than Call of Duty and its endless "KILL BROWN PEOPLE TO SAVE THE WORLD FROM TERROR!!!!" campaign. It's foolish to claim that the War on Terror is any different from a Jihad.

This post points out that terrorism and the ongoing War on Terror are common themes in video games that morally characterize terrorists as evil threatening enemies and contribute to the definition of what terrorism is and who the terrorists are (in this case, they are those with dark skin color). They do this by disseminating a range of problematic racialized stereotypes of the targeted groups (Saleem and Anderson 2013; Schulzke 2013a). However, another commenter published a post in response to the first one establishing similarities between jihad and the War on Terror:

A Jihad is a religiously motivated war. Terrorism is a tactic whereby you target civilians in order to exert internal pressure on an enemy. The War on Terror is a response to Jihadic terrorism. You aren't stupid enough to not see a difference here, are you? The coalition forces in Afghanistan and Iraq explicitly try to avoid killing civilians. Terrorists explicitly aim to kill civilians. The US military has the power to kill every last person in the middle east but does not desire to do so. Al Qaeda has the desire to kill every person in America but lacks the power. If all the US military had wanted to do was kill civilians, these wars would have been over 10 years ago.

These contrasting replies show how, within a community of practice around gaming, a controversial discussion produces knowledge that impacts participants' understanding and decryption of both offline world politics and armed conflicts, in this case, the differences and similarities between jihad, terrorism, and the War on Terror.

The second issue concerns the religious dimension of the game and the tensions surrounding Islam and jihad (tensions that the authors of this chapter also encountered in Mali). Several commenters expressed the view that the Muslim faith could be lived differently from the one conveyed through the "radical" video game:

Let me make this clear now, the affiliation between the usage of Qur'anic verses and ideologies of Islamic extremists, are NOT glorified within the Muslim society. The terms jihad and martyr are very very misused, in the society outside of Islam. I'm very disappointed to see a game like this out there, because as a Muslim, I'd ask, where are the positive vibe games that teach education, morals, determination, and humanistic qualities that Islam really teaches?

Another commenter added:

I would just like to clarify something many people seem to misunderstand, al Qaida is not a proper representative of Islam, as a matter of fact they do not represent it at all, they use the name of the religion to justify their ideas that have nothing to do with Islam.

This is also the reason why, when these issues are discussed in everyday life, most of our Malian interlocutors established distance between themselves and the jihadists by underlining the "radicalization" of these "extremist" fighters, their supposed religious beliefs, and the violence associated with them. As Mazzocchetti (2012) noticed, since the 11

September attacks and the responses of Western media and world political leaders to that event, Muslims have had to "constantly defend themselves against the link established between their religion and extremist practices or terrorist acts." The political and media coverage of this event, and of the terrorist attacks that followed it, further strengthened negative and aggressive perceptions, attitudes, and affect toward people perceived to be Muslims. A strong associative link was made between terrorism, violence, and Islam, one that used schematized stereotypic attributes (e.g., turbans, dark skin color, facial hair, AK-47s, deserts, and camels) to perpetuate the image of Muslims as terrorists (Saleem and Anderson 2013). Stereotypes of this kind have significant implications for representations of the self, the world, and intergroup relations, and for the performative engagement of cognition, affect, and behavior.

Finally, in his blog, Evan Narcisse highlighted the agency of local combatants: "Islamic Mali virtualizes the very real conflict in Mali, where local rebel forces have been fighting jihadi soldiers with help from the French military." This statement affirms that the Malian desert cannot be reduced to a battlefield between jihadist groups and France, a reduction that would convey a Western-centric imagination that portrays the West as the only bulwark against terrorism. Here, Evan Narcisse asserts that "local rebel forces" are fighting jihadist groups, a part of the complexity we observe on the Malian offline battlefield. However, this last point opened up the debate on the current conflicts in Mali and the multitude of armed groups whose alliances and loyalties are shifting and not always clear as several commenters noticed: "'where local rebel forces have been fighting jihadi soldiers with help from the French military' That looks like I mistake, or am I reading it wrong? The jihadists are the rebels, the French are helping the government fight the rebels." Another blogger added: "I was going to point out the same thing. The Malian army along with African allies and the French are fighting islamists and tuareg rebels."

These posts reassert the complexity of the Malian situation and produce a new theoretical bifurcation, that of the conspiracy theories circulating within and around that situation. In current popular debates in Mali, people are asking sharp questions about links between the French and the Malian governments, the various armed groups in the northern and the central parts of the country (including the "rebels"), and the obscure financial interests at stake with regard to mining prospects. Mali is debating, in other words, about who is manipulating whom and for what purpose. The reconquest of Kidal by French intervention forces alone, without the support of the Malian forces, fed widespread rumors of an alliance between France and the separatist movement and increased suspicions of French motives in northern Mali where France was accused of seeking a monopoly on the region's energy resources (see also Boilley 2005, 2011). Such rumors are part of the complex political landscape of insurgency in post-2011 Mali. The older rebel groups have been joined by new, largely Islamist, rivals: the relationships between the Malian army, non-state actors, and foreign intervention forces have not always been comfortable, or even clear. It has been alleged that when French troops took the town of Kidal, without the aid of Malian army personnel, they subsequently allowed the MNLA to not only remain in the town, but also patrolled with them and with Chadian troops (Rudolph 2015: 386). Such episodes create suspicions of proximity between various players that are officially opposed to each other: this is fertile ground for conspiracy theories.

Moreover, different posts refer to conspiracy theories by discussing the manufacture, origin, and model of the jet with the Al-Qaeda flag: "So they fly around in what looks like United states Lockheed F-117 Nighthawk stealth bombers?" Another poster added: "Well, in their defense, al-qaeda doesn't produce any fighter jets, so they had to buy one from an allied nation...HEY WAITAMINUTE!!!!" Another one commented: "I also learnt that France uses the Su-47!"[32] In discussing France's intervention in Mali, some commenters accused others of taking the French side, by saying that Evan Narcisse's blog "is propaganda as well, because it justifies the French invasion of Mali." This drew the derisive comment, "[y]es . . . France's invasion . . . that's [definitely] what just happened in Mali." A commenter responded more seriously that "Propaganda is defined as 'ideas, facts, or allegations spread deliberately to further one's cause or to damage an opposing cause' Do you honestly think Evan is trying to gain support for France's invasion?"

The comments quoted here evoke the ways conspiracy "theories" work, via the drawing of connections and comparisons within an atmosphere of suspicion. It is within this backdrop of renewed mistrust that each French move in Mali is observed and decrypted, and how France's motives in carrying out this intervention in Mali are interrogated. The suspicions aroused by such interrogations are neither frivolous nor facetious. Pierre Boilley (2005) reminds us that from Malian independence to today, the recurrent concept of a French conspiracy in Saharan regions has resurfaced at every point when violent events have involved Saharan populations, and pastoralist populations especially. Control of northern Mali would provide access to energy resources and rent-seeking opportunities: the military and diplomatic presence of rival powers such as France, the United States, Algeria, China, or Russia, gives rise to suspicions that their presence is best explained by reference to those resources and opportunities. When large private extractive companies investigate these areas, their activities remain opaque but perceptible to local Malian populations. For instance, in December 2017, when it was officially almost impossible for Western travelers to travel to northern Mali without a military escort (and when even trips under such escorts were heavily controlled), convoys of trucks owned by an Australian mineral company were regularly making the journey to the north. Despite the conflict, Malian citizens still suspected that this company was carrying on its prospecting activities on Malian soil with the assistance of national elites. A convoy of French trucks was also observed heading to the north, causing one of Deridder's interlocutors, who was working for a local NGO in Bamako, to comment: "We should not be taken for fools. We know that this is not humanitarian or military equipment. These discreet activities reinforce our feeling of country's exploitation by France in a context of high precariousness."

The French military intervention thus activated a set of imaginaries among Malian citizens, one focused on the historical exploitation of Malian resources by France, with the complicity of national and ruling elites. This set of imaginaries brought together narratives of the legacy of the colonial, and then the postcolonial state, and issues of energy resources, and used them to form a conspiracy theory. In the Malian case, we argue, conspiracy theories are ideological formations embedded in recurrent social experiences of power, violence, and injustice that have taken root in traumatic memories of various historical settings.

For decades, people in northern and central Mali have grown up with the idea that in case of need, the state would not be there to protect them, an idea confirmed by their concrete experiences of state power. Seen as a potential threat, the state is strongly associated with prebendary dynamics, especially among nomadic/transhumant pastoralists, who share this perception that the state has neglected and marginalized them since the time of Malian independence. This relation to the postcolonial state is marked by different forms of asymmetric power relationships, rumors, suspicions, and violence, in thrall to the specter of a French former colonial power grounded in the history of colonial exploitation. These are the many ingredients that feed mistrust, insurgency, and conspiracy theories, and they continue to play a major role in political dynamics today in the areas north of the Niger River. In Youwarou in early 2012, for example, all the municipality's civil servants evacuated the area because of the fear the presence of armed groups in the area provoked in them. The vacuum created by this retreat of state personnel left the population feeling alone and abandoned.

For people in search of sense or sometimes senselessness, this apprehension of the world in terms of conspiracy theories provides a way to grasp events and make them coherent. It allows them to escape from the position of victimhood by becoming creators of meaning (Abalakina-Paap et al. 1999; Mazzocchetti 2012). By doing so, believers in conspiracy theories place their concerns within a wider sociocultural and historical framework, one that enables them to expose the hidden forces that they believe animate their world by revealing and refracting the concealed logic of power (West and Sanders 2003). These are attempts to decode the cryptopolitics made of various global, regional, and local assemblages in a conflict-affected country like Mali. Drawing on the works of Marina Abalakina-Paap and colleagues (1999), West and Sanders (2003) thus deconstruct the common assertion that conspiracy theories provide simplified explanations of complex events. They underline the fact that, through their discursive imaginings, conspiracy theories make "the world more complex by calling attention to hidden and contradictory logics, by proposing alternative ways of understanding and engaging it" (West and Sanders 2003: 17).

As we have seen above in the Malian case, Western media too often neglect these elements when they reaffirm, explicitly or implicitly, simplistic and binary asymmetries that dangerously disqualify some subjectivities and political agencies. In doing so, they justify the French engagement in Mali, which is often locally understood as another expansion of the "racialized capitalism" (Gutiérrez Rodríguez 2018) experienced under French colonization. Concerning the controversies about *Muslim Mali* on the *Kotaku* website, it is therefore not surprising to observe in the same impetus both a denunciation of the negatively stereotyped analyses broadcast by Western media and a mobilization of elements that stem from both conspiracy theories and real historical settings overshadowed by French colonial power. This mobilization is put into motion to illustrate the messiness of everyday in/security discourse.

Conclusion

A primary goal of this chapter was to understand video games as popular artifacts with a specific particularity—their interactivity—that is constitutive of world politics. Gamers not only play video games but play with others and communicate about games with others. By playing and communicating within and about video games, they form communities of practice, which have a strong impact on learning, knowing, communicating, and socializing. Not only do these communities shape their members' understandings of the world (Zagal 2010) they may, by talking about the intersection of video games and world politics, elicit the interest of broader audiences like journalists. Therefore, we have argued, video games are part of the broader category of social media and should be studied to understand the cryptopolitics they embody and the meanings they produce when read in interrelation to other texts. We have thus looked at how intertextuality was performed and by whom to constitute meaning about *Muslim Mali*. We have unpacked some layers of encryption constitutive of the discursive digital network of which *Muslim Mali* is an interpretative junction.

This game has opened up a discursive digital space containing narratives, counternarratives, and several layers of encryption. The first layer of encryption concerns the video game itself, its narrative, its gameplay, and the digital space of affordances and limitations shaped by its procedural mechanics. While the French military intervention on the Malian battlefield was presented as timely and positive, this game reversed the moral line between "the good guys" and "the bad guys": the French forces were the invaders, and the player's avatar represented the resistance. *Muslim Mali* proposed a subversive digital cryptopolitics about a non-fictional conflict, one that inverted the dominant narrative employed by most of the Western commercial software staging the War on Terror. These latter video games usually present jihadists from a Western perspective as "bad guys" to be shot. The second layer of encryption we have identified concerned some US reports mocking the game, which were relayed in global media outlets. We have shown that these reportages are embedded into a racist and imperialist cryptopolitics embodied into in/security narratives, and whose roots lie within US and Western "coloniality of power" (Quijano 2000). They underscore some images of African Otherness that have serious implications for how Western media communicate information, feed social imagination, and encrypt local subjectivities, aspirations, nuances, and complexity. Finally, the digital space opened up by *Muslim Mali* has also allowed the emergence of counternarratives about the game: these resonate with arguments that are already frequent in Mali. Those arguments illustrate the messiness of everyday in/security discourses and denounce the negative stereotypes of Western media and do so by a mobilization of elements drawn from both conspiracy theories and the historical facts of colonialism.

In conclusion, looking to popular artifacts through intertextuality makes the off/online distinction less obvious. Knowledge produced online is performatively refracting understandings of Mali's current armed conflict. Instead of a simplistic opposition to the West, our chapter reveals complex power assemblages whose geopolitical interests define conflict-affected countries like Mali and enable us to situate *Muslim Mali* as one node among others in a network of diverse cryptopolitics that thereby transcends both on- and offline battlefields. However, digital media offer new forms of cryptopolitics through its technological opacity and globalized political imagination and inspires innovative ways of contesting its multiple layers of encryption. We conclude that this video game, *Muslim Mali,* is therefore part of ongoing postcolonial conversations that intersect with the current Malian armed conflict.

Marie Deridder is a postdoctoral researcher and a Marie Curie Fellow (MSCA-IF) at Uppsala University, Sweden.

Olivier Servais is Professor in Anthropology at UC Louvain.

Acknowledgment

This publication was supported by the European Union's Horizon 2020 research and innovation program, under the Marie Skłodowska-Curie grant agreement No 895859.

Notes

1. French troops were finally withdrawn from Mali early in 2022.
2. Her research in Youwarou focused on local politics. Her research in Bamako dealt with the migration-development-security nexus. She has, since then, kept in touch with some of her interlocutors on Facebook, a social media site.
3. See, for example, Jutta Weldes (1999); Kyle Grayson, Matt Davies, and Simon Philpott (2009); Anni Kangas (2009); Neumann and Nexon (2006).
4. According to Étienne Wenger (1998), a community of practice involves a collection of individuals who share a domain of interest for something they do, value their collective competence, and learn how to do it better as they interact regularly, even if they never know each other.
5. See US Army, "Army Career Match." Retrieved 15 January 2023 from www.americasarmy.com.
6. The United States has a history in this area: Tanfer Tunc (2007) explains how, in 1942, during the World War II, the famous film *Casablanca* was supported by the War Films division of the US Department of War. It presented a political and social propagandist commentary on World War II, one intended to counteract the US audiences' negative perception of the war.
7. See, for example, *Call of Duty Modern Warfare* series, *Call of Duty Black Ops* series, *Battlefield 3* and *4*, *Homefront,* which Nick Robinson (2015) studied as a lens to reveal key dynamics underpinning American exceptionalism in US foreign policy.

8. See, for example, Roger Stahl (2006); Johan Höglund (2008); Vit Sisler (2008); Nick Dyer-Witheford and Greig de Peuter (2009); Nina Huntemann and Matthew Thomas Payne (2009); Nick Robinson (2012, 2015); Muniba Saleem and Craig A. Anderson (2013); and Marcus Schulzke (2013a, 2013b).
9. See, for example, Gabriel Weimann (2006a: 123–129, 2006b); Hanna Rogan (2006); Brynjar Lia (2006).
10. See Miron Lakomy's article (2019) for a general review of these video games with a pro-jihadist inclination and a detailed description of their narratives and their gameplay.
11. See, for instance, David Lewis. "Analysis: Mali: From Democracy Poster Child to Broken State." *Reuters*, 24 April 2012. Retrieved 12 March 2021 from https://www.reuters.com/article/us-mali-idUSBRE83N09Q20120424.
12. The Malian government did not disarm the fighters coming back from Libya. Rumors said that the Algerian Red Crescent Society escorted these armed fighters to the Malian border. Once they had crossed this border, they would have been left to themselves.
13. In accordance with the United Nations Security Council Resolution 2100 of April 2013, the authority of the African-led International Support Mission in Mali (AFISMA) was transferred to the United Nations Multidimensional Integrated Stabilization Mission in Mali (MINUSMA).
14. Resolution 2085 adopted by the United Nations Security Council on 20 December 2012. Retrieved 11 September 2022 from http://unscr.com/en/resolutions/2085.
15. The Ansar al-Mujahideen website is an international forum promoting jihadist propaganda by broadcasting video, audio clips, and images related to jihad, as well as other jihad-related publications such as books, magazines, and more. This forum is also suspected of hiding sub-forums connecting jihadist groups with sympathizers around the world to carry out online jihadist activities. See, for instance, this press article connecting this forum to the organization of a thwarted terrorist attack in Brussels in 2010. "Deux opérations anti-terroristes en Belgique" [Two anti-terrorist operations in Belgium]. *Le Figaro*, 23 November 2010. Retrieved 9 September 2011 from https://www.lefigaro.fr/international/2010/11/23/01003-20101123ARTFIG00514-dix-interpellations-autour-d-un-projet-d-attentat-en-belgique.php.
16. See "In Response to French Military Campaign in Mali, Jihadis Design Video Game that Simulates Air-to-Air Shooting Down French Aircraft." *Memri*, 12 March 2013. Retrieved 9 September 2021 from https://www.memri.org/cjlab/in-response-to-french-military-campaign-in-mali-jihadis-design-video-game-that-simulates-air-to-air-shooting-down-french-aircraft. A video clip of the game is posted online: Red Pikeman. "Muslim Mali." *YouTube*, uploaded 18 January 2014 from https://www.youtube.com/watch?v=K5f1iNNSqkM.
17. The game mainly used Arabic. This translation has been checked with the help of a colleague who possesses relevant linguistic knowledge.
18. *Space Invaders* is a 1978 shooting game from the first generation of video games featuring spacecraft. In *Space Invaders*, the player aimed to destroy all enemy spaceships that were trying to invade the planet Earth. There was no way to win this game, as the objective was to resist as long as possible and score as many points as possible, by destroying the highest possible number of invaders. Even the highest-scoring player of *Space Invaders* would inevitably end up losing.

19. Among other online interactive entertainment expressing anti-Western and pro-jihadist inclination as new means of online jihad, Lakomy (2019) mentions *Quest for Bush* (*QfB*) released online (and for free) in 2006 by the Global Islamic Media Front, *Iraqi Resistance* (published in 2006), *Lion of Fallujah* (from 2007), or 2014's *Salil al-Sawarim*, a modified version of *Grand Theft Auto 5 G* (or at least of its trailer). These video games are all modified versions of already existing popular software developed mainly for desktop computers.
20. This assumption remains to be empirically investigated, which is not the aim of this chapter. Following Lakomy's caveat regarding the potential reception of his own article on jihadist propaganda through electronic entertainment (Lakomy 2019: 384), we caution that this chapter does not provide any conclusion as to the efficacy of any video games used by jihadists in their attempts to radicalize player communities and motivate them to follow jihadist goals. This is an issue that remains in need of empirical inquiry.
21. Kristin Deasy. "New Jihadi-Made 'Muslim Mali' Video Game Pits Militants against French Forces." *Agence France-Press*, 14 March 2013. Retrieved 12 March 2021 from https://www.pri.org/stories/2013-03-14/new-jihadi-made-muslim-mali-video-game-pits-militants-against-french-forces.
22. From 2009 to 2013, John Hudson was a senior reporter at Foreign Policy magazine where he covered the US State Department and the National Security Council, writing about politics and global affairs. Since 2018, he has been a US national security reporter at the *Washington Post* covering the State Department and diplomacy. See "John Hudson." *Washington Post*. Retrieved 30 September 2021 from https://www.washingtonpost.com/people/john-hudson/.
23. John Hudson. "Jihadis Create Retro 2-D Shooter Video Game." *Foreign Policy*, 12 March 2013. Retrieved 12 March 2021 from https://foreignpolicy.com/2013/03/12/jihadis-create-retro-2-d-shooter-video-game/.
24. Michael Peck is a US writer and journalist presenting himself as specialized in defense and national security issues with an interest in wargaming. See Michael Peck. "About." *Michael Peck: Writer and Journalist*. Retrieved 12 March 2021 from https://mipeck.com/about/.
25. Michael Peck, "Al Qaeda's Goofy Video Game Provokes Laughter, Not Terror." *Forbes*, 13 March 2013. Retrieved 12 March 2021 from https://www.forbes.com/sites/michaelpeck/2013/03/13/al-qaedas-goofy-new-video-game-provokes-laughter-instead-of-terror/?sh=c7841332734f.
26. However, contradictorily, this last point was an argument put forward by scholars to explain the jihadists' rapid progression and their seizure of northern Mali in 2012 (see section on The Beginning of the Offline War in Mali).
27. Evan Narcisse. "Islamic Extremists Made This Video Game." *Kotaku*, 13 March 2013. Retrieved 12 March 2021 from https://kotaku.com/islamic-extremists-made-this-video-game-5990392.
28. "About G/O Media." Retrieved 11 September 2022 from https://g-omedia.com/.
29. See, for instance, several blog posts written by Evan Narcisse on the theme of Blackness in the video games industry and published on the *Kotaku* website: "Video Games' Blackness Problem." *Kotaku*, 19 February 2015. Retrieved 15 January 2023 from https://kotaku.com/video-games-blackness-problem-1686694082; "Come On, Video Games, Let's See Some Black People I'm Not Embarrassed By." *Kotaku*, 29 March 2012. Retrieved 15 January 2023 from https://kotaku

.com/come-on-video-games-let-s-see-some-black-people-i-m-n-5897227; "This Is Why We Need More Black People Making Video Games." *Kotaku,* 1 March 2013. Retrieved 15 January 2023 from https://kotaku.com/this-is-why-we-need-more-black-people-making-video-game-31741439; "A Game That Showed Me My Own Black History." *Kotaku,* 19 December 2013. Retrieved 15 January 2023 from https://kotaku.com/a-game-that-showed-me-my-own-black-history-1486643518.

30. "What's a Kotaku? Who Works Here?" *Kotaku.* Retrieved 25 October 2021 from https://kotaku.com/about.
31. Stephen Totilo. "A Note about 'Brutal' Comments and a Kotaku for Everyone." *Kotaku,* 26 June 2013. Retrieved 25 October 2021 from https://kotaku.com/a-note-about-brutal-comments-and-a-kotaku-for-everyon-589637991#_ga=1.217962838.1910322999.1440343572.
32. The Su-47, or Sukhoi-47, was an experimental Russian-made fighter aircraft with forward-swept wings. It never entered general production. The French fighter jets depicted in *Muslim Mali* resemble it somewhat, just as the Al-Qaeda jet in the game resembles the US Nighthawk stealth bomber.

References

Abalakina-Paap, Marina, Walter G. Stephan, Traci Craig, and W. Larry Gregory. 1999. "Beliefs in Conspiracies." *Political Psychology* 20(3): 637–47.

Allen, R. 2011. "The Unreal Enemy of America's Army." *Games and Culture* 6(1): 38–60.

Andersson, R. 2019. *No Go World: How Fear Is Redrawing Our Maps and Infecting Our Politics.* Oakland: University of California Press.

Benjaminsen, Tor A., and Boubacar Ba. 2019. "Why do Pastoralists in Mali Join Jihadist Groups? A Political Ecological Explanation." *Journal of Peasant Studies* 46(1): 1–20.

Bergamaschi, I. 2014. "The Fall of a Donor Darling: The Role of Aid in Mali's Crisis." *The Journal of Modern African Studies* 52(3): 347–78.

Bernal, Victoria. 2014. *Nation as Network: Diaspora, Cyberspace, and Citizenship.* Chicago: University of Chicago Press.

Bertrand, M. 1992. "Un an de transition politique: de la révolte à la IIIe République" [A year of political transition: From the revolt to the Third Republic]. *Politique africaine* 47: 9–22.

———. 1999. "Décentralisation et culture politique locale au Mali : de la réforme territoriale au cas de Bamako" [Decentralization and local political culture in Mali: From territorial reform to the case of Bamako]. *Autrepart* 10: 23–40.

Bogost, Ian. 2006a. "Playing Politics: Videogames for Politics, Activism, and Advocacy." *First Monday.* https://doi.org/10.5210/fm.v0i0.1617.

———. 2006b. "Videogames and Ideological Frames." *Popular Communication* 4(3): 165–83. https://doi.org/10.1207/s15405710pc0403_2.

Boilley, Pierre. 2005. "Un complot français au Sahara? Politiques françaises et représentations maliennes" [A French plot in the Sahara? French policies and Malian representations]. In *Mali—France: Regards sur une histoire partagée,* ed. GEMDEV, 161–82. Paris: Karthala.

———. 2011. "Géopolitique africaine et rébellions touarègues. Approches locales, approches globales (1960, 2011)" [African geopolitics and Tuareg rebellions:

Local approaches, global approaches (1960, 2011)]. *L'Année du Maghreb* 7: 151–62.

Brachet, Julien. 2013. "Sahel et ahara: ni incontrôlables, ni incontrôlés" [Sahel and ahara: neither uncontrollable nor uncontrolled]. *Les dossiers du CERI*. Retrieved 15 January 2023 from https://www.sciencespo.fr/ceri/fr/content/dossiersduceri/sahel-et-sahara-ni-incontrolables-ni-incontroles.

Brachman, Jarret M. 2006. "High-Tech Terror: Al-Qaeda's Use of New Technology." *Fletcher Forum of World Affairs* 30(2): 149–64.

Clarke, B., C. Rouffaer, and F. Sénéchaud. 2012. "Beyond the Call of Duty: Why Shouldn't Video Game Players Face the Same Dilemmas as Real Soldiers?" *International Review of the Red Cross* 9 (886): 711–37.

Deridder, Marie. 2012. "Élections municipales dans le Delta intérieur du fleuve Niger (Mali) ou 'Ceux qui cherchent le pouvoir sont parmi nous'" [Municipal elections in the Inner Niger Delta (Mali) or "Those who seek power are among us"]. In *Interfaces empiriques de la mondialisation: African junctions under the Neoliberal development paradigm*, vol. 173, ed. D. De Lame and J. Mazzocchetti, 307–32. Tervuren: Musée royal de l'Afrique central, (MRAC), Studies in Social Sciences and Humanities.

———. 2013. "Processus électoraux, sécurisation des autorités traditionnelles et changement social dans une petite ville du Delta intérieur du fleuve Niger (Mali)" [Electoral processes, security of traditional authorities and social change in a small town in the Inner Niger Delta (Mali)]. In *La Modernité insécurisée: Anthropologie des conséquences de la mondialisation*, ed. C. Bréda, M. Deridder, and P-J. Laurent, 5-16. Louvain-la -Neuve: Academia-Bruylant.

———. 2019. "Invention du 'local,' élites politiques et décentralisation de l'État au Mali" [Invention of the 'local,' political elites and decentralization of the state in Mali]. In *Démocratie par le bas et politique municipale au Sahel*, ed. S. Hagberg, L. Kibora, and G. Körling, 145–62. Uppsala: Uppsala Papers in Africa Studies, no. 4, Uppsala University.

———. 2021. *Elites, élection et transformations du politique au Mali: "Ceux qui cherchent le pouvoir sont parmi nous."* Paris: Karthala.

Deridder, M., P-J. Laurent, and R. Konseiga. 2021. "Une anthropologie politique de la démocratie 'en pratique' au Sud du Sahara: Expériences malienne et burkinabè" [A political anthropology of democracy 'in practice' south of the Sahara: Malian and Burkinabè experiences]. *Anthropology and development* 52: 107–22. https://doi.org/10.4000/anthropodev.1187.

Deridder Marie, and Lotte Pelckmans, eds. 2020. "Perspectives ouest-africaines sur les politiques migratoires et sécuritaires européennes: West African engagements with the EU migration-development-security nexus." *Anthropology and Development*, 51. https://doi.org/10.4000/anthropodev.917

Deridder, M., L. Pelckmans, and E. Ward. 2020. "Reversing the Gaze: West Africa Performing the EU Migration-Development-Security Nexus. *Anthropology & Development* 51: 9–32.

Dyer-Witheford, Nick, and Greig de Peuter. (2009). *Games of Empire: Global Capitalism and Video Games*. Minneapolis: University of Minnesota Press.

Galloway, A. 2004. "Social Realism in Gaming." *Game Studies* 4(1). Retrieved 23 March 2021 from http://gamestudies.org/0401/galloway/.

Gary-Tounkara, D. 2013. "La gestion des migrations de retour, un paramètre négligé de la grille d'analyse de la crise malienne" [The management of return migration, a neglected parameter of the analysis grid of the Malian crisis]. *Politique africain* 2(2): 47–68.

Gavelle, J., J. Siméant, and L. Traoré. 2013. "Le court terme de la légi imité: prises de position, rumeurs et perceptions entre janvier et septembre 2012 à Bamako" [The short term of imitated legitimacy: Positions, rumors and perceptions between January and September 2012 in Bamako]. *Politique africaine* 2(2): 23–46.

Grayson, Kyle. 2013. "How to Read Paddington Bear: Liberalism and the Foreign Subject in *A Bear Called Paddington*." *British Journal of Politics and International Relations* 15(3): 378–93.

Grayson, Kyle, Matt Davies, and Simon Philpott. 2009. "Pop Goes IR? Researching the Popular Culture-World Politics Continuum." *Politics* 29(3): 155–63.

Gruffydd Jones, B. 2008. "The Global Political Economy of Social Crisis: Towards a Critique of the 'Failed State' Ideology." *Review of International Political Economy* 15(2): 180–205.

Gutiérrez Rodríguez, E. 2018. "The Coloniality of Migration and the Refugee Crisis: On the Asylum-Migration Nexus, the Transatlantic White European Settler Colonialism-Migration and Racial Capitalism." *Refuge: Canada's Journal on Refugees* 34(1): 6–28.

Hagberg, S., and G. Körling. 2012. "Socio-political Turmoil in Mali: The Public Debate Following the Coup d'État on 22 March 2012." *Africa Spectrum* 47(2–3): 111–25.

Höglund, Johan. 2008. "Electronic Empire: Orientalism Revisited in the Military Shooter." *Game Studies* 8(1). http://gamestudies.org/0801/articles/hoeglund.

Huntemann, Nina B., and Matthew Thomas Payne, eds. 2009. *Joystick Soldiers: The Politics of Play in Military Video Games.* London: Routledge.

Kangas, Anni. 2009. "From Interfaces to Interpretants: A Pragmatist Exploration into Popular Culture." *Millennium: Journal of International Studies* 38 (2): 317–43.

Lakomy, Miron. 2019. "Let's Play a Video Game: 'Jihadi' Propaganda in the World of Electronic Entertainment." *Studies in Conflict & Terrorism* 42(4): 383–406.

Lecocq, B., G. Mann, B. Whitehouse, D. Badi, L. Pelckmans, N. Belalimat, B. Hall, and W. Lacher. 2013. "One Hippopotamus and Eight Blind Analysts: A Multivocal Analysis of the 2012 Political Crisis in the Divided Republic of Mali." *Review of African Political Economy* 40(137): 343–57.

Lia, Brynjar. 2006. "Al Qaeda Online: Understanding Jihadi Internet Infrastructure." *Jane's Intelligence Review* 18: 14–19.

Mazzocchetti, Jacinthe. 2012. "Feelings of Injustice and Conspiracy Theory: Representations of Adolescents from an African Migrant Background (Morocco and sub-Saharan Africa) in Disadvantaged Neighborhoods of Brussels." *Brussels Studies* 63. https://doi.org/10.4000/brussels.1119.

Neumann, Iver B., and Daniel H. Nexon. 2006. "Introduction: Harry Potter and the Study of World Politics." In *Harry Potter and International Relations,* ed. Iver B. Neumann and Daniel H. Nexon, 1–23. Lanham, MD: Rowman & Littlefield Pub.

Nieborg, D. 2006. "Mods, Nay! Tournaments, Yay! The Appropriation of Contemporary Game Culture by the U.S. Military." *The Fibreculture Journal* 8. Retrieved 23 March 2023 from https://eight.fibreculturejournal.org/fcj-051-mods-nay-tournaments-yay-the-appropriation-of-contemporary-game-culture-by-the-u-s-military/.

———. 2010. "Training Recruits and Conditioning Youth: The Soft Power of Military Games." In *Joystick Soldiers: The Politics of Play in Military Video Games*, ed. Nina B. Huntemann and Matthew Thomas Payne, 53–66. New York: Routledge.

Pelckmans, Lotte. 2015. "Fragmentation of (in-)Security Actors in Mali: The Case of Douentza." In *Insights from Eastern Africa and Sahel: Protection and (in)Security beyond the State*, ed. Kasper Hoffman and Louise Wiuff Moe. Copenhagen: DIIS.

Perraton, C., M. Fusaro, and M. Bonenfant, eds. 2011. *Socialisation et communication dans les jeux vidéo* [Socialization and communication in video games]. Montréal: Presses de l'Université de Montréal.

Pype, Katrien. 2018. "The Devil Is in the Rumba Text: Commenting on Digital Depth." In *Palgrave Handbook for Media and Communication Research in Africa*, ed. B. Mutsvairo, 245–62. Houndmills: Palgrave.

Quijano, A. 2000. "Coloniality of Power and Eurocentrism in Latin America." *International Sociology* 15(2): 215–32.

Robinson, Nick. 2012. "Videogames, Persuasion and the War on Terror: Escaping or Embedding the Military-Entertainment Complex?" *Political Studies* 60: 504–22.

———. 2015. "Have You Won the War on Terror? Military Videogames and the State of American Exceptionalism." *Millennium—Journal of International Studies* 43(2): 450–70.

Rogan, Hanna. 2006. *Jihadism Online: A Study of How Al-Qaida and Radical Islamist Groups Use the Internet for Terrorist Purposes.* Kjeller: FFI.

Rowley, C., and J. Weldes. 2012. "The Evolution of International Security Studies and the Everyday: Suggestions from the Buffyverse." *Security Dialogue* 43(69): 513–30.

Rudolph, J. R. Jr. 2015. *Encyclopedia of Modern Ethnic Conflicts*, 2nd edition. Santa Barbara, CA: ABC-CLIO,

Saleem, Muniba, and Craig A. Anderson. 2013. "Arabs as Terrorists: Effects of Stereotypes within Violent Contexts on Attitudes, Perceptions, and Affect." *Psychology of Violence* 3(1): 84–99.

Sanders, Todd. 2003. "Imaging the Dark Continent: The Met, the Media and the Thames Torso." *Cambridge Anthropology* 23(3): 53–66.

Schulzke, Marcus. 2013a. "Being a Terrorist: Video Game Simulations of the Other Side of the War on Terror." *Media, War & Conflict* 6(3): 207–20.

———. 2013b. "The Virtual War on Terror: Counterterrorism Narratives in Video Games." *New Political Science* 35(4): 586–603.

Seiffert, Jens, and Howard Nothhaft. 2015. "The Missing Media: The Procedural Rhetoric of Computer Games." *Public Relations Review* 41(2): 254–63.

Servais, O. 2020. *Jeux vidéo, nouvel opium du peuple?* [Video games, opium of the people?] Paris: Karthala.

Shaw, I. G. R. 2010. "Playing War." *Social & Cultural Geography* 11(8): 789–803.

Siméant, J. 2014. *Contester au Mali: Formes de la mobilisation et de la critique à Bamako* [Contesting in Mali: Forms of mobilization and criticism in Bamako]. Paris: Karthala.

Sisler, Vit. 2008. "Digital Arabs: Representation in Video Games." *European Journal of Cultural Studies* 11(2): 203–20.

Solomon, H. 2013. "Mali: West Africa's Afghanistan." *RUSI Journal* 158(1): 12–19.

Stahl, R. 2006. "Have You Played the War on Terror?" *Critical Studies in Media Communication* 23(2): 112–30.

Stenersen, Anne. 2008. "The Internet: A Virtual Training Camp?" *Terrorism and Political Violence* 20(2): 215–33.

Torres-Soriano, Manuel R. 2014. "The Hidden Face of Jihadist Internet Forum Management: The Case of Ansar Al Mujahideen." *Terrorism and Political Violence* 28(4): 735–49.

Tunc, Tanfer Emin. 2007. "Casablanca: The Romance of Propaganda." *Bright Lights Film Journal* 55.

Weimann, Gabriel. 2006a. *Terror on the Internet: The New Arena, the New Challenges.* Washington, DC: United States Institute of Peace Press.

———. 2006b. "Virtual Training Camps: Terrorists' Use of the Internet." In *Teaching Terror: Strategic and Tactical Learning in the Terrorist World,* ed. James J. F., 110–32. Forest. Lanham, MD: Rowman & Littlefield.

Weldes, Jutta. 1999. "Going Cultural: Star Trek, State Action, and Popular Culture." *Millennium: Journal of International Studies* 28(1): 117–34.

Weldes, Jutta, and Christina Rowley. 2015. "So, How *Does* Popular Culture Relate to World Politics?" In *Popular Culture and World Politics: Theories, Methods, Pedagogies,* ed. Federica Caso and Caitlin Hamilton, 11–33. Bristol: E-International Relations Publishing.

Wenger, Étienne. 1998. *Communities of Practice: Learning, Meaning, and Identity.* Cambridge: Cambridge University Press.

West, H. G., and T. Sanders. 2003. "Power Revealed and Concealed in the New World Order." In *Transparency and Conspiracy: Ethnographies of Suspicion in the New World Order,* ed. H. G. West and T. Sanders, 1–37. Durham, NC: Duke University Press Books.

Younas, M. A. 2014. "'Digital Jihad' and Its Significance to Counterterrorism." *Counter Terrorist Trends and Analyses* 6(2): 10–17.

Zagal, J. P. 2010. *Ludoliteracy: Defining, Understanding and Supporting Games Education.* Pittsburgh, PA: ECT Press.

Zelin, Aaron. Y. 2013. "The State of Global Jihad Online. A Qualitative, Quantitative, and Cross-Lingual Analysis." *Policy Analysis,* Washington Institute for Near East Policy. Retrieved 15 January 2023 from https://www.washingtoninstitute.org/policy-analysis/state-global-jihad-online.

CHAPTER 5

Algorithmic Power in a Contested Digital Public

Cryptopolitics and Identity in the Somali Conflict

Peter Chonka

Ongoing conflict in Somalia is conventionally understood in terms of a struggle between an internationally backed Federal Government of Somalia (FGS) and the Islamist militancy of Harakaat Al Shabaab Al Mujahideen (Al Shabaab). However, this basic alignment of actors intersects with a far more complex configuration of domestic and external political actors including regional/autonomous state administrations, local militia, African Union-mandated forces, and neighboring/international state actors. Al Shabaab—as a clandestine militant network and parallel form of governance—has often been described by local political commentators as working toward agendas that intertwine with those of a multitude of other political/military actors and identities across the region. In recent history, many of these cryptopolitical narratives have taken the form of different (and sometimes contradictory) conspiracy theories/beliefs that employ highly sensitive rhetoric around the contested history of Somalia's state collapse and the discursive construct of "clan" affiliation. Some of these conspiracies are articulated through demonstrably "fake" news published online by anonymous producers in the region and in the diaspora. However, these narratives can have tangible impacts on the stance and communications of "official" political actors, in what remains a highly contested security environment. Online platforms enable the spread and impact of these narratives but are not simply neutral spaces for the engagement of political actors and commentators. Instead, the chapter argues that it is also increasingly important to consider both human and nonhuman influences on the Somali-language digital public in which these cryptopolitical discourses play out. Different forms of algorithmic power may structure and encourage particular types of information retrieval that both reflect and influence dynamics of political or military contestation in the Somali Horn of Africa.

Cryptopolitical understandings of Al Shabaab's militancy can be understood in relation to three factors. First, they have their roots in the unreconciled legacies of the wider and longer Somali conflict (the period before and after state collapse in 1991) and the distinctive (if disputed) anthropological discussion of clan differences as "invisible" among a regional population who largely identify in ethno-linguistic and socio-religious terms as Somalis and Muslims (Ali Ahmed 1995; Besteman 1998; Lewis 1998, 2004). Second, conspiracy theorization is also engendered by the complex realities of violent power projection by both local and external actors in Somalia and the remarkable robustness and reach of Al Shabaab's networks of parallel governance. The third factor, the chapter argues, relates to the nature of the modern Somali-language "digital public" in which these cryptopolitical narratives circulate and are debated. The chapter outlines a regionally and politically fragmented network of media producers that include "state" broadcasters, private local, transnational news organizations and diaspora commentators, all of which are intertwined through ubiquitous social media platforms and practices of online information retrieval through search engine algorithms.

Recent discussions of digital "cryptopolitics" have foregrounded encryption as a core technology of internet security—protecting data and (potentially) "stabilising the power of the state" in an anarchic and transnational digital realm (Monsees 2019: 2). Although this chapter focuses on the digital public of debates around the Somali conflict and state reconstruction, "cryptopolitics" here is understood more in relation to its earlier use to describe hidden agendas of factional politics (Rigby 1969). Central here is the idea that political actors are working in clandestine fashion toward particular goals and are part of wider—but often invisible—networks. Through conspiracy narratives, commentators make links and build networks of relationships. In this sense, the process is analogous to the structuring of the Internet, through which many of these theories are articulated. However, this digital public is not merely an open forum within which commentators publish and compete for attention. Access to content is mediated through technologies such as search engines. These are underpinned by commercial algorithms that enable or encourage user access to particular sources of information. Features such as search engine autocomplete "predictions" can influence the type of content searched for and accessed. They themselves make associations between different keywords and fields, based on a variety of factors that may include previous user searches.

The opaque and inscrutable nature of these algorithms makes them cryptopolitical technologies in and of themselves. Highlighting one example of Somali-language autocomplete search prediction, the chapter demonstrates how search algorithms may encourage users to "uncover" information relating to controversial identity markers of clan—the same types of markers that have been frequently engaged in cryptopolitical narratives around Al Shabaab and wider Somali political dynamics.

The chapter demonstrates the nature and significance of cryptopolitical conspiracy theorization to the recent history of ongoing political fragmentation in Somalia, and then problematizes the algorithmic power of search engines in this African-language digital public as a potentially important factor shaping understandings of identity and narratives of conflict. As such, I first outline relevant discussions in the anthropological and historical literature that engage with identity construction and political contestation in Somalia. This is followed with an introduction to local structures of digital media production. To demonstrate how the digital public becomes an important arena for identity-based regional contestation, I analyze several (predominantly Somali-language) texts that have disseminated specific conspiracy claims—coming from anonymous "journalists," named commentators, as well as prominent politicians. A case for the "offline" or "real-world" salience of these types of narratives is made by linking the texts to security dynamics that have been documented in relation to the ongoing conflict and the evolution of Al Shabaab as an organization. The data analyzed in this section is largely derived from my PhD fieldwork in different sites of media production in Somalia/Somaliland and the diaspora around 2015 and my previous experience monitoring Somali-language media in my role as an interpreter for an international humanitarian organization.

That digital platforms are conducive arenas for the circulation of conspiracy theories or other forms of mis/disinformation is hardly a novel finding nor one peculiar to the Somali digital public. However, after the chapter makes the case for the importance of such narratives for understandings and practices of violence within the Somali conflict, it then introduces another element in the digital semantic context that should also be factored into accounts of the Internet's impact on "fragile states": external search engine engagement with local language content. The chapter builds on the previous structural analysis of conflict media production with consideration of potential algorithmic influences on debates and practices of popular information retrieval. I present a systematic case study that examines how search engine "autocomplete" suggestions/predictions currently engage with Somali-language input and present users with keywords relating to "clan."

Consideration of how algorithms make visible or encourage user engagement with certain types of information provides a new lens through which to explore the broader concept of digital cryptopolitics that is the subject of this volume. The analysis around a specific digital practice relating to identity politics brings to light an emergent (and challenging) field for critical engagement with algorithmic power in conflict-affected states. Scholarship in this area has hitherto overwhelmingly focused on Western and English-language contexts and scrutiny must be expanded to explore the structuring effects of algorithmic technologies—such as globally ubiquitous search engines—on transnational African-language digital publics and discourses in conflict zones.

Historical Roots of Contemporary Cryptopolitics

Somalia has been without an empirically sovereign state exercising control over the entirety of its territory since the collapse of Siyaad Barre's military regime in 1991. The civil war of the 1980s fractured the country along multiple regional and clan-based fault lines that remain salient and (to a large extent) unreconciled to this day. Distinctive in the wider continental context, the Somali Horn of Africa is home to a population that largely identifies (ethnically) as Somali, speaks dialects of the Somali language, and are Sunni Muslims. A swathe of "Somali" territory stretches beyond the boundaries of Somalia into Djibouti, eastern Ethiopia, and northeastern Kenya. That these territories were not incorporated into the post-independence Republic of Somalia in 1960 was largely the result of prior histories of colonial contestation and boundary creation in which Britain, Italy, France, and Ethiopia played important roles (Barnes 2007; Clifford 1936).

Relatively high levels of ethno-linguistic commonality through the region should not be taken as an indicator of social homogeneity. Somali society is characterized by a range of cleavages that engage minority-racial, ethnic and caste-type distinctions, and the lineage "system" of clan affiliation and customary law that historically helped structure social relations among a predominantly nomadic pastoral population. These are all disputed (and, at times, essentializing) characterizations of "Somali society" that have been fiercely debated in the wider anthropological and Somali Studies literature (Ali Ahmed 1995; Besteman 1998; Lewis 1998). Nonetheless, there has come to be broad scholarly recognition that the idea of "clan" has never remained static. Instead, processes of economic and political transformation from the colonial encounter through the post-independence state-building era fundamentally altered the political logics of the lineage system in ways unrecognizable from the pastoral context that was the backdrop for earlier ethnographies of Somali societies (Samatar 1989, 1992)

Three points within the clan and society debate are particularly salient for this chapter's discussion of cryptopolitical conspiracy narratives in digital and real-world arenas of conflict. First, the sharing of a standardized dominant dialect of Somali is central to the functioning of the transnational media spaces that serve as channels for debate across the multiple borders of the Somali Horn. In comparison to apparently greater heterogeneity in Somalia's neighboring multi-ethnic states such as Ethiopia and Kenya, the relatively high level of ethno-linguistic and socio-cultural homogeneity between Somalis from the main clan families has meant that differences between these groups have been described as "invisible" (Lewis 2004).[1] This notion of "invisibility" is important to consider in relation to the wider concept of cryptopolitics and conspiracy and the ways certain modern media technologies (e.g., search engine algorithms) facilitate—and potentially encourage—an uncovering of information pertaining to individuals and associated markers of identity.

The second point is that Somali politics in recent history has been understood by many local actors in terms of clan affiliation. This has been quasi-institutionalized in the so-called 4.5 quota system that has allocated political representation at the federal level on the basis of four main "clan families" and a half share for so-called minority populations. Despite attempts over the last decade to facilitate one-person-one-vote elections for Parliament and the Presidency, transfers of power have continued to be undertaken through indirect processes involving clan representatives and electoral delegates, a fraction of the wider population who vote for parliamentary seats allocated according to the 4.5 formula (these MPs in turn vote for presidential candidates, most recently in 2022). Some scholars argue that institutionalizations of "tribal" identity simply reflect the internalization of external narratives about the apparently primordial origins of clan within an essentialized Somali society that date back to colonial-era anthropological studies (Kapteijns 2004). Nonetheless, there remains a tension in the formulation of this 4.5 quota system (itself highly disputed) and general taboos in political discourse around the explicit public mentioning of clan identities (Kapteijns 2012).

These tensions are themselves related to the wider history of the Somali conflict. Although Siyaad Barre's "scientific socialist" regime (1969–1991) embarked on a "modernist" project of (literally) burying clan identities (Tahir 2016: 84), the repressive nature of his rule both required and encouraged the widely perceived development of a particular (and clan-based) inner circle of power-holders (Compagnon 1995). In facing growing opposition, the regime responded by effectively mobilizing and militarizing the same clan cleavages that it had once railed against in the name of Somali ethno-nationalism and the irredentist project of unifying the territories of "Greater Somalia." Armed opposition to the regime came to be organized along clan lines, not as a result of overriding primordial attachments to lineage groups but because of the ways in which the regime had manipulated such wider divisions (Kapteijns 2012), and the logistical advantages that were presented to armed movements in their engagement of clan elders and customary law (Compagnon 1998). After Barre was overthrown in 1991, the civil war continued in the south-central regions and violence was often enacted along clan lines. Lineages (even loosely) associated with the former regime were "cleansed" from the capital (Kapteijns 2012), southern ethnic and racial minorities—particularly in agro-pastoralist areas—suffered disproportionately from the predations of armed groups (Besteman and Cassanelli 2000). This period (from the late 1980s till the mid-1990s) of mass violence, humanitarian crisis, and the "destruction" (*burburkii*) of the state has had profound implications for the modern territorial and political-social map of Somalia. To a large extent, what occurred through that period was the displacement and relocation of large numbers of people to areas (*deegaano*) traditionally associated with their clan groups (Hoehne 2016). This had the longer-term impact of crystallizing certain clan-territorial boundaries that had historically been characterized by a significant level of blurring, overlap, and mobility (Cassanelli 2015).

These processes contributed to the emergence of the post-1991 political authorities that this chapter discusses in relation to narratives of Al Shabaab's (later) militancy. These various secessionist, regional, or insurgent administrations require some historical introduction. The Republic of Somaliland in the northwest declared its independence from Somalia in 1991, largely as a reaction to the mass violence unleashed by the southern Mogadishu-based regime. Throughout the course of the civil war, Somaliland's capital, Hargeisa, was almost entirely destroyed by the regime in its offensives against northern rebels (Omaar 1993). Many in Somaliland have described this as a "genocide" carried out against the clan-family that predominates in the northwest (Jhazbhay 2009). Although sub-clans of this clan-family dominate politics in Somaliland, some other groups outside this lineage have been partially incorporated into Somaliland's (relatively democratic) independent political project.

The Puntland State of Somalia was established in the northeastern part of the Somali Horn in 1998. Puntland became a refuge for many people (including those hailing from the broad clan-family of deposed dictator Siyaad Barre) fleeing early 1990s violence in south-central Somalia (Marchal 2010). Puntland has remained largely autonomous since then and, like Somaliland, developed its own governing institutions and armed forces. Unlike Somaliland, Puntland now considers itself to be a Federal Member State of Somalia Federal Republic. Nonetheless its relationship with the FGS in Mogadishu has often come under serious strain. Somalia's other, more recently formed, federal member states (Jubbaland, Southwest State, Galmudug, and Hirshabelle) all took formal shape under the auspices of the wider (UN-backed) federalization project undertaken by the internationally recognized FGS in Mogadishu. The FGS came into power under President Hassan Sheikh Mohamoud in 2012, after the expulsion of Al Shabaab from the capital the previous year. Under the subsequent presidency of Mohamed Abdulaahi Farmaajo (2017–2022) these center-periphery relations continued to be tested. Contestation has related to a lack of constitutional clarity on the federal division of responsibilities and revenue between the FGS and the federal member states (Somali Public Agenda 2018). Hassan Sheikh Mohamoud retook the presidency in May 2022, the culmination of a delayed, disputed, and protracted indirect electoral process for the legislature and executive. At the time of writing, center-periphery tensions over fiscal federalism remain.

International patronage is also an important factor in political fragmentation, for instance in relation to the engagement of the United Arab Emirates and Saudi Arabia (which have often dealt directly with the federal member states, and de facto independent Somaliland), and Turkey and Qatar (which have tended to maintain closer links with the FGS in Mogadishu). Turkey's humanitarian, diplomatic, and security-sector training support has been vital to the FGS since its formation in 2012. As such, Somalia has become an important arena for wider Gulf/Middle East rivalries. This has manifested itself in regional port/infrastructure development (Roble 2017) and extensive training to various federal and regional forces. Many other actors are involved in such military capacity building, such as British and EU trainers, as well as private security companies. Overall, however, the FGS has faced difficulties in consolidating the Somali National Army (SNA) and integrating regional forces into its command structures (Williams 2019). The FGS still exerts limited authority beyond Mogadishu. Although Al Shabaab has lost significant amounts of urban territory since 2012 under African Union (AMISOM), SNA, and US military pressure, it maintains an active presence in many rural areas and the ability to continue to launch deadly conventional and asymmetric attacks across the south-central region (and Puntland).

This brings us to Al Shabaab's campaign itself and the parallel systems of governance it operates. The distinctiveness of the organization's strong, pervasive, widespread, and clandestine institutions is fundamental to popular imaginations of its cryptopolitical agency and its instrumentalization of social cleavages. Al Shabaab rose to power in Somalia in the wake of the (US-backed) Ethiopian overthrow of the Union of Islamic Courts (UIC) in 2006 (Barnes and Hassan 2007; Hansen 2013). From the mid-1990s onward, the UIC had emerged as a somewhat "organic" alliance of local Islamic judicial authorities and business actors in many urban centers across south-central regions (Ahmad 2015). By the middle of the first decade of the twenty-first century, it was seen by many Somalis as constituting a relatively legitimate governance experiment that neutralized the power of warlords who had emerged through the 1990s, and improved general security conditions in cities such as Mogadishu (Kapteijns 2010). The specter of organized Islamist governance across its historically disputed border was troubling to the Ethiopian government, which effectively leveraged post-9/11 fears of Al-Qaeda penetration in the region to secure US support for an invasion. This violent regime change proved highly unpopular with many Somalis, and Al Shabaab—hitherto one armed faction within the wider courts system—positioned itself as a "nationalist" resistance movement and ultimately succeeded in expanding its administrative power even further than that previously held by the UIC. An ambiguous Ethiopian withdrawal and propping up of an unpopular Transitional Federal Government gave Al Shabaab the opportunity for this expansion. However, by 2011, multilateral international support for anti-Islamist operations had ramped back up to the level that AMISOM—the African Union's now longest serving "peace support" operation (Williams 2018)—was able to expel Al Shabaab from Mogadishu. This set the scene for the installation of the Somali Federal Government and successive SNA/AMISOM taking of other south-central cities and towns from the group.[2]

Al Shabaab's insurgency has continued, and the group continues to penetrate security measures in Mogadishu in its high-profile attacks against military, governmental and civilian targets. It attempts to justify the latter in terms of their association with the state, intelligence or foreign interests (Chonka 2018). Although Al Shabaab's targeting has not been entirely indiscriminate (Warner and Chapin 2018), the group has lost a significant amount of the popular support it once enjoyed in its engagement with foreign forces on Somali soil. Relevant to the analysis that follows is the way that Al Shabaab has evolved as a multi-faceted and clandestine military and administrative network across the Somali territories and beyond. This has consistently been evidenced in security, humanitarian, and policy-orientated literature on the Somali context over the last decade. Al Shabaab maintains governance institutions in areas that it still controls and extracts significant revenue. Truckers in south-central Somalia, for instance, have reported preferring to travel along Al Shabaab-controlled routes due to their more regular taxation of goods, in comparison to multiple local militias aligned with the regional states and/or the federal government (United Nations Monitoring Group on Somalia and Eritrea 2017: 40). "Taxes" are levied on a wide array of businesses throughout Somalia (with the likely partial exception of Somaliland), while some of the poorest agriculturalists in central regions have been hit by extortive extractions. Al Shabaab also administers a parallel judicial system in many areas, including, reportedly, districts in and around Mogadishu (Bananay 2017). The organization's intelligence/counterintelligence arm, the Amniyat, is widely feared, both within the group and in wider society. The group has maintained a tight ideological core (despite internal purges and leadership changes) and also engages in practices akin to organized crime. Almost uniquely in modern Somali politics, Al Shabaab has often maintained a degree of cross-clan representation in its decision-making structures,[3] although centralization due to military pressure may have altered this and influenced the development of a rival Islamic State affiliate in Somalia (Hiraal Institute 2018).[4]

Cryptopolitics and Conspiracy in the Digital Public

Al Shabaab's militancy at times maps onto—or is imagined to conspiratorially intersect with—the regional fragmentations of political power across the Somali territories. The chapter now outlines the digital media environment in which these political-regional-clan narratives have often been debated across regional and international borders. It then discusses media texts that have both advanced and attempted to debate and debunk conspiracy theories around Al Shabaab's crypto-militancy. While these texts mostly date from the period of Hassan Sheikh Mohamoud's first presidency, similar types of cryptopolitical narrative were expressed throughout the term of his successor (President Farmaajo), where Al Shabaab violence continued and was often linked by commentators to broader political or commercial disputes (Elder 2022).

Local and diasporic understandings of political change and conflict in Somalia are debated across a Somali-language digital public of multiple overlapping media networks and social media platforms. Elsewhere I have outlined a broad typology of these media producers (Chonka 2019) drawing distinctions between (1) Somali-language media networks that are headquartered in the global diaspora and broadcast via TV, radio, and Internet news across all of the territories of the Somali Horn (e.g., BBC Somali Service or Universal TV); (2) "State" broadcasters of the various administrations that claim authority in different parts of the territory (e.g., Somali National TV, Puntland TV, Somaliland National TV); (3) private locally headquartered media houses that have the capacity to broadcast across the whole territory (e.g., online) but often have sectional audiences (e.g., media consumers who identify with particular regions/administrations and who may be located in the region or in the wider global diaspora); and (4) the media production of Al Shabaab itself and its affiliates/sympathizers (Chonka 2016). Importantly, ubiquitous social media platforms such as Facebook interlink many of these different networks and producers and individual commentators/politicians use these spaces to publish and publicize their work. Similar to other African contexts, political authorities across the region have recognized the security implications brought by increasing access to social media and the potential for (mis/dis)information to spread rapidly (Hassan and Hitchen 2019; Srinivasan, Diepeveen, and Karekwaivanane 2019). The capacity of authorities to regulate this media ecology varies widely, however authorities in Somaliland have blocked access to social media around election times (Walls et al. 2018), and the federal government in Mogadishu has recently emphasized their willingness to restrict access to such platforms in its attempt to hold national school examinations.[5]

Within this wider media ecology, certain administrations have carved out their own publics to debate "internal" politics. Somaliland-based media, for instance, cover developments inside the de facto independent republic that relates to its own political institutions and processes—"Somalia" here is very much defined as a foreign country. Nonetheless, even in Somaliland, multimedia transnational Somali-language broadcasting is consumed widely by citizens. It is within this broader Somali digital public that Somaliland articulates its status and claim to independence. Within these media spaces the different political directions of secessionist or autonomous administrations are also disputed. It is in relation to these discursive contests that the article examines the specter of Al Shabaab, as expressed in narratives from various political actors across (and between) the different regions in the post 2012 period of federal state reconfiguration.

One conspiracy narrative that has found periodic expression in macro-political debates involves Somaliland's alleged complicity with (or even active support for) Al Shabaab, as a means to perpetuate instability in southern Somalia and therefore bolster Hargeisa's claim to secession and international recognition. Such accounts often focus on the fact that Somaliland has not been a recent target of Al Shabaab operations (since large-scale bombings of state, Ethiopian, and UN interests in 2008), and that former leaders of the organization—such as deceased Emir Ahmed Abdi Godane—hailed from the region itself. This supposed relationship was outlined in a highly questionable (English-language) article that appeared in February 2016 on the (now defunct) Kenyamedia.net website. Entitled "The Nexus between Somaliland and Al Shabaab," the article's byline featured two named "Swedish Investigative Journalists." These individuals do not appear to exist, and it is unclear who the producers of the piece actually were. Although now irretrievable on the original site, copies of this article continue to circulate on other Somali websites,[6] in the same manner that much other digital content is copied and pasted across multiple locations. Of course, digital platforms also provide the spaces and tools for other commentators and "investigative journalists" to debunk such content, as was the case with the "nexus" piece in question. In this case, the website Solaportal.com presented evidence that these writers were fake, casting doubt on the claims made.[7]

Although the dubious "nexus" piece did not directly engage with narratives of clan, conspiracy theorization of this sort has intersected with wider clan/territorial narratives engaging with conflict in southern Somalia. Somali-language polemics such as that written in 2014 by an individual purporting to be an elder in the conflicted Lower Shabelle region (in southern Somalia where the conflict with Al Shabaab has been particularly acute) reference multiple external actors described in controversially explicit clan terms. Somaliland was labeled derisively as "Isaaq-land" (in reference to the predominant clan-family in the northwest), and the writer alleged their agents' involvement in the Shabelle conflict, and wider Mogadishu politics as a means to prevent state-building in the south and advance the interests of Somaliland.[8] The writer employed the colorful description of Isaaq MPs—for him "secret agents" of Somaliland—sitting around in hotels in Mogadishu plotting against Somali "unity" (this trope plays on the fact that there are politicians in the Somali capital who hail from Somaliland, but who nominally "represent" the northwest regions in *Somalia's* parliament). Although this piece constituted an extreme and convoluted form of clan conspiracy-based argumentation, it nonetheless shares many rhetorical features with other similarly written polemics in Somali cyberspace. Different vocabularies, idioms, or euphemisms of clan here interplay with nationalist tropes of Somali cultural, religious, or linguistic homogeneity in the face of externally manipulated political fragmentation—in which Al Shabaab is seen to play a clandestine role.

Such conspiracy narratives could be dismissed as the inevitable ephemera of the vast digital spaces that provide platforms for fringe voices and seemingly unlimited scope for the propagation of misinformation. Nonetheless, just as scholars in the west are increasingly cognizant of the cumulative impact of "fake news" and "toxic" digital subcultures on "mainstream" political debate and electoral processes (Allcott and Gentzkow 2017; Gruzd and Roy 2014; Persily 2017; Wodak, Mral, and Khosravinik 2013), the Somali context also provides examples of how such narratives could be seen to both reflect and potentially influence "official" political stances.

An instructive case here relates to the conflicted relationship between the administrations of autonomous Puntland and secessionist Somaliland, which over the last decade has manifested in open hostilities in the regions of Sool and Sanaag that are disputed between them (Hoehne 2015). Clashes around the strategic village of Tukaraq in May 2018 were an escalation of these tensions and claimed the lives of dozens of soldiers on both sides. In the context of these long-running disputes with Somaliland, Puntland authorities have invoked the conspiratorial specter of Al Shabaab. The group has long maintained a presence in Puntland (particularly in the mountainous regions along the northern coast and close to the important port city of Bosaaso) and has carried out asymmetric and conventional attacks against Puntland state and military targets. Officially aligned against all Somali state actors, Al Shabaab considers Puntland to be an "apostate" administration, in league with foreign intelligence services and favorably aligned with UN-backed "stabilization" plans for Somalia. The Puntland authorities, for their part, have on several occasions made public statements to the effect that external Somali political actors (including Somaliland) have been supporting Al Shabaab as a proxy to undermine their control of the northeast.[9] In January 2015, those allegations from Puntland's Security Minister—while not backed up with specific evidence—related to a controversy over Somaliland's impounding of a ship containing international military cargo at the port of Berbera. I have previously documented how this incident was also accompanied by a flurry of dubious reporting and misleading images that circulated online at the time (Chonka 2019), and the Puntland Security Minister here expressed concerns that such equipment could be channeled by Somaliland to Al Shabaab in the Galgala hills.

Puntland authorities have also accused the Federal Government of Somalia (in President Hassan Sheikh Mohamoud's first term) of facilitating Al Shabaab operations in its territory. As such, another Puntland Security Minister in 2016 accused the FGS in Mogadishu of allowing Al Shabaab forces to enter Puntland in order to destabilize its territory.[10] He claimed that this was related to Puntland's dissatisfaction with the 4.5 system of clan representation (being used at the time for parliamentary selection) advocated by the Mogadishu-based government. Around that period, a prevalent conspiracy theory in Puntland claimed that Hasan Sheikh-era FGS authorities in Mogadishu were manipulating or even directing Al Shabaab attacks for clan-political goals. The targeted killings of Daarood Members of Parliament (linked in these narratives with their "home territory" of Puntland) were alleged to be part of a "Hawiye" conspiracy against Puntland in the process of the reconstruction of a federal government. At that time, a popular Puntland-orientated news site published an article called "Muuq-disho" that played on the name of the capital as an "image of killing" and other puns to signify collusion between Al Shabaab ("Al Habaab/the lost") and the Dam Jadiid faction (or "Dulmi Jadiid"—the "new oppression") associated with the president.[11] Although such accounts tended to feature much more in the way of rhetorical flourish than evidence, they epitomized contrasts being drawn between clan "home" territory (*deegaan*) and the apparent dangers of the Mogadishu political environment.[12]

The wider conflict with Al Shabaab in Somalia is not only played out via regional forces such as Puntland or the Somali "National" Army, but also engages a wide array of foreign security "partners." In a highly opaque operating environment, various forms of security patronage and cooperation are open to accusations of manipulation and hidden agendas. For instance, Puntland security/intelligence agencies were themselves accused by the Galmudug regional administration in September 2016 of feeding US forces false intelligence that resulted in an airstrike against the latter's militia near the city of Galkacyo. Puntland and Galmudug dispute their border (and the city of Galkacyo itself is divided along clan-political lines) and Galmudug authorities alleged that Puntland actors had led US forces to believe that their troops were Al Shabaab operatives.[13] Further south, in regions such as Lower Shabelle, other botched raids involving US forces on the ground have also been attributed to false "human intelligence." A SNA/US Special Forces joint raid in the village of Bariire in August 2017 led to deaths of ten civilians (including children) and subsequent investigative reporting alleged that clan-political motivations lay behind misleading information that precipitated the operation.[14]

The Lower Shabelle region has itself been a particularly complex theater of operations for various clan militias, African Union and US forces, the Somali National Army, and Al Shabaab. The latter has itself proved adept at taking advantage of long-standing communal grievances from populations that consider themselves to be indigenous to the region against the encroachment of powerful Hawiye sub-clans into southern regions. This has a long history that stretches back into post-colonial industrial agricultural developments, post-state collapse predations of marauding militias (Besteman and Cassanelli 2000; DeWaal 2007), and more recent discontent around the role of the SNA—itself often structured around clan groupings—in extending political and economic power from nearby Mogadishu into the region. In this context, credible reports emerged in that period of SNA soldiers "moonlighting" as Al Shabaab operatives for financial gain and clan-motivated attacks on civilians by combined groups of SNA, clan-militiamen, and Al Shabaab fighters.[15]

All of the above narratives of conspiracy—some of which are grounded in stronger evidence than others—are partly engendered by Al Shabaab's organizational profile and the clandestine networks through which it operates. Important here are its aforementioned mechanisms for financing. A lack of regulation and relative ease of mobile money payments across the territory (as well as Al Shabaab's renowned use of SMS messaging for extortion) have meant that a wide variety of businesses have needed to pay the organization to continue functioning (Mubarak 2020). As such, it is frequently possible for commentators to imagine ways in which conspiratorial relations are enacted through flows of finance and information across a spectral regional network.

This section has presented a series of snapshots of narratives that connect Al Shabaab's militancy to various complex and contested political relationships involving regional and clan identities. These narratives have been frequently debated in the "real-world" political context of the ongoing reconfiguration of the Somali state, and in a digital public of media production across various political boundaries within and beyond the region. A myopic focus on "clan" politics—as a primordial signifier and determinant of conflict—is a deeply problematic approach (Kapteijns 2004; Samatar 1992, 2006). I engage the concept here only in the sense that its contested and ambiguous position in local political discourse render it a frequently engaged trope for conspiracy theorization in the digital public. Tensions are manifest in the relationship between its taboo status in acceptable public discourse (not always respected in online debates) and its continued institutionalization in certain political structures—such as the 4.5 quota formula for clan representation in Somalia's legislature. Conspiracy narratives link various actors with different types of (often hidden) agendas, and often present themselves as making the invisible visible. The following selection continues this discussion of invisibility, taboo, and cryptopolitics but argues that analysis of controversial content in the digital public also requires consideration of the ways in which nonhuman actors (such as algorithms) may affect how people search for and retrieve information about a conflicted context.

Identity Politics and Algorithmic Power

Studies of online discourse globally have increasingly emphasized how sensational, controversial, and polarizing content can come to have disproportionate impacts on wider information environments (Allcott and Gentzkow 2017). Often this is discussed in terms of the power of "fake news" and other forms of "clickbait" that are driven by the commercial logics of internet traffic advertising revenue (Bakir and McStay 2018; Gray, Bounegru, and Venturini 2020). Also important are the ways in which social media platforms "curate" content into user's "newsfeeds" through algorithms that predict what those users will respond positively toward—thus creating "echo chambers" or "filter bubbles" that reduce users' exposure to alternative viewpoints (Bennett and Pfetsch 2018; Bozdag and van den Hoven 2015). This burgeoning literature reminds us that online platforms are not neutral spaces where ideas have an equal capacity to circulate and compete. Instead, nonhuman elements—like the algorithms that underpin social media platforms or search engines—play a significant role in directing users' behavior and providing access to certain types of information. Understanding the circulation of controversial cryptopolitical conspiracy theories in the Somali-language digital public requires similar consideration of the influence of such platform structures. Studies of these dynamics in non-Western/non-English-language digital spaces have largely been lacking, and the "black box" nature of proprietary algorithms makes it difficult to identify specific ways content in African indigenous languages is being processed by the platforms on which people search and access such content. Nonetheless, this section is able to pinpoint an example where a clear "algorithmic power" (Bucher 2018) is identifiable and demonstrates how this may reinforce or encourage online engagement with the cryptopolitical discourses of clan and conspiracy highlighted above. Presented here is a specific and systematic case study on digital information retrieval and

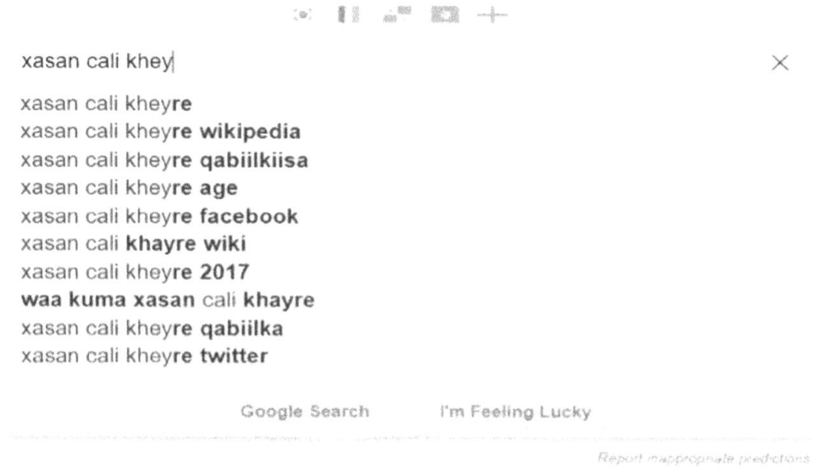

Figure 5.1. Selection of Google autocomplete predictions (18 June 2019). © Peter Chonka.

the role of Google's search engine query "autocomplete" algorithm, which offers users predictions in relation to their typed query. This data illuminates ways these technologies have the potential play into cryptopolitical understandings of political agency and the challenges they present to understandings of ethnic identity formation or construction.

While undertaking fieldwork in Somalia, I came across the phenomenon whereby entering the (Somali) name of a male political figure (for instance, the then Somali prime minister) into the Google search engine produced the following type of selection of autocomplete predictions (see Figure 5.1).

Aside from completing the spelling of his name and suggesting a search for his Wikipedia entry, the third autocomplete prediction is "*qabiilkiisa*," Somali for "his clan." Prompted by this experience, I later designed a systematic test to enter search terms for ten male Somali politicians (all contemporary, except former president Siyaad Barre) and to record the autocomplete predictions the algorithm presented. Out of the ten names, similar clan-related keywords were suggested for six of these. For three women prominent in Somali politics, one returned a clan-specific keyword prediction in the test. Recognizing the potential for the researcher's past digital traces to influence the operation of the algorithm, I conducted this experiment not only on my personal computer in the UK (which I frequently use to access Somali-language online material), but also on a UK colleague's computer, who had never accessed any Somali-language content). Although I had first noticed this

Author's computer (UK)													
Date of search	03.06.2019			Suggested/predicted Google autocomplete search term									
Full Name (Somali)	Position	User search input	M/F	1	2	3	4	5	6	7	8	9	10
Muuse Biixi Cabdi	President of Republic of Somaliland	Muuse Biixi	M	abdi	snm	hooyadii	**qabiilkiisa**	**waa qoloma**	twitter	iyo farmaajo	age	**qabiilka**	
Cabdiweli Maxamed Cali Gaas	Former Puntland President	Cabdiweli Gaas	M	wikipedia	taariikhda	madaxweyne	**qabiilka**	dr	gaas	gaas			
Maxamed Cabdilaahi Farmaajo	President of Somalia	farmaajo	M	twitter	somalia	wife	age	kheyre	iyo kheyre	pic	book	news	
Xasan Sheikh Maxamuud	Former President of Somalia	Xasan Sheikh	M	muumin	maxamuud	facebook	**qabiilka**	cali nuur	wikipedia	**abgaal**	jigjiga	iyo xaaskiisa	
Axmed Maxamed Islaam	President of Jubbaland	Axmed Madoobe	M	**qabiilkiisa**	2006	pictures	youtube	images	kismaayo	photos	iyo qalbi dhagax	wikipedia	
Shariff Xasan Sheikh Aden	Former president of SouthWest state	Shariff Sakiin	M	n/a									
Edna Aadan	Internationally renowned doctor in Somaliland	Edna Aadan	F	ismail	hospital	book	university	foundation	desert island discs	half the sky	quotes	a woman of firsts	midwife
Siyaad Barre	Former President of Somalia (1969-1991)		M	**iyo isaaq**	iyo diinta	sawiro	hooyadiis	quotes	iyo salaad gabeyre	1969	video	history	
Fowsiya Yuusuf Xaaji Aadan	Politician who has served for Somalia and Somaliland	fowsiya yuusuf	F	xaaji aadan									
Ayaan Xirsi Cali	Controversial, internationally famous writer	ayaan xirsi	F	cali	magan	oo dhimatay	hirsi ali	**qabiilka**	waa tuma				
Xasan Cali Kheyre	Somalia Prime Minister	Xasan Cali	M	kheyre	**qabiilkiisa**	kheyre		age	mire	geesey	maxamed wasiirka ...	twitter	wikipedia
Xasan Daahir Aweys	Former Al Shabaab ideologue (under house arrest)	xasan daahir	M	2017	2018	sheekh	taariikhda						

phenomenon when I was physically present in Somalia, a colleague in Mogadishu also conducted the same test for me on their computer in order to take into account any potential impact of location on the data returned.[16] The results showed minimal difference between the autocomplete predictions. This can be seen in Figure 5.2, which presents all of the keywords and autocomplete predictions across the three tests. As the searches were not completed (and the users did not enter the "*qabiil*" search terms themselves), they did not contribute to the further tendency of the algorithm to suggest these results—a recursive feature of the algorithmic phenomenon I return to below. Furthermore, none of the suggested keywords included in the sample shown below had derived from any of my (or my colleague's) previous searches. Google autocomplete predictions that are informed by a user's past searches are generally highlighted in purple, and include the option to remove them. Screenshots were saved from every search (thirty-six in total) and none include "previously searched for" keywords.

Because the tests all used the Somali spellings of the names, it is highly likely that the users whose searches had initially generated these terms were Somali speakers. The particular male figures whose names were entered were chosen given their high profile in contemporary and historical Somali politics. Women are significantly underrepresented in elite Somali politics and there are fewer well-known female figures. The three women included in this search

Figure 5.2. Autocomplete results of three search tests (clan-related suggested keywords highlighted in bold). © Peter Chonka.

engine test each have distinct profiles and have generated political debate or controversy: Dr. Edna Aadan is a former first lady of Somalia, a renowned physician and women's health advocate and also a vocal supporter of Somaliland's independence; Fowsiya Yuusuf Haji Aadan is a female politician who (uniquely) has served in both Somaliland and Somalia's governments; Ayaan Hirsi Ali is a writer of Somali descent who currently lives outside of Somalia and is well known (and highly controversial) in the region for her critical writings on Islam.

In most cases the autocomplete keywords appear to relate to a question—suggesting that a user employ that keyword to search for the clan-identity of the individual. In one case (for former president Hassan Sheikh Mohamoud), the autocomplete predictions include the actual clan identification of that individual. In the case of Siyaad Barre (former president and head of 1969–1991 military regime), the clan-related keywords are "iyo Isaaq" (English: and the Isaaq [clan]). Barre did not hail from this clan, and it is likely that this suggested keyword relates to users' intended retrieval of historical information about the Barre regime's activities in the northwest and mass violence against the Somali National Movement (SNM) rebels (and civilians) who were predominantly from the Isaaq. Of the three women included in the sample, Ayaan Xirsi Cali was the only one for whom the autocomplete returned a clan-related question keyword. For Dr. Aadan, all of the returned autocomplete predictions were in English. This is potentially indicative of her high international profile and the fact that the spelling of her first name is the same in both English and Somali—therefore English-language queries about her may also feed into the data that is then returned as autocomplete predictions to both Somali-speaking and non-Somali-speaking users. The same may also be true for President "Farmaajo"—his distinctive nickname can be spelled the same in English and Somali (being derived from the Italian for "cheese"), and this could blur the lines between the influence of search terms generated by both Somali and non-Somali-speaking Google users.[17]

How, then, should these autocomplete search keyword predictions be understood? How might they be significant within practices of political/identity information retrieval in the Somali digital public? From one perspective, the phenomena illustrates simply that some people *do* search for the clan affiliations of prominent political figures, indicating that this is information of interest to Somali-speaking internet users. The algorithm (presumably) operates by aggregating and ranking associated keywords that are "common and trending" in the searches of other Google users.[18] This is a presumption in that the precise parameters of the (proprietary) algorithm are not publicly accessible.

Google describes the autocomplete function as providing "predictions" as opposed to "suggestions" for search terms. Of course, this is a largely semantic distinction and one that may break down in the actual users' experience of searching (Miller and Record 2017). Imagine, for instance, that a user is searching for general information about an individual and not specifically anything to do with "clan." However, after seeing that "prediction" the user may then become inclined to focus their search on that particular keyword. Once that autocompleted search is clicked, it feeds back into the "trend" of searches for that topic. This recursive feedback loop would thus make it more likely that subsequent users will encounter similar "predictions."

Racist and sexist tendencies revealed (and amplified) through search engine technologies have become an important focus for scholars scrutinizing the impact of Google's (almost) global monopoly over information retrieval (Becker and Stalder 2010). Safiya Umoja Noble's work (2013, 2018) highlights how "porn-ified" racial identities are reflected and reinforced through searches for "black girls" (see also Baker and Potts 2013). Pip Thornton (2018) examines the ways language itself is commoditized through the value of keywords to marketers, explaining why a search for "WAGs" [male footballers' wives and girlfriends] with the term "sexist" will return results instead for the "sexiest" women. All of this research builds on the fundamental (but not always popularly understood) fact that Google searches are not neutral returns of what exists "out there" online. Search algorithms are instead (crypto)political technologies in and of themselves in that their operations are influenced by (largely invisible) dynamic keyword bidding processes by advertisers and significant amounts of human labor (Bilić 2016).

As for the autocomplete function (as opposed to the subsequent return of search results), Google itself recognizes the risk of "inappropriate" predictions: those that are "sexually explicit," "hateful," "violent," or related to "dangerous and harmful activity."[19] Here Google uses a "feedback" tool that allows users to flag predictions of this nature and thus polices the operation of autocomplete. The extent to which this can be policed is a complicated question and would depend on (1) the capacity for Somali-language digital content to be machine read (currently this is relatively limited); (2) the human resources a technology company like Google would invest in content moderation for such a context (a pressing question elsewhere); and (3) the input of Somali-language internet users in drawing attention to such data. Regardless, for Google to imply that this function constitutes a "prediction" rather than a "suggestion" of search terms seems to be a misleading obfuscation of a potentially more profound algorithmic power in an unstable context. Elsewhere, colleagues and I—while analyzing misogynistic autocomplete suggestions for gendered keyword suggestions in various East African languages—describe inequalities in the capacity and inclination of Western technology companies to adequately monitor the interaction of their tools with marginalized languages as a form of digital colonialism (Chonka, Diepeveen, and Haile 2023).

Content moderation is undoubtedly a complicated, contextually dependent, and difficult task. Therefore, it is important to examine the extent to which the automatic appearance of such clan-related keywords would be considered "inappropriate" in the Somali digital public. If we regard clan differences to be, in part, "invisible"; and if we understand the (contested but important) role that clan has played in historical violence in the Somali context, alongside the taboos that exist around the public expression of these identities, then it is conceivable that individuals in the digital age would use Google to attempt to retrieve this type of information. This raises wider questions about the role of search engines in the shaping of historical memories around conflict. In the Somali context, there is no reconciled or "official" narrative of a civil war which is, in some senses, ongoing. Nor is there an agreed "national" curriculum on modern Somali history. These factors only increase the potential significance of information technologies, particularly for younger generations.

These digital practices of historical information retrieval are transnational in scope. The autocomplete data discussed in the test above has primarily been generated by Somali-speaking internet users (given that the search terms all used Somali spellings of names). It is less clear whether the majority of these users were located in the Horn of Africa or in the global Somali diaspora. Although diaspora contributions to civil society and post-conflict investment and reconstruction efforts in Somalia/Somaliland have long been recognized (I. Ahmed 2000; Majid 2018), the role of foreign-resident Somalis in discursively or materially fueling conflict "back home" is also a theme of diaspora literatures (Osman 2017). Indeed, many of the most controversial or inflammatory commentators on Somali affairs (and potentially some of those highlighted in the earlier part of this chapter) may be based outside of the region, and social media increasingly facilitates their engagement in day-to-day politics in the Horn of Africa. A different discourse relevant to this phenomenon relates to the oft-expressed perception that many (particularly young) Somalis abroad have "lost" cultural connections with the region and may be less familiar with particular lineage identities, either with regard to their own families or in the context of historical debates about Somalia. This is evidenced through the common practice of *dhaqan-celis* (or "cultural rehabilitation") where diaspora youths are sent to the Horn to (re)acclimatize to Somali cultural norms (Tiilikainen 2011). It is possible that such individuals use search engines to retrieve "cultural" or "historical" data about Somalia, including queries relating to clan. Regardless, if external users make up a significant proportion of those deploying Somali search terms in this way, then their particular keyword habits may influence the recursive algorithmic dynamics of the technologies, which can return similar results to users whether they are in London or Mogadishu (as the search testing here demonstrated). This new potential form of diasporic influence could become ever more salient in the Horn of Africa itself, as local access to the internet increases and larger numbers of people engage with Internet search engines to retrieve information. The issues raised here are somewhat speculative, given limits to researchers' access to the (proprietary) Google data that could more precisely illuminate how Somali-language search practices actually work and who/where the users are. Nevertheless, the data presented above does point to a potential vector of transnational and algorithmic influence on local political discourse that has not yet been considered in the fields of diaspora media studies or conflict analysis.

Finally, from an anthropological perspective on (political) identity formation, it is necessary to highlight the potential for these opaque influences to add new elements into old debates around ethnicity in African political contexts (Berman 1998; Eller and Coughlan 1993; Tilley 1997). Whether "tribal" identity is an underlying or primordial attachment; something instrumentalized by elites for political or economic ends, or whether these ideas are all constructed through language and enactments in everyday settings; digital technologies are emerging as another element of recursive influence—potentially feeding back and amplifying particular framings of questions around cryptopolitical identities.

Conclusion

This chapter has analyzed two phenomena relating to the digital cryptopolitics of the Somali conflict. The first part provided a comparative analysis of narratives of conspiracy relating to ongoing conflict that circulate within the (transnational) Somali digital public. The second part examined a very specific feature of this media ecology as an example of the potential impact of algorithmic power on the retrieval of information linked to related identities. The argument here is that analyses of contentious digital debates in conflict-affected contexts need to begin to consider the role of digital platform structures and the ways they engage with African indigenous-language data.

The chapter has not intended (and is not able) to demonstrate a clear causal link between algorithmic features of search engines or social media and the perpetuation and evolution of conspiracy beliefs that engage "invisible" identities and agendas. Instead, it has demonstrated how features of the conflict context are conducive to cryptopolitical understandings of actors and agency. These relate to a particular history of constructions and fragmentations of ethno-national political identity; a divided but transnational digital media space in which these experiences continue to be debated; the wide array of different forces involved in the reconfiguration of the Somali state; and the evolution of Al Shabaab as a clandestine militant network across the region. The chapter's subsequent discussion of the search engine "autocomplete" results *does not* expose a popular Somali predilection for clan-related search keywords—indeed, Google's claim that this tool simply reflects what others have searched for in its "prediction" is deeply problematic in that this ignores the cumulative recursive impact of making visible a particular option for information retrieval. What it *does* illustrate are emerging forms of algorithmic power that have the potential to shape a digital public that is already characterized by multiple uses (and abuses) of information relating to an ongoing and historically unreconciled conflict. Consideration of digital algorithmic power adds another dimension to debates over the nature and enactment of cryptopolitical identity politics in African contexts. The potential transnational influence of diasporic information retrieval practices—combined with the increasing local prevalence of Internet connectivity in the Horn—mean that these technologies are in urgent need of further scrutiny. The expansion of the scope of scholarship on the politics of "search" beyond the West and the English-speaking world is essential here.

Peter Chonka is a Lecturer in Global Digital Cultures in King's College London's Department of Digital Humanities. His research explores how information and communication technologies affect mobility, politics, activism, and conflict in the Horn of Africa.

Notes

1. An exception here relates to the Af Maay dialect, significantly different from the Af Maxaa Tiri dialects formalized as "standard Somali." Af Maay dialects are commonly associated with the Digil and Mirifle (aka "Raxanweyn") clan family, one of the four "main" clan families represented in the 4.5 system described above (the other three main clan families are the Daarood, Dir, and Hawiye).
2. AMISOM was re-mandated as the African Union Transition Mission in Somalia (ATMIS) in April 2022. It is supposed to hand over all security responsibilities to Somali forces by 2024.
3. A "most wanted" list of Al Shabaab leaders published in 2015 by the FGS included clan affiliations, illustrating a diversity of backgrounds across the major Somali "clan-families." See "Dowladda Federaalka Soomaaliya oo lacag dul dhigtay 11 hogaamiye oo ka tirsan Al-shabaab" [The federal government puts money on the heads of 11 Al Shabaab leaders]. *Halgan.net*, 9 April 2015. Retrieved 16 January 2023 from http://halgan.net/2015/04/dowladda-federaalka-soomaaliya-oo-lacag-dul-dhigtay-11-hogaamiye-oo-ka-tirsan-al-shabaab/.
4. Some local reports—based on interviews with defectors—suggested that some of those leaving the south to join an Islamic State affiliate in Puntland were disaffected with Al Shabaab, whose leadership they perceived as increasingly dominated by Hawiye sub-clans. See Hiraal Institute (2018: 5).
5. "Goodaax Barre: waxaan heysanaa awood saacad kasta aan ku jooji karno baraha bulshada" [Goodax Barre: We have the ability at any hour to stop social media]. *Radio Kulmiye*, 27 May 2019 (No longer online, copy in author's possession).
6. Peter Wolfson and Greta Backstrom. 2016. "Somalia: The Nexus between Somaliland and Al-Shabaab." Sun Times, 16 February. Retrieved 16 January 2023 from http://sunatimes.com/articles/3743/Somalia-The-Nexus-between-Somaliland-and-Al-Shabaab (original Kenyamedia.net link no longer active, copy in author's possession).
7. Sola Portal, 17 February, 2016. "Wada shaqeynta Somaliland iyo Al-Shabaab ee la yiri waxaa soo soo qoray wariyaal Swedish ah maxaa ka jiraa? Sola investigates" [What's going on with this alleged cooperation between Somaliland and Al Shabaab written by Swedish Journalists? Sola investigates]. *Sola Portal*, 17 February. Retrieved 16 January 2023 from http://solaportal.com/Archive/2016/2/56solaportal.
8. Axmed Sheekh Maxamed. 2014. "Dagaallada Shabeellaha yaa hurinaya?" [Who's fueling the conflict in the Shabelle regions] *Keyd Media online*, June 14. (No longer online, copy in author's possession).
9. *Xog-doon*. 2015. "Puntland oo ku eedeysay Somaliland inay taageerto xoogaga Al-Shabaab ee Galgala" [Puntland accuses Somaliland of supporting Al Shabaab in Galgala]. *Mogadishu*, 31 January.
10. Horn Cable TV. 2016. "Puntland Oo Xukuumada Somaliya Ku Eedaysay Galitaanka Alshabab Gudaha Puntland" [Puntland accuses the government of Somalia over the Al Shabaab incursion inside Puntland]. YouTube, uploaded 15 March. (No longer online, copy in author's possession).
11. Ahmed Yusuf Ahmed, "Muuq-disho", *Dunida Online*, March 29, 2015 (No longer online, copy in author's possession).

12. Muuse Xaji Abees. 2014. "Digniin culus ku socota xildhibaanada daarood" [Strong warning to Daarood MPs]. *Dunida Online*, 20 July. (No longer online, copy in author's possession).
13. Abdi Sheikh. 2016. "US Accused of Killing 22 in Misdirected Somalia Airstrike." *Reuters*, 28 September. Retrieved 16 January 2023 from https://www.reuters.com/article/us-somalia-security/u-s-accused-of-killing-22-in-misdirected-somalia-air-strike-idUSKCN11Y0UC.
14. Christina Goldbaum. 2017. "Strong Evidence that U.S. Special Operations Forces Massacred Civilians in Somalia." *The Daily Beast*, 29 November. Retrieved 16 January 2023 from https://www.thedailybeast.com/strong-evidence-that-us-special-operations-forces-massacred-civilians-in-somalia.
15. United Nations Monitoring Group on Somalia and Eritrea, report S/2016/919 (October 2016) Annex 7.5. p. 161.
16. Thanks to Mahad Wasuge for his assistance with this.
17. This highlights the limits of the technique in exploring auto-complete returns for a wider range of relevant keywords: only terms with distinct Somali spellings (e.g., names) will likely give Somali language predictions. For example, for "Al Shabaab" (same spelling in English and Somali), auto-complete predictions are returned in English, given that the organization has been widely googled by a global audience.
18. Danny Sullivan. 2018. "How Google Autocomplete Works in Search." *Google*, 20 April. Retrieved 16 January 2023 from https://www.blog.google/products/search/how-google-autocomplete-works-search/.
19. Ibid.

References

Ahmad, Aisha. 2015. "The Security Bazaar: Business Interests and Islamist Power in Civil War Somalia." *International Security* 39(3): 89–117.

Ahmed, Ali J., ed. 1995. *The Invention of Somalia*. Trenton, NJ: The Red Sea Press.

Ahmed, Ismail I. 2000. "Remittances and Their Economic Impact in Post-War Somaliland." *Disasters* 24(4): 380–89.

Allcott, Hunt, and Matthew Gentzkow. 2017. "Social Media and Fake News in the 2016 Election." *Journal of Economic Perspectives* 31(2): 211–36.

Baker, Paul, and Amanda Potts. 2013. "Why Do White People Have Thin Lips?" Google and the Perpetuation of Stereotypes via Auto-complete Search Forms." *Critical Discourse Studies* 10(2): 187–204.

Bakir, Vian, and Andrew McStay. 2018. "Fake News and the Economy of Emotions: Problems, Causes, Solutions." *Digital journalism* 6(2): 154–75.

Bananay, Mustafe. 2017. "Can Military Might Alone Defeat al-Shabaab?" IPI Global Observatory. Retrieved 21 March 2018 from https://theglobalobservatory.org/2017/03/al-shabaab-amisom-extremism-afgoye/.

Barnes, Cedric. 2007. "The Somali Youth League, Ethiopian Somalis and the Greater Somalia Idea, c.1946–48." *Journal of Eastern African Studies* 1, 2(2007): 277–91.

Barnes, Cedric, and Harun Hassan. 2007. "The Rise and Fall of Mogadishu's Islamic Courts." *Journal of Eastern African Studies* 1(2): 151–60.

Becker, Konrad and Felix Stalder. 2010. *Deep Search: The Politics of Search beyond Google*. BoD–Books on Demand.

Bennett, Lance W., and Barbara Pfetsch. 2018. "Rethinking Political Communication in a Time of Disrupted Public Spheres." *Journal of Communication* 68(2): 243–53.

Berman, Bruce, J. 1998. "Ethnicity, Patronage and the African State: The Politics of Uncivil Nationalism." *African Affairs* 97(388): 305–41.

Besteman, Catherine. 1998. "Primordialist Blinders: A Reply to IM Lewis." *Cultural Anthropology* 13(1): 109–20.

Besteman, Catherine, and Lee Cassanelli, eds. 2000. *The Struggle for Land in Southern Somalia: The War Behind the War.* Washington, DC: Westview.

Bilić, Paško. 2016. "Search Algorithms, Hidden Labour and Information Control." *Big Data & Society* 3(1). https://doi.org/10.1177/2053951716652159.

Bozdag, Engin, and Jeroen van den Hoven. 2015. "Breaking the Filter Bubble: Democracy and Design." *Ethics and Information Technology* 17(4): 249–65.

Bucher, Tania. 2018. *If . . . Then: Algorithmic Power and Politics.* Oxford: Oxford University Press.

Cassanelli, Lee. 2015. *Hosts and Guests: A Historical Interpretation of Land Conflicts in Southern and Central Somalia.* Nairobi: Rift Valley Institute.

Chonka, Peter. 2016. "Spies, Stonework, and the Suuq: Somali Nationalism and the Narrative Politics of pro-Harakat Al Shabaab Al Mujaahidiin Online Propaganda." *Journal of Eastern African Studies* 10(2): 247–65.

———. 2018. "New Media, Performative Violence, and State Reconstruction in Mogadishu." *African Affairs* 117(468): 392–414.

———. 2019. "News Media and Political Contestation in the Somali Territories: Defining the Parameters of a Transnational Digital Public." *Journal of Eastern African Studies* 13(1): 140–57.

Chonka, Peter, Stephanie Diepeveen, and Yidnekachew Haile. 2023. "Algorithmic Power and African Indigenous Languages: Search Engine Autocomplete and the Global Multilingual Internet." *Media, Culture & Society* 45(2): 246–65. https://doi.org/10.1177/01634437221104705.

Clifford, E.H.M. 1936. "The British Somaliland-Ethiopia Boundary." *The Geographical Journal* 87(4): 289–302.

Compagnon, Daniel. 1995. *Ressources Politiques, Regulation Autoritaire et Domination Personnelle en Somalie* [Political resources, authoritarian regulation and personal domination in Somalia]. Pau: Francois Constantin Publisher.

———. 1998. "Somali Armed Units: The Interplay of Political Entrepreneurship and Clan-based Factions." In *African Guerrillas,* ed Christopher Clapham, 73–90. London: James Currey.

DeWaal, Alex. 2007. "Class and Power in a Stateless Somalia." Social Science Research Council 20.

Elder, Claire. 2022. "Logistics Contracts and the Political Economy of State Failure: Evidence from Somalia." *African Affairs* 121(484): 395–417.

Eller, Jack D., and Reed Coughlan. 1993. "The Poverty of Primordialism: The Demystification of Ethnic Attachments." *Ethnic and Racial Studies* 16(2): 183–202.

Gray, Jonathan, Liliana Bounegru, and Tommaso Venturini. 2020. "'Fake News' as Infrastructural Uncanny." *New Media & Society* 22(2): 317–41.

Gruzd, Anatoliy, and Jeffrey Roy. 2014. "Investigating Political Polarization on Twitter: A Canadian Perspective." *Policy & Internet* 6(1): 28–45.

Hansen, Stig J. 2013. *Al-Shabaab in Somalia: The History and Ideology of a Militant Islamist Group, 2005–2012.* London: Hurst.

Hassan, Idayat, and Jamie Hitchen. 2019. "The 'Propaganda Secretaries' behind Nigeria's 2019 Election." *Mail & Guardian*, 18 April. Retrieved 25 June 2019 from https://mg.co.za/article/2019-04-18-00-nigerias-propaganda-secretaries.

Hiraal Institute. 2018. *Taming the Clans: Al Shabaab's Clan Politics.* Mogadishu: Hiraal Institute.

Hoehne, Markus V. 2015. *Between Somaliland and Puntland: Marginalization, Militarization and Conflicting Political Visions.* Nairobi: Rift Valley Institute.

———. 2016. "The Rupture of Territoriality and the Diminishing Relevance of Cross-cutting Ties in Somalia after 1990." *Development and Change* 47(6): 1379–411.

Jhazbhay, Iqbal. 2009. "Somaliland: The Journey of Resistance, Reconciliation and Peace." *African Safety Promotion: A Journal of Injury and Violence Prevention* 7(1): 50–76.

Kapteijns, Lidwien. 2004. "IM Lewis and Somali Clanship: A Critique." *Northeast African Studies* 11(1): 1–23.

———. 2010. "Making Memories of Mogadishu in Somali Poetry about the Civil War." In *Mediations of Violence in Africa*, ed. Lidwien Kapteijns and Annemiek Richters, 25–74. Leiden: Brill.

———. 2012. *Clan Cleansing in Somalia: The Ruinous Legacy of 1991.* Philadelphia: University of Pennsylvania Press.

Lewis, Ioan, M. 1998. "Doing Violence to Ethnography: A Response to Catherine Besteman's Representing Violence and 'Othering' Somalia." *Cultural Anthropology* 13(1): 100–8.

———. 2004. "Visible and Invisible Differences: The Somali Paradox." *Africa* 74(4): 489–515.

Majid, Nisar. 2018. *Remittances and Vulnerability in Somalia.* Nairobi: Rift Valley Institute.

Marchal, Roland. 2010. "The Puntland State of Somalia: A Tentative Social Analysis." Paris: Science Po. Retrieved 25 June 2019 from: https://hal-sciencespo.archives-ouvertes.fr/hal-01044642.

Miller, Boaz, and Isaac Record. 2017. "Responsible Epistemic Technologies: A Social-Epistemological Analysis of Autocompleted Web Search." *New Media & Society* 19(12): 1945–63.

Monsees, Linda. 2019. *Crypto-politics: Encryption and Democratic Practices in the Digital Era.* Routledge.

Mubarak, Mohamed 2020. *A Losing Game: Countering Al-Shabab's Financial System.* Mogadishu: Hiraal Institute.

Noble, Safiya U. 2013. "Google Search: Hyper-visibility as a Means of Rendering Black Women and Girls Invisible." *InVisible Culture* (19). https://ivc.lib.rochester.edu/google-search-hyper-visibility-as-a-means-of-rendering-black-women-and-girls-invisible/.

———. 2018. *Algorithms of Oppression: How Search Engines Reinforce Racism.* New York: New York University Press.

Omaar, Rakiya. 1993. "The Best Chance for Peace." *Africa Report* 38(3): 44–48.

Osman, Idil. 2017. *Media, Diaspora and the Somali Conflict.* London: Palgrave MacMillan.

Persily, Nathaniel. 2017. "The 2016 US Election: Can Democracy Survive the Internet?" *Journal of Democracy* 28(2): 63–76.

Rigby, T. H. 1969. "CryptoPolitics." In *Communist Studies and the Social Sciences: Essays in Methodology and Empirical Theory*, ed. Frederic Fleron, 116–28. Chicago: University of Chicago Press.

Roble, Muhyadin A. 2017. "'Neutral' Somalia Finds Itself Engulfed in Saudi Arabia-Qatar Dispute." *African Arguments,* 16 August. Retrieved 17 August 2017 from https://africanarguments.org/2017/08/16/neutral-somalia-finds-itself-engulfed-in-saudi-arabia-qatar-dispute/.

Samatar, Abdi I. 1989. *The State and Rural Transformation in Northern Somalia, 1884–1986.* Madison: University of Wisconsin Press.

———. 1992. "Destruction of State and Society in Somalia: Beyond the Tribal Convention." *The Journal of Modern African Studies* 30(4): 625–41.

———. 2006. "Debating Somali Identity in a British Tribunal: The Case of the BBC Somali Service." *The Arab World Geographer* 9(1): 40–73.

Somali Public Agenda. 2018. "Options for Political Reconciliation in Somalia." *Somali Public Agenda,* 25 September. Retrieved 20 December 2018 from https://somalipublicagenda.org/options-for-political-reconciliation-in-somalia/.

Srinivasan, Sharath, Stephanie Diepeveen, and George Karekwaivanane. 2019. "Rethinking Publics in Africa in a Digital Age." *Journal of Eastern African Studies* 13(1): 2–17.

Tahir, Abdifatah I. 2016. "Urban Governance, Land conflicts and Segregation in Hargeisa, Somaliland: Historical Perspectives and Contemporary Dynamics." Ph.D. dissertation, Brighton: University of Sussex.

Thornton, Pip. 2018. "Geographies of (Con) Text: Language and Structure in a Digital Age." *Computational Culture* 6. http://computationalculture.net/geographies-of-context-language-and-structure-in-a-digital-age/.

Tiilikainen, Marja. 2011. "Failed Diaspora: Experiences of Dhaqan Celis and Mentally Ill Returnees in Somaliland." Nordic *Journal of African Studies* 20(1): 71–89.

Tilley, Virginia. 1997. "The Terms of the Debate: Untangling Language about Ethnicity and Ethnic Movements." *Ethnic and Racial Studies* 20(3): 497–522.

United Nations Monitoring Group on Somalia and Eritrea. 2017. Report to the Security Council, S/2017/924, November 2017.

Williams, Paul D. 2018. *Fighting for Peace in Somalia: A History and Analysis of the African Union Mission (AMISOM), 2007–2017.* Oxford: Oxford University Press.

———. 2019. "Building the Somali National Army: Anatomy of a Failure, 2008–2018." *Journal of Strategic Studies* 43(3): 366–91.

Warner, Jason, and Ellen Chapin. 2018. "Targeted Terror: The Suicide Bombers of al-Shabaab, Combating Terrorism Center at West Point." *Combating Terrorism Center at West Point,* 13 February. https://ctc.usma.edu/targeted-terror-suicide-bombers-al-shabaab/.

Walls, Michael, Conrad Heine, Andrea Klingel, Carrie Goggin, Ahmed Farag, and Susan Mwape. 2018. *International Election Observation Mission: The Limits of Consensus? Report on the Somaliland Presidential Election 13th November 2017.* London: Development Planning Unit, The Bartlett, University College London.

Wodak, Ruth, Briditte Mral, and Majid Khosravinik, eds. 2013. *Right-Wing Populism in Europe: Politics and Discourse.* London: Bloomsbury Publishing.

CHAPTER 6

The Cryptopolitics of Digital Mutuality

Daivi Rodima-Taylor

"WhatsApp Stokvels Are Back and You're Probably Being Scammed!"[1] screamed a newspaper headline in South Africa in 2020.[2] "New WhatsApp Scam Doing the Rounds in South Africa," announced another.[3] "WhatsApp 'Stokvels' Are a Scam & Don't Be Tempted to Join Telegram or Signal 'Stokvels' Now . . ." implored a third.[4] "WhatsApp stokvels are all the buzz at the moment. It starts with a promise that if you invest R1,000, you're likely to end up with a R6,000 payout but many think it's nothing more than elaborate pyramid scheme that will end in tears," explained one of the news articles. Another one conveyed the warning of the chairman of the National Stokvel Association of South Africa who advised that "fraudsters were using the popularity of stokvels to take advantage of gullible and vulnerable people. 'People will take chances and we can only warn people not to fall for things that have not been tested. Stokvels have been tried and tested for many years.'"[5]

These heated opinions illustrate the contentious response around the growing popularity of WhatsApp-mediated savings groups in Africa. While a share of scams is certainly occurring, this also highlights the controversy around the foray of the digital medium of messaging apps into the territory of informal savings groups that are central to many African economies. In Kenya, an estimated one-third of the adult population belongs in a savings group (Gichuru 2014), while in South Africa, about 810,000 stokvel groups mobilize around 11 million participants and manage up to R50 billion (over US$3 million) a year (Pillay 2022). The groups are also increasingly popular among the diaspora and migrant communities, mobilizing remittances and facilitating social support (Ardener 2010; Hossein 2017; Rodima-Taylor 2022a). My chapter explores this paradoxical partnership between a BigTech platform and these informal initiatives that offer alternatives to those excluded from formal finance and addresses the novel questions that this poses about digital media, cryptopolitics, and the civic spaces of resistance and change in Africa.

Transnational migrants increasingly rely on internet-based social media and chat apps to keep up connections with kin and friends in their countries of origin—including Facebook, WhatsApp, Skype, Facetime, Snapchat, Twitter, and Google Hangout (Plaza and Plaza 2019). People celebrate family events, rituals, and national holidays, and they exchange information about news and politics through newsgroup debates, list serves, and website postings. These digital platforms are also used to pool money and mobilize remittances—migrants' money transfers to their families and friends.

At the same time, the messaging platforms also facilitate applications that are less constructive and peaceful. To some degree, these relate to general trends observed around the spreading digital platforms. In recent years, a significant rise has been noted in pyramid schemes and "get-rich-quick" scams globally, particularly as related to electronic media (Comaroff and Comaroff 2001: 22). A recent Consultative Group to Assist the Poor (CGAP) report notes that such fraudulent digital investment schemes often claim to be "mutual aid networks that mimic the informal savings groups and village banks that people in such markets are used to" (Chalwe-Mulenga, Duflos, and Coetzee 2022: 21). John Comaroff and Jean Comaroff suggest that arising from a "promiscuous mix of scarcity and deregulation," these schemes feature in many "occult economies" of the Global South. Such economies have emerged with the recent expansion of speculative global investment—an expression of the unregulated excess of "casino capitalism" where the globalized markets, electronic media and finance capital have fueled speculative venture enterprise (2001: 7; see also Strange 1986). They resonate especially hard in the developing economies where postcolonial disappointments disrupt the neoliberal narratives of progress.

My chapter suggests that the spreading digital media platforms play a significant role in mediating the new "hidden economies"—with diverse effects that can lead to empowerment as well as marginalization. Advances in communication technologies have transformed the ways the hidden is mediated through diverse media and public spaces. Secrets have been seen as intricately connected to power and social control. While concealed knowledge can be instrumental in manipulating the boundaries of belonging, secrets could also constitute a powerful tool of resistance (Manderson et al. 2015; Simmel 1906). Both public spaces as well as publics themselves are transformed through the acts of revealing secrets. Publics are convened and civic life reshaped through the practices of disclosure of hidden information (see also Warner 2002). While the rapidly diversifying contemporary media is affecting the practices of concealment and disclosure, it is also reconfigured through the practices of revealing information and addressing the publics. Critical media studies have highlighted the gradual transformation of the meaning of transparency and revelation with the ongoing multiplication of outlets for new forms of public communication (Manderson et al. 2015; see also Jones 2014). The democratization of the means of publicity has also amplified political calls for transparency (Nutall and Mbembe 2015: 318). New digital communication technologies enable new tools for people to counteract surveillance, and these tools have often been associated with power contestations and potentially subversive communication. At the same time, they have also created new means for concealment, deception, and exclusion.

It is also important to bear in mind the integral connectedness of online and offline modalities in these power negotiations occurring through new media. Victoria Bernal's study of African diasporas (2014) highlights the significance of cyberspace in contemporary politics and demonstrates the existence of multiple forms of territoriality and extraterritoriality that do not correspond to a neat division of online versus offline or nations versus the Internet. Both virtual and offline spaces are socially constructed as well as political.

My chapter explores the cryptopolitics of the emerging digital mutuality in Africa as facilitated by encrypted chat apps. It argues that the popularity of digital messaging apps such as WhatsApp in Africa presents an intriguing paradox: while it is part of the BigTech dynamic of global data capture by increasingly monopolistic service providers (see Nothias 2020), it is increasingly used to mediate informal, local livelihood initiatives and collectivities. This chapter focuses on the use of WhatsApp for providing a digital medium to informal savings groups as well as fundraising initiatives. While there is more information available about the role of such encrypted chat apps in advancing political participation and dissent, little is known yet about the dynamics of their mobilization toward these everyday livelihood causes, and the broader consequences of this engagement to civic activism and emerging digital peer-based collectivities. My chapter aims to address this research gap and raise areas for further investigation.

The first section of the chapter provides an overview of existing scholarly debates about the role of encrypted messaging apps in advancing digital activism. It then proceeds to examine the use of WhatsApp in mobilizing savings groups and crowdfunding initiatives in Kenya and South Africa that have emerged as local, informal alternatives to the initiatives advanced by dedicated FinTech platforms and commercial banks (see Langley and Rodima-Taylor 2022; Rodima-Taylor 2022b).[6] Instead of assuming that WhatsApp engenders group cohesion and frictionless cooperation because it enables greater privacy than open social media platforms or allows broader outreach than place-bound savings groups, my analysis suggests that it is important to examine the social and historical embeddedness of both mutuality and the digital infrastructures. The chapter discusses the complexities of the notion of "digital publics" in an era of Big Data, highlighting the need to situate the conversations around digital resistance and agency in the Global South within a framework of coloniality in its past and present forms. The concept of coloniality refers to the continuing effects of historical colonization that endure into the present day, and the repressive power patterns that are heightened and transformed through the ongoing "data coloniality" of financial technology platforms (Couldry and Mejias 2021; Mohamed, Png, and Isaac 2020).

The next section discusses the development of crypto-publics as novel digitally mediated collectivities (Johns 2020; see also Vidan and Lehdonvirta 2019), problematizing some features of such techno-communities in the light of empirical cases from Africa. It highlights the importance of examining the evolving digital structures as multilevel sociotechnical assemblages that bring together diverse formal and informal, online and offline, physical and "peopled" infrastructural elements (Rodima-Taylor and Grimes 2019). The chapter argues that to understand the role of encrypted messaging platforms in facilitating social activism and peer group cohesion, we need to look at new and old mutualities, social imaginaries, local institutions and cultural repertoires, as well as the complex materialities of infrastructures with their historical embeddedness. My chapter integrates perspectives from social anthropology, media studies, and science and technology studies and draws on historical and ethnographic accounts, reports, and working papers from financial and development industries, news media articles, and policy documents and memos. The analysis is also informed by my background of longitudinal field research in East Africa on informal savings groups and financial inclusion. The article contributes to the study of social media and data politics in the Global South, and presents novel perspectives on civil society, migration, and the increasingly borderless African informal economies.

Encrypted Chat Apps and Digital Collectivities

Encrypted messaging platforms, such as Telegram, Signal, and WhatsApp, are often seen as enabling safe spaces for their users that are hidden from repressive state monitoring. WhatsApp, a digital messaging and voice call service, has become a foremost platform for mediating conversations and resource pooling around livelihood issues in many regions of the Global South. Designed to work on low-cost phones in contexts of limited bandwidth, the app has a big following in Africa where it has been rolled out in thirty-two countries since 2014. It became the most popular messaging application globally by 2015 and has emerged as the primary means of Internet communication in much of Latin America, South East Asia, and large parts of Europe and Africa (Malik 2022; Metz 2016).

The platform enables voice and video calls, messages, and sharing of images and documents.[7] It allows users to form groups of over two hundred members and enables personal communication among them. The service is accessible from computers, smart phones, as well as certain feature phones. The "simplicity, reliability and accessibility" of the app make it especially relevant for the users in the Global South where mobile phones are more widespread than computers for online connectivity (Treré 2020). Due to its group functionality, it has been likened to social media rather than regular text-messaging services. At the same time, differently from publicly visible social media platforms such as Twitter or Facebook, communication on WhatsApp can be seen by only a designated group of people. Encrypted chat apps thus incorporate the qualities of both a public social media platform and a private messaging service, by allowing group conversations while limiting the audience able to access them. The perceived privacy of the app is further enhanced by its end-to-end encryption feature that was introduced in 2016.

This has contributed to a growing use of the platform for political mobilization in many countries where freedom of public speech is restricted (Milan and Treré 2019). In the contexts of repressive state surveillance of open media platforms, such semi-public messaging services are becoming a "critical infrastructure" for social activists (Johns 2020). As users shift to these platforms from public-facing social media such as Facebook and Twitter, encrypted chat apps have given rise to new types of publics—"crypto-publics," suggests Amelia Johns (2020). The apps may therefore not just affect individual privacy but enable new forms of collective freedom from surveillance and novel activist mobilization. The notion of crypto-publics has been shaped by discourses on cryptographic technologies and currencies, and the vision of cryptography as a technology that ensures privacy "as not only a personal right but a public good" (2020). Parallels can therefore be drawn between the political mobilizations within WhatsApp and open-source software technologies.

The ability of encrypted chat apps to build solidarity between users has been attributed to their propensity to advance "informal and depoliticized conversations" (Pang and Woo 2019). In many groups that did not start out as openly political, casual everyday conversations turned out to be instrumental for further cooperation. Stefania Milan and Sergio Barbosa (2020) argue that WhatsApp is facilitating the rise of a new type of political subject—"WhatsApper," whose engagement with political issues emerges gradually in an "intimate and familiar context," facilitated by ever-accessible mobile phones. Mobilization builds organically on people's lived experiences and feelings as they go through the app-mediated process that encourages emotional exchanges. Chat group activities inspire joint responsibility: "WhatsApp 'private groups' are associated with a stronger sense of belonging rather than network-based Facebook" (2020).

These qualities of the encrypted chat apps seem of particular relevance for building the virtual solidarity necessary for the functioning of online contribution groups and networks—which we will examine in more detail in the following section with the example of material from East and Southern Africa.

WhatsApp as a Tool of Mutual Security in Africa

The Rise of WhatsApp Savings Groups

The recent rise of WhatsApp in the political and economic lives of Africans has been unprecedented. In countries such as Kenya, WhatsApp has grown from a "tool for interpersonal communication into a group channel for engagement within families, companies and even for holding religious services" (Kimega 2021). Its use has skyrocketed during the COVID pandemic that restricted in-person meetings. Banks and other formal sector businesses are moving onto WhatsApp while transitioning away from website chat boxes or physical branches (Kivuva 2021). Commercial banks in Kenya have introduced banking services on WhatsApp for balance inquiry, bill payments, and money transfers. Zamara Group[8] recently announced WhatsApp access to its digital pension plan and funeral insurance that target customers in the informal sector: "We are using a channel that more than 12 million Kenyans use. This is the app we use to communicate with our friends, family and connect with brands and businesses. Now you can use WhatsApp to enrol, join a pension plan, save and take out insurance" (Kivuva 2021). Such service is especially likely to offer solutions to the estimated 17 million Kenyans that are currently without insurance or pension solutions (Mwita and Okwemba 2021). The *Business Daily Africa* article notes that social media channels "including Telegram, Instagram and Facebook have become common with companies for onboarding customers and services" (Kivuva 2021).

The power of social media is also evident in the recent governmental efforts in Africa to impose social media restrictions during contentious election campaigns—including in countries such as Cameroon, Congo, Uganda, Tanzania, Guinea, Togo, Benin, Mali, and Mauritania (Kene-Okafor 2021). It is significant that the Zambian government reportedly prioritized cutting WhatsApp on the day of general elections in August 2021 (Campbell 2021), highlighting the perceived importance of that platform in organizing and channeling social dissent.

Facebook and WhatsApp have also emerged as primary instruments to help people keep in contact with their overseas family and kin. These platforms are used by migrants to connect them to familiar people and cultural practices (Plaza and Plaza 2019). They also serve to "solidify linkages of obligation" within transnational kin networks, motivating people to send back remittances. Mobilizing remittances as well as saving and pooling money increasingly occur through digitally powered transnational networks that draw on various social media and payment apps.

I suggest that the WhatsApp platform is used to extend digitally the informal networks of mutual security that have historically served as a powerful expression of cryptopolitics for migrants marginalized from formal financial sector opportunities. These networks build on the principles of rotating savings-credit associations (ROSCAs) and are widespread among migrant communities for mobilizing funds. Haitian migrants in Toronto create such informal financial cooperatives that they are familiar with from their communities of origin, to counter their racialized exclusion from the formal financial sector (Hossein 2017). Tapping into their cultural networks and personal friendships, the "Toronto's Banker Ladies" change Canada's social economy through these incremental, everyday activities—and teach commercial banks that "banking can be done by ordinary women who collect and share funds among members in a way that is caring and supports individual and community projects" (2017: 39). Knowing that such peer-to-peer lending systems may invite scrutiny from the formal sector and could be criticized as being illegal, the women keep their activities under close guard (2017: 39). I suggest that the formation of such informal—and frequently secretive—collectivities to counteract social exclusion constitutes an act of cryptopolitics.

Describing the popularity of rotating savings groups among the Cameroonian diaspora in the United Kingdom and United States, Shirley Ardener (2010) notes that for many migrants, the groups offer viable alternatives to sub-prime, high-interest bank loans and predatory payday lending. Many diaspora members pool money for building homes in their countries of origin where they can retire. The savings groups also function as a "private health insurance company" for their members. Participating in these groups is driven by more than economic need; many wealthier members have joined to show their solidarity as "sons and daughters of the soil" (Ardener 2014: 5). Through membership in diaspora ROSCAs, people enhance their social reputations and professional identities. Migrants can belong to several rotating groups, producing a network of overlapping circles, with "lace-like support networks covering large areas of England" (2014: 6). Similar patterns emerge among the Cameroonian diaspora in the United States: Ardener's informant in Massachusetts belongs to multiple ROSCAs, putting her in contact with several hundred fellow Cameroonians across the country (2010). Through such groups, "migrants can quickly settle in and make their way" (Ardener 2014: 6). I suggest that these groups can be seen as important sites of cryptopolitics where people counteract their exclusion by relying on these culturally familiar grassroots collectivities that enable new types of affinities and serve novel goals.

A growing number of such groups manage their affairs online by means of WhatsApp. In South Africa, for example, WhatsApp and Facebook are among the most popular social media apps among low-income internet users (Reichel et al. 2020). As the app already serves as a widespread means of communication among young people in many areas of Africa, its recent use for savings group management has skyrocketed. In Kenya, easy socialization and instant payouts are seen as a major draw of the app that does not demand much data or airtime, argue Paul Kariuki and Lizzy Ofusori (2017). Recent research among informal savings groups in the Western Cape, South Africa, found that group members drew extensively on various forms of information and communication technology, including "mobile phones, spreadsheet applications (Excel), mobile banking, social media communications (mostly WhatsApp) and e-mail" when managing their group activities (Tsibolane, Nokwazi, Van Belle 2019: 35). The most popular form of digital media used for group management was WhatsApp, viewed as a means to "save time and money when you want to be in touch with people" (2019: 42). WhatsApp stokvels usually utilize some sort of electronic payment solutions, such as mobile payments—eWallet or Instacash—or electronic bank fund transfers (Menze and Tsibolane 2019).

Frequently, planning an online savings group would start on Facebook where group members introduce themselves, and then move to WhatsApp as a more private communication platform (Menze and Tsibolane 2019). As members do not meet in person and may not know each other outside their group activities, important social safeguards are missing that secure the functioning of traditional, offline savings groups. Digital groups lack regular interaction around their goals and procedures. Communication often remains minimal: "Yes announcements are made on the WhatsApp group but it's mostly reminders or enquiries about the payments" (2019: 9). These digital money pooling networks can bring together people from different regions of the country and diaspora abroad, eliminating many aspects of common language and understanding. They can therefore facilitate deceptive bonds between people who do not know each other well. While it has been argued that savings groups utilizing WhatsApp and Facebook may develop "new forms of socio-cultural ties that extend the traditional meaning" of the groups and facilitate "previously non-existent social bonds" (Menze and Tsibolane 2019), it is not clear that this has been the case so far. Significant limitations of the app to advance social ties among the members have been noted: "The use of WhatsApp for communication in stokvels, and the restrictive rules that typically govern what can be discussed and not discussed on the group chat, negatively impacts the free flow of casual communication characteristic of traditional stokvels" (2019: 11).

Stories of endemic scams and failures of online savings groups abound. In South Africa, the "WhatsApp stokvels" (sometimes referred to as "WhatsApp-Gifting"—a phenomenon that has seen rapid rise in the past few years) have recently been plagued by media reports about fraudulent activities and quick collapses (see Mavundza 2020; Moodley 2019; Pijoos 2019). What started as members of existing stokvels using social media to ease communication has quickly become a trend of online-only groups, some of which served as "get-rich-quick" schemes for their organizers. These digital groups became widespread in South Africa in 2019, inviting people to join and contribute certain amounts of money—usually around R200 (around US$13.00)—while offering bigger payouts, often up to R6,000 (around US$400.00) within a short time period. Many of them left their trusting contributors stranded when group administrators disappeared with the money. The National Stokvel Association of South Africa has cautioned residents about the high likelihood of the "WhatsApp stokvels" being pyramid schemes, where those joining first may get their payout but latecomers would lose their money (Kgophane 2020). Many of the victims are unemployed and economically vulnerable. Such electronic scams build on the trusted reputation of traditional stokvels, but also damage that reputation when the breach of trust becomes evident (Lindeque 2019). Similar reports about possible scams[9] perpetuated by the members of WhatsApp-mediated digital savings groups can be found in Kenya (Mvowa 2022).

Scams can be particularly prevalent in savings groups with large, anonymous memberships. Recently, over 230,000 investors in the Up Money grocery stokvel[10] were reportedly swindled and bank accounts containing over R18 million (about US$1.2 million) were frozen by the National Consumer Commission of South Africa (Githathu 2020). Prospective members were solicited over social media with promised meat and grocery packs and required to pay a one-time joining fee of R180 (US$12.00) and recruit five new participants. Promises included getting access to cheaper grocery prices with bulk buying. Some of the money, however, was transferred to private accounts of the savings scheme's director and used for purchasing luxury vehicles for group organizers.

The platform can also be vulnerable to hacking and outsiders can use specially crafted messages to sabotage the network, take over someone's account, or delete some of the information (Kariuki and Ofusori 2017: 257). Privacy concerns also abound, and these can be quite different from those in the Global North. While social media platforms enable companies to profit from extracting user information and selling it to third parties, this was not the main concern of platform users in South Africa (Reichel et al. 2020). Instead, users were worried about who could see their messages and how this would affect their social standing, particularly among their elders and superiors. Concerns about physical safety also affected what and how users posted on social media. People often concealed their locations to avoid kidnapping when living in high-crime areas (2020: 1). Scams leading to robberies proliferated, and phone sharing and theft added to security concerns. Users in developing countries are particularly vulnerable to privacy breaches, often posting large amounts of personal data without knowledge of who can access it and how. Many social media users were unaware how to use privacy settings and left them on default (2020: 1). WhatsApp was perceived as more private and easier to control than Facebook in that regard, but stories about hacking and information stealing were still widespread in users' accounts.

The scams around digital savings groups are not just a feature of the Global South. There have been recent reports from UK about loan sharks targeting victims through WhatsApp and Facebook groups. While local WhatsApp groups have proliferated during the pandemic, "creating community ties and support networks," these are increasingly penetrated by criminals offering members short-term loans with abruptly increasing interest rates (Tapper 2021). Such online scams may particularly affect low-income communities with high volumes of recent migrants.

Whatsapp as Alternative Tool for Crowdfunding

In addition to assisting existing or new savings groups in their regular efforts to pool money, WhatsApp is also becoming a preferred tool for (one-time) digital fundraising in many African societies. Frankline Matanji (2020) reports that crowdfunding has become widespread in Kenya through the reliance of fundraisers and contributors on the WhatsApp platform, in conjunction with M-Pesa mobile money service. One of the reasons for WhatsApp's popularity as an informal fundraising platform is the fact that the chat app is already in wide use for everyday communication. Fundraising calls get the attention of many people by directly reaching their inboxes. In addition to these "strong ties" between the primary members the network, fundraising calls indirectly engage with the "weak ties" of secondary contacts of every group member with their own networks. The process of digital fundraising entails "creating a WhatsApp group with a title, adding friends, from either your phonebook or friends of friends and updating an appealing narrative to members explaining why they should contribute" (2020: 245). Group links can be shared with other WhatsApp users, thereby expanding the circle of contributors. The group treasurer shares updates on contributions and defaulters, encouraging people to contribute. The WhatsApp communicative model enables group members to receive messages jointly, while also building on the ease of one-on-one conversations. As communication on the platform is not public, it enables sufficient privacy regarding the cause and contributors of the fundraising event, while still allowing visibility within the group to facilitate accountability. WhatsApp-based fundraising is on the rise in many sectors of society and employed for business projects, events and ceremonies, medical emergencies, and educational expenses. Matanji documents frequent use of WhatsApp fundraising among students at Kisii University in Kenya to fund education-related costs. Kenyan politicians also increasingly turn to WhatsApp to mobilize voters to assist with public sector expenditures (2020: 245–46).

Digital crowdfunding became popular in Kenya after the #1MilliForJadudi campaign in August 2015 that aimed to raise KSh1 million (Kenyan shillings) (approximately US$10,000) to help fund a cancer patient's surgery in India. The campaign that drew on online blogs as well as Twitter and Facebook went viral within hours of launching it, and within three days, had managed to raise US$71,000, which had been contributed by Kenyans all over the country. The money was collected through M-Pesa mobile money contributions.[11] This campaign demonstrated the effectiveness of spontaneous online funding pleas in conjunction with social media platforms and digital payment technologies, enabling private citizens to effectively reach wider publics to mobilize monetary assistance.

The potential of WhatsApp and similar encrypted chat apps for crowdfunding remains significant in Africa, as the continent faces a strong prevalence of foreign-based dedicated crowdfunding platforms—with only an estimated one-third of the total funded amounts coming from African-based platforms (N'Guessan, Alegre, and Berbegal-Mirabent 2019: 288). Most of the African-based platforms are active within their respective countries only,[12] with very few Pan-African platforms (Hiller 2017: 65).

Potentially, crowdfunding technologies in Africa are likely to successfully harness diaspora philanthropy, as many diaspora members are interested in donating for the social benefits of a community broader than kin and family (Chao et al. 2020). Insufficient regulatory frameworks as well as unreliable internet connection are the main impediments. Due to the widespread adoption of mobile money and low rate of penetration of traditional financial institutions, crowdfunding initiatives in Africa frequently leverage mobile technology and build on SMS-messaging and mobile chat apps such as WhatsApp to mobilize fundraising (2020). Offline methods of fundraising remain important in such settings.

At the same time, however, the digital medium is likely to introduce a new competitive aspect to collective fundraising endeavors—and possibly cause changes in traditional fundraising mechanisms. People turn to crowdfunding when their formal and informal "conventional safety nets" fail them, but crowdfunding is more than just "friendfunding," argue Sumin Lee and Vili Lehdonvirta at the example of medical crowdfunding in the United States: the funding is not need-based but rather depends on one's entrepreneurial abilities to "outcompete rivaling needfuls" (2022: 1151).

The Infrastructures of Cryptopolitics

These cases reveal that the emerging crypto-publics in Africa are constituted through multiple materialities and communicative forms, including the offline spaces of self-help groups with their social and historical embeddedness, and new digital interfaces with their BigTech connectivities. This highlights the importance of examining the evolving digital structures as multilevel and fragmented sociotechnical assemblages that bring together diverse formal and informal, online and offline, physical and peopled infrastructural elements (Rodima-Taylor and Grimes 2019). Mediated by encrypted chat apps, the poor and marginal exercise their agency through self-help groups and networks, carving out new civic spaces in the process. This links to the prevailing conceptualization of the public sphere as a mediated space for citizens to voice and share their opinions about public affairs (Habermas 1992, see also Johns 2020 for a nuanced critique). New communicative technologies may therefore foster a new, virtual public sphere that similarly allows freedom of expression.

The realities are more complex, however. First, as feminist and decolonial critiques have pointed out, the concept of public sphere has historically evolved around the "male bourgeois public sphere" that instituted a number of exclusions (Frazer 1992). Marginalized social groups created their own oppositional counter-publics as "parallel discursive arenas" (see also Warner 2002). The rise of digital technologies with their proprietary platforms have fragmented the public spaces even further. Johns has suggested that social media platforms should not be seen as neutral enablers of civic discourse, but as expressive of institutional power exercised through algorithms (2020). The "backstage media channels" such as encrypted messaging services, on the other hand, may allow safe spaces to negotiate internal differences and affirm solidarity, away from public scrutiny and manipulative news media. I suggest, however, that these assumptions about encrypted apps as enabling activism and solidarity need to be questioned, too. Instead of assuming that encrypted chat apps engender alternative public spheres, we should ask what kinds of new and old solidarities and inequalities the technology fosters and builds upon.

The democratic potential of people enacting their rights in society through digital technologies has been distorted by the ubiquitous data collection by technology companies and governments, argue Arne Hintz, Lina Dencik, and Karin Wahl-Jorgensen (2017). Those who control people's personal data gain unprecedented insights into people's lives, resulting in an unequal power dynamic (2017: 733). Big Data is continuously generated and scalable, processed through software-empowered machine learning that detects patterns and builds predictive models (Kitchin 2014: 9). Datafication—the processes by which the system and lifeworld are transmuted into data—can thus be seen as a fundamental shift in contemporary society (Beraldo and Milan 2019). Critical approaches to datafication have highlighted the colonial heritage of modern technology, situating it within the broader history of European colonial powers aggregating global resources that gave rise to industrial capitalism. Coloniality can be traced in the extraction of value through data that can be compared to historical land grabs, suggest Nick Couldry and Ulises Mejias (2021: 10–11). The concept of coloniality thus refers to the continuing effects of historical colonization that endure to the present day. Automated, data-driven systems can extend the biases and privileges of algorithmic oppression in society (Mohamed et al. 2020:665). The following sections of the chapter explore the broader infrastructural embeddedness of the self-help groups as well as digital platforms, with attention to the legacies of power inequalities, and discuss the characteristics of the emerging digital publics as they strive to negotiate these.

Savings Groups and the Histories of Mutuality

Instead of assuming that WhatsApp engenders group cohesion and frictionless administration just because it enables greater privacy than open social media platforms or allows wider outreach than place-bound savings groups, I suggest that it is important to examine the broader social histories of the mutual help groups as well as the digital infrastructures that they are increasingly part of. Self-help groups can be found in many areas of Africa, including the *chama* groups of Kenya, *isusu* of Nigeria, and *stokvel* of South Africa (Ardener and Burman 1995; Ardener 2010). A considerable rise has occurred in these groups with the neoliberal restructuring reforms of the 1980s–1990s, with a decline in formal sector employment and state-funded producer cooperatives (Rodima-Taylor 2014; Tripp 1997). As my two-year fieldwork in northeast Tanzania revealed, a variety of self-help groups were widespread among the Kuria people. These built on the norms of cooperation that had emerged in the distant past for sharing agricultural labor, transitioning from large "festive" work parties to regularly mobilized, smaller work groups. As an informant told me: "Nowadays we have much more old-time groups than in the past" (Rodima-Taylor 2014: 553). While many of them had retained the element of rotating farm work, they were also active in non-agricultural ventures such as carpentry, brick-making or tailoring, managing a group farm plot or retail kiosk, and many had joint credit arrangements (most often rotating savings-credit). The groups provided new opportunities for marginalized social groups, such as women and youth. They assisted women with farm work and cash income, allowing them more independence especially in polygynous households. Through their group membership, people constructed their social personhood through the practices claim-making and extending debt (Rodima-Taylor 2014). Group affairs and mutual loan contributions were concealed from the public, and informal bylaws frequently included sanctions against revealing them to outsiders. By providing new economic and social opportunities for women and young people marginalized from the men's sphere of cattle wealth, these groups constituted a conducive site for cryptopolitics—as well as an important venue for negotiating people's increasingly unstable livelihoods.

Similar self-help groups (locally called *chama*) are also proliferating in neighboring Kenya: according to recent estimates, there are around 300,000 *chama* groups in the country, circulating over US$3 billion (Chidziwizano et al. 2020). The groups are widespread among both genders and many of them also manage joint business projects (Mwangi and Kimani 2015; Nyataya 2016). Informal savings groups are also popular in South Africa where they emerged in the era of colonial displacement. In 2019, 10 million people saved through stokvel groups and 45 percent of the population belonged to an informal burial society (Shipalana 2019). The evolvement of these groups has been shaped by the country's colonial history. Stokvels emerged with the labor migration of many Black South Africans into gold and diamond mines in the early 1900s and spread across the country with the migration of Black women as urban domestic and industrial workers (see Rodima-Taylor 2022b).

Both Kenya and South Africa carry the legacies of White settler economies where the colonizing population inhabited the African territories, appropriating land and labor. It is therefore important to remember that the ideologies and practices of mutuality, while building on customary norms, are not static. Rather than merely embodying timeless sentiments of sharing and reciprocity, savings groups in those countries have been impacted by the extractive coloniality of European settler economies and later neoliberal restructuring that has fueled the informal economy and over-indebtedness. The new digital initiatives that claim to build on the "traditional" mechanisms of risk sharing and local cosmologies of "unity" could render the groups more vulnerable.

The BigTech Implications of WhatsApp Groups

While WhatsApp may offer its users in Africa more autonomy and flexibility than dedicated fundraising or savings group management platforms, the fact that it is owned by a foreign BigTech company could complicate the dynamic. WhatsApp started in California in 2009 and was acquired by Facebook (now Meta Platforms) in 2014. As a recent *Guardian* article claims: "Across Africa, Facebook *is* the internet" (Malik 2022). The Free Basic service launched in 2015 is an application that provides access free of data charges to a variety of local news and information platforms and Facebook itself.[13] Free Basic has faced opposition in several countries, where it has been critiqued for insufficient transparency in selecting services available on the app and restricting the development of local startups (Nothias 2020). Partly in response to the backlash from digital rights activists, Facebook has recently focused more on engagement with civil society organizations and assisting local software developers (2020). Facebook and WhatsApp have thus contributed to facilitating free speech and civic activism in countries with oppressive regimes.

Recent media reports discuss Facebook's plans to transform its huge global user base into a "profit center" by motivating retailers to sell goods and services inside the WhatsApp application (Wagner 2020). For Facebook, WhatsApp therefore presents a chance to diversify its business as well as deepen control over a brand and its customer: "'Instagram and Facebook are the storefront' . . . 'WhatsApp is the cash register.'" There are also plans to further consolidate the business-consumer interface within WhatsApp—an important new line of revenue for Facebook—by enabling consumers to process payments inside the app, thereby turning the messaging service into a WeChat-like digital storefront. The payment aspect of WhatsApp already operates on a limited scale in some countries.

The ongoing commercialization of the WhatsApp platform may raise broader concerns about the growing influence of Western-owned companies in African communicative space. Michael Kwet (2019: 9) suggests that the emerging global architecture of the digital economy is shaped by structural inequality as BigTech companies exercise monopoly power over rent and user data extraction, making it difficult for the local firms to compete with the incumbents. At the same time, encrypted chat apps continue to offer autonomous and empowering spaces to civil society activists as well as savings group members in Africa—suggesting a fertile terrain for further research into these emerging synergies.

The Ambiguities of the Digital Public Sphere

Ambiguities also surround the effects of the digital medium to the socialities of the savings groups. Considering that many self-help groups have turned to social media, in particular to encrypted chat apps, to manage their affairs and extend outreach, one may assume that the digital connective modality is well suited to the needs of these informal collectivities. However, it has been noted that the ease of digital communication comes with undesired side-effects. Matanji (2020: 246) points out that one of the downsides of digital crowdfunding is isolation: "People who used to see one another physically, talk and chat and laugh in traditional Harambees no longer exist. This technological advancement has led to family ties being broken and people moving away from a collectivist society. The price of efficient fundraising is replacing the face-to-face interactions." I suggest that this erasure of in-person communication can fundamentally alter the dynamic that has defined offline savings groups. B. Njeru (2018) points out that informal savings groups (*chama*) in western Kenya operate in a highly oral space. In South African stokvels, despite complex written group constitutions, interpersonal communication between group members was central for upholding its laws (Hutchison 2020).

In my field observations of Kuria self-help groups in neighboring Tanzania, I similarly noted the central importance of oral negotiations in group affairs (Rodima-Taylor 2014). Most of the groups had elaborate written bylaws, and their rules and hierarchies constituted a creative mix borrowed from the traditional social institutions of Kuria clans and more recent administrative structures of the socialist era. While there was a tension between the more indirect mode of "customary" decision-making and the "statutory" hierarchical model of negotiating differences, it was the consensus-based model that prevailed most of the time. Written documents carried symbolic significance and were used to legitimize the groups with local administrative bureaucracy, but they offered little formal recourse for disputes. Group bylaws were subject to a constant reinterpretation in daily practice (2014: 563). This shows a fundamental disconnect between the offline modalities of savings group management and the ways that communication tends to be structured in digitally mediated savings groups.

Evidence from recent studies of the emerging "digital publics" in East Africa testifies to the enduring importance of the form and function of traditional public assemblies in shaping the new online spaces. In Swahili communities, *baraza* signified a place for regular public gatherings. The new digital publics or "cyberbaraza" that emerged during the 2015 Zanzibar presidential elections enabled alternative ways of political participation by contesting dominant political discourses, suggests Irene Brunotti, while its form remained molded by the "discursive tradition of Swahili orature" (2019: 25). Baraza had mediated the Kenyan state through a rhetoric that recast the daily concerns of citizens into moral themes, while at the same time also rendering these narratives debatable (Haugerud 1995: 193–96). Discussing the complexity of the evolving "political personhood" in Kenya, Duncan Omanga (2019) suggested that while offline forums such as county assemblies and committees failed to encourage meaningful participation in local governance, WhatsApp groups made information more accessible and enabled safer dissent. George Ogola (2019) argues that the disruption created by social media platforms in Kenya is partial and piecemeal—facilitating "pockets of indiscipline" and encouraging popular participation, while staying limited by costly computer and internet access, and lacking digital literacy. Social media therefore remains situated within the existing, unequal structures of economic opportunity and can reproduce offline divisions and marginalities (2019).

Uncertain Crypto-Publics: Code, Community, and Politics

When discussing the potential of encrypted chat apps to enable new types of collectivities built on peer solidarity—including WhatsApp-empowered savings groups or fundraising endeavors—it may be helpful to draw parallels with the types of crypto-publics that emerge with cryptographic technologies and currencies. Blockchain technology can facilitate organizations where individuals cooperate on a peer-to-peer basis, with no need for centralized management structures. These techno-communities where connections are formed through cryptographic protocols can be viewed as a technological advancement of commons-based peer production systems that are based on "sharing resources and outputs among widely distributed, loosely connected individuals" (De Filippi and Wright 2018: 136). Their activities are governed by algorithmic "smart contracts," and governance relies on group consensus rather than formal hierarchy (2018: 137). Such systems for "human and machine coordination" in decision-making seek to bypass the "messiness of human relationships, legal contracts, and leaky information flows" (Dupont 2019: 194).

In applying the cryptographic protocol, technology thus appears autonomous—erasing the work of governance and politics (Vidan and

Lehdonvirta 2019). The trustlessness of the blockchain is therefore not just material (as giving priority to certain gatekeepers and infrastructures) but also discursive—expressed in the commitment of the users to the social imaginary of trustworthy code and algorithmic regulation. The "trust in code" discourse, however, can be seen as inspired by a binary perspective on modernity and transition—one that views modernity as a shift from traditional social ties to centralized, formal institutions that become mediators of "impersonal economic relationships." Cryptographic authentication technologies thus come to replace both personal ties and formal institutions (2019).

While cryptocode is often viewed as a "fundamentally democratic process" that results from peer production (2019: 45), Gili Vidan and Vili Lehdonvirta point out that this promise of trustlessness is an ongoing process of discursive maintenance by powerful actors in the network. Open-source software communities could be seen as recursive publics that construct themselves as such through the sharing of source code at the basis of a moral and technological order. Such publics emerge as "organized around the ability to build, modify, and maintain the very infrastructure that gives it life in the first place" (Kelty 2008). The infrastructures of cryptographic trustlessness are therefore not just material but also discursive, with collective imaginaries and narratives playing an important role.

We could therefore say that the emerging digital crypto-publics bring along hierarchies and group templates from offline spaces, but may also fall victim to a new type of technocratic governance that obscures the location of power and encourages trust in the (hidden) code. Easy deception can follow. The combination of offline and online spaces remains important and is a frequently overlooked aspect of the new types of online communications. I suggest that the search for technologically mediated trust may be more pervasive in societies that are subject to chronic political and economic instabilities, with unreliable administrative and financial infrastructures. People in such settings are more dependent on online, fragmented, and privately managed alternatives. It can thus be expected that the technology-driven alternatives become increasingly central in the livelihoods of the marginal and displaced populations in the Global South. At the same time, these spaces remain of a "hybrid" nature, incorporating online and offline, material and discursive dimensions. It is therefore important to acknowledge the hidden political dimensions of the new digitally empowered publics, and the continued inequalities that may play out in their material infrastructures and power relations.

Conclusion

My chapter explored the cryptopolitics of informal savings groups and contribution networks in two African countries—South Africa and Kenya—as mediated through encrypted digital messaging platforms. It argued that the emerging crypto-publics are constituted through multiple materialities and communicative forms, including the offline spaces of self-help groups with their social and historical embeddedness, and new digital platforms with their BigTech connectivities. Mediated by encrypted messaging apps, the poor and marginal exercise their agency through self-help groups and networks, carving out new civic spaces. The article argues that such spaces always involve important and interconnected offline and online, and material and human modalities. It offers new perspectives to the formation of the digital public sphere through attention to cryptopolitics, and advances new approaches for analyzing it.

WhatsApp has rapidly become one of the most widely used digital platforms in the Global South. This has been attributed to its peculiar features that allow it to accommodate large groups as well as private chat messaging on its platform. It has been suggested that especially in the contexts of repressive states, such "semi-public chat apps" may constitute critical infrastructures for social activism (Johns 2020). While some studies focus on the role of WhatsApp in advancing political activism, this chapter argued that an important use case of the platform has been overlooked so far. In several African countries, WhatsApp is increasingly central for mobilizing online savings groups as well as used for fundraising for a variety of causes, both public and private. It has also emerged as a primary platform connecting the diaspora with their home communities in the Global South through mobilizing remittances and facilitating everyday conversations and often features as an essential part of transborder care networks.

In existing research, the platform's ability to mediate informal and depoliticized conversations has been highlighted as a reason for its effectiveness in mobilizing new connections as well as inspiring collective action (Pang and Woo 2019). By forging connections between "the vernacular and the political" (Milan and Barbosa 2020), such encrypted messaging apps may give rise to a new type of political subject that builds on the joint responsibility advanced in the chat groups. The notion of crypto-publics links encryption to digital resistance and citizenship, and such publics have been viewed as counteracting the ongoing datafication and challenging the power of bureaucracies (Johns 2020).

This leads us to the question about the nature of the present-day digital publics as mediated through social media platforms. Data coloniality connects to the enduring effects of historical colonization in the Global South (Couldry and Mejias 2021). My chapter argues therefore that when analyzing the data coloniality of social media, it should be seen as integrally connected to other kinds of coloniality—calling for an integrated approach to offline and online dimensions of these processes. In order to study the algorithmic coloniality (Mohamed et al. 2020) in the Global South through a "de-Westernized" epistemic lens, the chapter suggested attention to the sociotechnical infrastructures with their physical and peopled dimensions that channel the construction of mutuality both online and offline. My chapter examined the "contentious politics of data" (Beraldo and Milan 2019) with the example of WhatsApp as mobilizing collective action around people's livelihoods and harnessing their customary collectivities of savings groups and mutual support networks. These have a long history and have been integrally related to the unstable economies shaped by colonialism. In the present day, the savings groups continue providing mutual support and manage risk among low-income people domestically, as well as offer innovative solutions for the diaspora to counteract their economic and social marginalization. On the other hand, digital groups have also become fodder for rapidly spreading new scams and get-rich-quick schemes, and increasingly attract high-interest online loan offers. While social imaginaries abound about the integrative function of the savings schemes among strangers, there is little evidence to support that. The chapter also revealed an important disconnect between the offline modalities of savings group management and the ways communication tends to be structured in digitally mediated savings groups.

Instead of assuming that WhatsApp engenders group cohesion and frictionless cooperation because it enables greater privacy than open social media platforms, my chapter thus argues that it is important to examine the histories and social embeddedness of the offline mutualities it channels and the broader political economies of the digital infrastructures involved. As part of the ubiquitous Facebook platform, WhatsApp encapsulates the extractive dynamic of BigTech global data capture. At the same time, it has also emerged as a local alternative to digital group accounts increasingly offered by commercial banks and FinTech platforms and dedicated crowdfunding services that in Africa are still dominated by Western-owned companies and developmental paradigms. As the chapter revealed, successful fundraising campaigns frequently draw on WhatsApp and combine the online platform with offline contribution networks and mobile payment channels, demonstrating the continued importance of integrating the diverse existing modalities of financial management in local livelihoods. More research is needed into the rapidly growing use of encrypted chat apps and other social media platforms for facilitating the informal collectivities of the "hidden economies" in the Global South.

Crypto-publics as digitally mediated collectivities frequently advance social imaginaries that highlight trust in code and community, as we learned. Social imaginaries, however, can also lead to alternative epistemologies and local agendas of change—those inspired by decolonial thinking and "working toward epistemic justice" (Milan and Treré 2019: 328). While in contemporary Western-centered conceptualizations of datafication, local people have been relegated to the margins as passive objects of surveillance, the social imaginaries of the Global South may thus allude to alternative ways of thinking about digital information that emerge in the fringes. Such imaginaries inspired by "grassroots data practices" (2019: 329) may therefore contain novel paradigms of resistance and autonomy. These may reveal alternative ways of imagining borderless cooperation among relatives and existing and new friends in the global diaspora, while building on people's own initiatives and circumventing formal sector exclusion—and countless other instances of cryptopolitics advanced by people both online and off.

Daivi Rodima-Taylor is a social anthropologist and researcher at the African Studies Center of the Pardee School of Global Studies of Boston University. Her research focuses on African informal economies, financial technology and social media platforms, and migration and remittances. She has conducted longitudinal field research in East Africa and published in journals including *Africa, African Studies Review, Global Networks, Social Analysis, American Ethnologist, Journal of International Relations and Development, Environment and Planning: Politics and Space, Geoforum, Global Policy,* and *Review of International Political Economy.* Her recent publications include the co-edited volume *Land and the Mortgage: History, Culture, Belonging* (Berghahn Books, 2022) and the co-edited special issue *Fintech in Africa* (*Journal of Cultural Economy,* 2022).

Notes

1. Informal savings groups in South Africa.
2. Mavundza (2020).
3. "New WhatsApp Scam Doing the Rounds in South Africa." *BusinessTech,* 9 October 2019. Retrieved 16 January from https://businesstech.co.za/news/mobile/345424/new-whatsapp-scam-doing-the-rounds-in-south-africa/.

4. Ntombizakhona. 2021. "WhatsApp 'Stokvels' Are A Scam and Don't Be Tempted To Join Telegram or Signal 'Stokvels' Now . . . How To Start A Stokvel." *Search Medium*, 16 January. Retrieved 16 January from https://studentanalyst.medium.com/whatsapp-stokvels-are-a-scam-amp-don-t-be-tempted-to-join-telegram-or-signal-stokvels-8b503a4dafef.
5. Pijoos (2019).
6. See also Paul Langley and Andrew Leyshon (2020) on platform intermediation as premised on multisided value extraction and rapid scaling, which can foster oligopolies and change the competitive basis of retail finance.
7. *WhatsApp*. Retrieved 16 January 2023 from https://www.whatsapp.com/.
8. The Zamara Fahari Retirement Plan account is a platform backed by Kenya's Retirement Regulatory Authority (RBA) and the Insurance Regulatory Authority (IRA).
9. Samrack. "Kate wa Gladys, a Kenyan Woman Who Runs Multiple WhatsApp Chamas Reportedly Arrested over Fraud Allegations." *Samrack: Diaspora News and Updates*, 29 August. Retrieved 16 January 2023 from https://samrack.com/kate-wa-gladys-a-kenyan-woman-who-runs-multiple-whatsapp-chamas-reportedly-arrested-over-fraud-allegations/.
10. The "retail stokvels" in South Africa are savings groups that pool money to obtain bulk groceries from retailers at a discount. Retailers target such stokvels as their regular clients, developing business models that include storage space, discounts, and special payment systems (Lappeman et al. 2019).
11. "Kenyans surpass the #1MilliforJadudi target and raise Sh6 million." *Nairobi News*, 6 August 2015. Retrieved 16 January 2023 from https://nairobinews.nation.co.ke/32265/.
12. While there is a scarcity of statistical data about the present state of crowdfunding platforms as a more general category in Africa as well, foreign-based platforms are still prevalent also in that overall sector, covering about 64 percent of the crowdfunding platforms operating in Africa in May 2020 (Adjakou 2021).
13. *Meta Connectivity*. Retrieved 16 January 2023 from https://www.facebook.com/connectivity/#what-s-free-basics-.

References

Adjakou, Oloutchegoun. 2021. "Crowdfunding: Genesis and Comprehensive Review of Its State in Africa." *Open Journal of Business and Management* 9: 557–85.

Ardener, Shirley. 2010. "Microcredit, Money Transfers, Women, and the Cameroon Diaspora." *Afrika Focus* 23(2): 11–24.

Ardener, Shirley. 2014. "Credit Unions and Money Clubs (ROSCAs)." *Anthropology Today* 30(4): 3-6.

Ardener, Shirley, and Sandra Burman (eds). 1995. *Money-Go-Rounds*. Oxford and Washington DC: Berg Publishers.

Beraldo, Davide, and Stefania Milan. 2019. "From Data Politics to the Contentious Politics of Data." *Big Data & Society* July–December: 1–11.

Bernal, Victoria. 2014. *Nation as Network: Diaspora, Cyberspace, and Citizenship*. Chicago: University of Chicago Press.

Brunotti, Irene. 2019. "From *Baraza* to *Cyberbaraza*: Interrogating Publics in the Context of the 2015 Zanzibar Electoral Impasse." *Journal of Eastern African Studies* 13(1): 18–34.

Campbell, Ian Carlos. 2021. “WhatsApp, Twitter, and Facebook are Reportedly Blocked in Zambia during Its Presidential Election.” Retrieved 5 October 2022 from https://www.theverge.com/2021/8/12/22621875/whatsapp-twitter-facebook-blocked-zambia-presidential-election.

Chalwe-Mulenga, Majorie, Eric Duflos, and Gerhard Coetzee. 2022. *The Evolution of the Nature and Scale of DFS Consumer Risks*. Washington, DC: CGAP.

Chao, Emmanuel James, Priscilla Serwaah, Prince Baah-Peprah, and Rotem Shneor. 2020. “Crowdfunding in Africa: Opportunities and Challenges.” In *Advances in Crowdfunding*, ed. Rotem Shneor, Liang Zhao, and Bjørn-Tore Flåten, 319–40. London: Palgrave MacMillan.

Chidziwisano, George, Susan Wyche, and Rellikson Kisyula. 2020. “SmartChama: Designing Collaborative Digital Financial Systems for Chama Groups in Kenya.” In Proceedings of the 2020 International Conference on Information and Communication Technologies and Development (ICTD2020). Association for Computing Machinery, New York, NY, USA, Article 13, 1–12. https://doi.org/10.1145/3392561.3394641

Comaroff, John, and Jean Comaroff, eds. 2001. *Millenial Capitalism and the Culture of Neoliberalism*. Durham, NC: Duke University Press.

Couldry, Nick, and Ulises Mejias. 2021. “The Decolonial Turn in Data and Technology Research: What Is at Stake and Where Is It Heading?” *Information, Communication & Society*. https://doi.org/10.1080/1369118X.2021.1986102.

De Philippi, Primavera, and Aaron Wright. 2018. *Blockchain and the Law: The Rule of Code*. Cambridge, MA: Harvard University Press.

Dupont, Quinn. 2019. *Cryptocurrencies and Blockchains*. Cambridge: Polity Press.

Frazer, Nancy. 1992. “Rethinking the Public Sphere: A Contribution to the Critique of Actually Existing Democracy.” In *Habermas and the Public Sphere*, ed. Craig Calhoun, 109–42. Cambridge, MA: MIT Press.

Gichuru, Mercy. 2014. *Strategic Planning in Investment Groups (Chama) in Nairobi County*. MBA thesis. Nairobi: University of Nairobi.

Githathu, Mwangi. 2020. “Over 230,000 Investors in the Up Money ‘Stokvel’ Swindled.” *IOL*, 5 August. Retrieved 5 October 2022 from https://www.iol.co.za/capeargus/news/over-230-000-investors-in-the-up-money-stokvel-swindled-8a9261c0-beca-4de6-bac8-fa8e173df7a4.

Habermas, Juergen. 1992. “Further Reflections on the Public Sphere.” In *Habermas and the Public Sphere*, ed. C. Calhoun, 109–42. Cambridge, MA: MIT Press.

Haugerud, Angelique. 1995. *The Culture of Politics in Modern Kenya*. Cambridge: Cambridge University Press.

Hiller, A. 2017. “An Empirical Analysis of Crowdfunding in Sub-Saharan Africa.” Ph.D. dissertation. Leipzig: Leipzig Graduate School of Management.

Hintz, Arne, Lina Dencik, and Karin Wahl-Jorgensen. 2017. “Digital Citizenship and Surveillance Society.” *International Journal of Communication* 11: 731–39.

Hossein, Caroline. 2017. “Fringe Banking in Canada: The Collective Economies of Toronto’s ‘Banker Ladies.’” *ANSERJ* 8(1): 29–43.

Hutchison, Andrew. 2020. “Uncovering Contracting Norms in Khayelitsha Stokvels.” *The Journal of Legal Pluralism and Unofficial Law* 52 (1): 3-27.

Johns, Amelia. 2020. “‘This Will Be the WhatsApp Election’: Crypto-publics and Digital Citizenship in Malaysia’s GE14 election.” *First Monday* 25(12). https://doi.org/10.5210/fm.v25i12.10381.

Jones, Graham. 2014. “Secrecy.” *Annual Review of Anthropology* 43: 53–69.

Kariuki, Paul, and Lizzy Ofusori. 2017. "WhatsApp-operated Stokvels Promoting Youth Entrepreneurship in Durban, South Africa." *ICEGOV '17: Proceedings of the 10th International Conference on Theory and Practice of Electronic Governance*, 253–59. https://doi.org/10.1145/3047273.3047397.

Kelty, Christopher. 2008. *Two Bits: The Cultural Significance of Free Software*. Durham, NC: Duke University Press.

Kene-Okofor, Tage. 2021. "WhatsApp and Other Social Media Platforms Restricted in Zambia amidst Ongoing Elections." *Yahoo! Finance*, 12 August. Retrieved 5 October 2022 from https://ca.finance.yahoo.com/news/whatsapp-other-social-media-platforms-143333617.html.

Kgophane, Karabo. 2020. "Warning: WhatsApp Stokvel Makes a Comeback in 2020." *The South African*, 5 July. Retrieved 5 October 2022 from https://www.thesouthafrican.com/technology/whatsapp-stokvel-2020/.

Kimega, Godfrey. 2021. "Kenyans Behaving Badly on WhatsApp Groups." *The Star*, 29 August. Retrieved 5 October 2022 from https://www.the-star.co.ke/sasa/lifestyle/2021-08-29-kenyans-behaving-badly-on-whatsapp-groups/.

Kitchin, Rob. 2014. "Big Data, New Epistemologies and Paradigm Shifts." *Big Data & Society* April–June: 1–12.

Kivuva, Elizabeth. 2021. "Zamara Targets WhatsApp Users with Digital Pension Plan." *Business Daily*, 7 December. Retrieved 5 October 2022 from https://www.businessdailyafrica.com/bd/markets/capital-markets/zamara-targets-whatsapp-users-with-digital-pensions-plan-3644884.

Kwet, Michael. 2019. "Digital Colonialism: US Empire and the New Imperialism in the Global South." *Race & Class* 60(4): 3–26.

Langley, Paul, and Andrew Leyshon. 2020. "The Platform Political Economy of FinTech: Reintermediation, Consolidation and Capitalisation." *New Polit. Econ.* 26(3): 376–88.

Langley, Paul, and Daivi Rodima-Taylor. 2022. "FinTech in Africa: An Editorial Introduction." *Journal of Cultural Economy* 15(4): 387–400.

Lappeman, James, Jemma Litkie, Shrya Bramdaw, and Abigail Quibell. 2019. "Exploring Retail-Oriented Rotating Savings-Credit Associations: Festive Season 'Stokvels' in South Africa." *The International Review of Retail Distribution and Consumer Research* 30(3): 331–58. https://doi.org/10.1080/09593969.2019.1667853.

Lee, Sumin, and Vili Lehdonvirta. 2022. "New Digital Safety Net or Just More 'Friendfunding'? Institutional Analysis of Medical Crowdfunding in the United States." *Information, Communication & Society* 25(8): 1151–75.

Lindeque, Mia. 2019. "WhatsApp Stokvels: How Fraudsters Use Group Chats to Steal Money." *EWN*, 9 October. Retrieved 5 October 2022 from https://ewn.co.za/2019/10/09/whatsapp-stokvels-how-fraudsters-use-group-chats-to-steal-money.

Malik, Nesrine. 2022. "How Facebook Took Over the Internet in Africa—And Changed Everything." *The Guardian*, 20 January. Retrieved 5 October 2022 from https://www.theguardian.com/technology/2022/jan/20/facebook-second-life-the-unstoppable-rise-of-the-tech-company-in-africa.

Manderson, Lenore, Mark Davis, Chip Colwell, and Tanja Ahlin. 2015. "On Secrecy, Disclosure, the Public, and the Private in Anthropology." *Current Anthropology* 56 (S12): S183–90.

Matanji, Frankline. 2020. "WhatsApp and Mobile Money: Ameliorating Crowdfunding for Social Change in Kenya." *Asia Pacific Media Educator* 29(2): 237–48.

Mavundza, Bombi. 2020. "WhatsApp Stokvels Are Back and You're Probably Being Scammed." *Business Insider*, 1 July. Retrieved 5 October 2022 from https://www.businessinsider.co.za/whatsapp-stokvel-scams-2020-6.

Menze, Aviwe, and Pitso Tsibolane. 2019. "Online Stokvels: The Use of Social Media by the Marginalized." *CONF-IRM 2019 Proceedings*. 26. https://aisel.aisnet.org/confirm2019/26/.

Metz, Cade. 2016. "Forget Apple vs. the FBI: WhatsApp Just Switched on Encryption for a Billion People." *Wired*, 5 April. Retrieved 5 October 2022 from https://www.wired.com/2016/04/forget-apple-vs-fbi-whatsapp-just-switched-encryption-billion-people/.

Milan, Stefania, and Sergio Barbosa. 2020. "Enter the WhatsApper: Reinventing Digital Activism at the Time of Chat Apps." *First Monday* 25(1). https://doi.org/10.5210/fm.v25i12.10414.

Milan, Stefania, and Emilio Treré. 2019. "Big Data from the South(s): Beyond Data Universalism." *Television & New Media* 20(4): 319–35.

Mohamed, Shakir, Marie-Therese Png, and William Isaac. 2020. "Decolonial AI: Decolonial Theory as Sociotechnical Foresight in Artificial Intelligence." *Philosophy & Technology* 33: 659–84.

Moodley, Clinton. 2019. "How WhatsApp Groups Are Ruining the Travel Stokvel's Reputation." *IOL*, 24 October. Retrieved 5 October 2022 from https://www.iol.co.za/travel/travel-news/how-whatsapp-groups-are-ruining-the-travel-stokvels-reputation-35772880.

Mvende, Mwova. 2022. "Unsuspecting Kenyan Women Losing Millions in Whatsapp, Facebook Chamas." *Bizna*, 18 October. Retrieved 5 October 2022 from https://biznakenya.com/facebook-chamas/.

Mwangi, J., and E. Kimani. 2015. "Factors Influencing Participation of Men and Women in Informal Finance Groups." *Int Journ Hum Soc Stud.* 3(1): 42–48.

Mwita, Martin, and Charles Okwemba. 2021. "Regulators Back WhatsApp Pension Plan Targeting Informal Sector." *The Star*, 8 December. Retrieved 5 October 2022 from https://www.the-star.co.ke/business/kenya/2021-12-08-regulators-back-whatsapp-pension-plan-targeting-informal-sector/.

N'Guessan, Marie, Ines Alegre, and Jasmina Berbegal-Mirabent. 2019. "Crowdlending: A Global Phenomenon Arrives to Sub-Saharan Africa." In *Globalization and Development. Contributions to Management Science*, ed. Nezameddin Faghih, 285–306. Cham: Springer.

Njeru, B. 2018. "Communication as Organization: An Exploration of a Constitution of Chamas in Kenya." *Journal of Media Critiques* 4(14): 153–70.

Nothias, Toussaint. 2020. "Access Granted: Facebook's Free Basics in Africa." *Media, Culture & Society* 42(3): 329–48.

Nuttall, Sarah, and Achille Mbembe. 2015. "Secrecy's Softwares." *Current Anthropology* 56 (S12): S317–24.

Nyataya, I. 2016. "Women Self-help Groups Enhancing Women's Development Processes in Kenya." *IJRSA* 2(2): 18–25.

Ogola, George. 2019. "#Whatwouldmagufulido? Kenya's Digital 'Practices' and 'Individuation' as a (Non)Political Act." *Journal of Eastern African Studies* 13(1): 124–39.

Omanga, Duncan. 2019. "WhatsApp as 'Digital Publics': The *Nakuru Analysts* and the Evolution of Participation in County Governance in Kenya." *Journal of Eastern African Studies* 13(1): 175–91.

Pang, Natalie, and Yue Ting Woo. 2020. "What about WhatsApp? A Systematic Review of WhatsApp and Its Role in Civic and Political Engagement." *First Monday* 25(12). https://doi.org/10.5210/fm.v25i12.10417.

Pillay, Vernon. 2022. "Saving, the Truly South African Way." Retrieved 9 February 2023 from https://www.iol.co.za/business-report/economy/saving-the-truly-south-african-way-a-look-at-stokvels-and-tax-free-savings-accounts-8631d37d-a935-4306-89b9-5224a62da71c.

Pijoos, Iavan. 2019. "Don't Fall for the R200 WhatsApp Stokvels Scam, Association Warns." Times Live, 9 October. Retrieved 5 October 2022 from https://www.timeslive.co.za/news/south-africa/2019-10-09-dont-fall-for-the-r200-whatsapp-stokvels-scam-association-warns/.

Plaza, Dwaine, and Lauren Plaza. 2019. "Facebook and Whatsapp as Elements in Transnational Care Chains for the Trinidadian Diaspora." *Genealogy* 3(2): 15. https://doi.org/10.3390/genealogy3020015.

Reichel, Jake, Fleming Peck, Mikako Inaba, Bisrat T. Moges, Brahmnoor S. Chawla, and Marshini Chetty. 2020. "'I Have Too Much Respect for My Elders': Understanding South African Mobile Users' Perceptions of Privacy and Current Behaviors on Facebook and WhatsApp." SEC '20: Proceedings of the 29th USENIX Conference on Security Symposium, 1949–66.

Rodima-Taylor, Daivi. 2014. "Passageways of Cooperation: Mutuality in Post-socialist Tanzania." *Africa* 84(4): 553–75.

———. 2022a. "Sending Money Home in Conflict Settings: Revisiting Migrant Remittances." *Georgetown Journal of International Affairs* 23(1): 43–51.

———. 2022b. "Platformizing Ubuntu? FinTech, Inclusion, and Mutual Help in Africa." *Journal of Cultural Economy* 15(4): 416–35.

Rodima-Taylor, Daivi, and William Grimes. 2019. "International Remittance Rails as Infrastructures: Embeddedness, Innovation and Financial Access in Developing Economies." *Review of International Political Economy* 26(5): 839–62.

Shipalana, Palesa. 2019. *Digitising Financial Services: A Tool for Financial Inclusion in South Africa?* SAIIA Occasional paper 301.

Simmel, George. 1906. "The Sociology of Secrecy and of Secret Societies." *American Journal of Sociology* 11(4): 441–98.

Strange, Susan. 1986. *Casino Capitalism.* Oxford: Blackwell.

Tapper, James. 2021. "Loan Sharks Target New Victims via Whatsapp and Facebook." *The Guardian,* 9 May. Retrieved 5 October 2022 from https://www.theguardian.com/money/2021/may/09/loan-sharks-target-new-victims-via-whatsapp-and-facebook.

Treré, Emilio. 2020. "The Banality of WhatsApp: On the Everyday Politics of Backstage Activism in Mexico and Spain." *First Monday* 25(12). DOI: https://doi.org/10.5210/fm.v25i12.10404.

Tripp, Aili. 1997. *Changing the Rules: the Politics of Liberalization and the Urban Informal Economy in Tanzania.* Berkeley and Los Angeles CA: University of California Press.

Tsibolane, Pitso, Biyela Nokwazi, and Jean-Paul W. Van Belle. 2018. *Domestication of ICTs in Community Savings and Credit Associations (Stokvels) in the Western Cape, South Africa.* Conference: Making ICT Research Locally Relevant. South Africa.

Vidan, Gili, and Vili Lehdonvirta. 2019. "Mine the Gap: Bitcoin and the Maintenance of Trustlessness." *new media & society* 21(1): 42–59.

Warner, Michael. 2002. *Publics and Counterpublics.* New York: Zone Books.

Wagner, Kurt. 2020. "Facebook Sees WhatsApp as Its Future, Antitrust Suit or Not." *Bloomberg,* 9 December. Retrieved 5 October 2022 from https://www.bloomberg.com/news/features/2020-12-09/facebook-fb-plans-to-turn-messaging-app-whatsapp-into-a-moneymaking-business.

CHAPTER 7

This Dictatorship Is a Joke

Eritrean Politics as Tragicomedy

Victoria Bernal

In a repressive system, the truth is dangerous for both ruler and ruled, and cryptopolitics flourish. Repression operates in part through complicity and duplicity as Gail Kligman's (1998) brilliant study of Romania under Ceaucescu makes clear. In the case of Eritrea, official narratives, orchestrated public rallies in Eritrea and in the diaspora, and pro-government posts to Eritrean websites present one picture (Bernal 2014; Hepner 2009). A different picture emerges from the experiences of daily life in Eritrea, posts on opposition websites, journalistic reports on international news outlets, and the findings of international organizations. To describe conditions this way, however, makes it sound as if the contradictions are clear and stand external to society. Things are far more complicated for Eritreans because repression does not simply produce opposition; it produces uncertainty, complicity, duplicity, and ambivalence. It also produces humor, which is the focus of this chapter.

Cryptopolitics permeate Eritrean society as fear compels people to dissimulate and perform support for the regime that is not genuine (T. Woldemikael 2009). In David Bozzini's (2013: 48) words, there is in Eritrea "a necessary double game, manifested in the distinction between a public and a hidden discourse—a duplicity that can be overcome only by exile." Amanda Poole similarly describes social life in Eritrea as "characterized by a pervasive sense that everything done publicly, and perhaps privately, was under observation, subject to suspicious scrutiny, capricious interpretation, and punishment. And nearly everything, beneath the surface, seemed to hold within itself a double meaning" (2013: 77). A UN inquiry found "systematic, widespread and gross human rights violations have been and are being committed in Eritrea under the authority of the Government" and that "Information collected on people's activities, their supposed intentions and even conjectured thoughts are used to rule through fear in a country where individuals are routinely arbitrarily arrested and detained, tortured, disappeared or extrajudicially executed" (UN Office of the High Commissioner for Human Rights 2015). A UN Commission of Inquiry on Human Rights accused Eritrea's government of crimes against humanity and reported that Eritrea practices a shoot-to-kill policy on Eritreans who try to leave the country.[1]

Eritreans respond to these tragic conditions in many ways, including through comedy. Why do people choose humor as one response to soul-crushing oppression? What makes such humor funny, and, aside from producing mirth, what possible effects might such humor create? What is distinctive about political humor compared to serious politics? These questions animate this analysis of Eritrean humor that focuses, in particular, on jokes Eritreans produce and circulate about President Isaias Afewerki. I approach humor as a form of cryptopolitics. Through its structure of double meanings and ambiguity, moreover, I argue that humor works in part as critical discourse about representation. In considering what it means that Eritreans choose to laugh about some of the political suffering they and their compatriots endure, I suggest that the structure of comedy, how things are made funny, which involves copying with a twist, has a particular resonance with dictatorship, which, like humor, involves insincere performances and distorted logics.

This chapter explores contemporary Eritrean political humor that circulates online in texts and videos and also by word of mouth inside Eritrea and among the diaspora. Zeroing in on jokes about President Isaias Afewerki helps get to the essence of dictatorship in the figure of the dictator. Isaias Afewerki is independent Eritrea's first and only president, a guerrilla hero of the victorious independence struggle that ended in 1991, and the individual who has done the most to shape Eritrean national political culture. The analysis draws on material posted by Eritreans on diaspora websites, Twitter accounts, jokes that were told to me, and jokes collected and translated for me by Eritrean interlocutors. The analysis draws on my long-term research on Eritrean politics including four sojourns in Eritrea, the first in 1981 and the most recent in 2016 and extensive observations of activities on Eritrean diaspora websites.

The essay is organized as follows: "Under Isaias: Cryptopolitics Territory" describes the character of the regime and the quality of life it produces. "Humor as Politics: What's in a Joke?" explores theories about humor as a genre of expression and its political significance. I then turn to an analysis of "Dictatorship and Duplicity" before focusing on President Isaias and Eritreans, humorous responses to his regime.

Under Isaias: Cryptopolitics Territory

Life inside Eritrea's borders is defined by the attempt of the Isaias regime to leave no sphere of activity outside state control. Some Western media outlets call Eritrea "the North Korea of Africa" for its state-controlled media and severe state practices.[2] Eritreans are subject to indefinite years of national service with no control over their assignment and only token payment. There is no constitution, and the ruling party allows no space for civil society (Riggan 2009; T. Woldemikael 2013). The regime's exercise of power, moreover, is often unpredictable and seemingly irrational. Sometimes this is rather farcical as when censors at Eritrea's Ministry of Information refused to allow Eritrean singer Ghirmay Andom to release an album of love songs, arguing that: "When the country is facing lots of adversaries, it is unjustifiable to consistently sing about romance."[3]

Walking around Asmara, Eritrea's capital city, one can see the heavy-handed state management of the economy reflected in the austere atmosphere of the city compared to other African cities that are enlivened by the hustle and bustle of a myriad of microenterprises that spill into public space. As I meandered the urban landscape in the summer of 2016 there were no hawkers or street vendors plying their trade on the streets of Asmara, only children here and there selling chewing gum, a few scattered beggars, and on some street corners people selling the seasonal treat, cactus fruit. Many shops were closed for lack of goods and lack of customers according to a couple of merchants with whom I spoke. The nakfa (Eritrean currency) had recently been devalued and shopkeepers could not afford to restock their goods. The regime of Isaias Afewerki no longer espouses the Marxism that informed the politics of national liberation in Eritrea, yet the regime has something of the flavor of the old socialist regimes that similarly attempted to centrally control political culture, close borders, and isolate the population from outside influences.

One of the starkest and most contentious policies is the national service requirement that takes young teenagers from their families to receive training and complete their final year of high school in a remote military camp. Young people are then retained indefinitely in national service. Often referred to as Sawa (the name of the first remote training camp), this policy has been likened to slavery by Eritrean organizations based in the diaspora because of its unlimited time frame. Young people I talked with who had completed their training and were performing national service work described conditions in the camps in terms of inadequate food, poor health care, and harsh corporal punishment that left one individual I met with a permanent injury. When I asked one person whether they had cried on the bus to Sawa, they said "we were all crying."

Eritreans pride themselves on stoicism and resilience, but a new sense of depression, resignation, or even perhaps despair seemed palpable during my visit in 2016. At the extreme were numbers of mentally ill individuals who roamed the streets. Someone explained to me that the state decided it could no longer afford to keep them institutionalized and simply released them. Several years have since passed, and I hear that people not in their right minds are still wandering the streets. As one Eritrean quipped, "Insanity here starts at the top. We have a crazy leader. He has driven us crazy. All the sane people have left the country."

In a post on the Eritrean diaspora website Asmarino titled "Eritrea: Why I Am Optimistic about 2015," the author, while comparing the Isaias regime to a psychopath, points to humor as a reason for optimism. He argues that:

> the public becomes increasingly astute in identifying the deficiencies and underlying pathological web maintaining the system. A shared language against the system develops . . . one of the earliest signs is the rise in humour . . . an irreverent humour against the system that shackles society . . . (rings a bell does it?) . . . eventually people wake up to the reality that pathocrats are not impressive or admirable but malicious incompetents and begin to disobey them turning the tables by identifying the pathocrat's weaknesses and exploiting them . . . when this starts it can be said that pathocracy, or in our case pfdj [the ruling party], is indeed in its twilight . . . (Asmarino 24 December 2014, ellipses and parentheses original, bracketed material added)

Eritrean political humor contributes to and complements diverse forms of serious politics that seek to pressure, persuade, resist, or undermine the Isaias regime. Dissent and protest activities can be pursued openly only outside Eritrea's borders, and therefore outspoken and organized opposition happens among Eritrean diaspora communities. Websites established by Eritreans in the diaspora, in particular, serve as a public sphere where freedoms of expression not possible within Eritrea can be exercised (Bernal 2014). Inside the country, subtler forms of resistance involve obstruction, avoidance, and indiscipline (Bozzini 2013). Humor can take subtle forms and operate underground. Verbal jokes, like rumors, require no authorship and can circulate anonymously. Political jokes may even draw authority from the fact that they cannot be tied to a particular individual whose motives and knowledge might then be impugned. A joke originates with someone at a given place and time, but jokes that circulate do so independent of their original author and context; jokes survive by invoking a social condition that audiences recognize. Jokes about President Isaias relate to a figure with whom all Eritreans are familiar.

Humor as Politics or What's in a Joke?

This study draws on and contributes to a growing body of new scholarship on humor in anthropology (Boyer and Yurchak 2010; Carty and Musharbash 2008; Goldstein 2003; Hasty 2005; Haugerud 2013; Mole 2013; Pype 2015; Trnka 2011). It further develops themes and arguments I began to formulate in an earlier article (Bernal 2013). Much of the scholarship cited above explores the entanglement of humor in power relations. Donna Goldstein's notion of "laughter out of place" draws attention to the paradox of how tragedy can be met with humor. Through her analysis, humor can be seen as a denial of passive victimhood, serving poor women in Rio de Janeiro as a way of expressing and understanding their experience. Goldstein observes that "humor both masks and reveals . . . the very structures and hierarchies on which the humor depends" (2003: 273). This meme of Isaias Afewerki as Hitler could be understood as unmasking the president's true character as a ruthless dictator.[4]

One of the great puzzles of humor is how it can unmask if it must rely on what we already know in order for us to get the joke. Slavoj Žižek points to this conundrum when he writes that "comedy relies on the gesture of unveiling" while noting that funniest of all is when "after removing the mask, we confront exactly the same face as that of the mask" (2005). This dynamic of humor, which I argue unmasks by drawing attention to the mask, is at work in an Isaias joke told to me by a young man during my 2016 stay in Eritrea. He explained that at one point the government had closed down all the truck repair shops (which like virtually every business of any consequence in Eritrea were run by the government). The joke says that "when truckers went to complain to President Isaias, asking 'why have all the repair shops been closed?,' Isaias replied, 'I don't know. They shut down mine, too.'" The humor in this joke lies in the way it builds on mythic anecdotes that have circulated about Isaias Afewerki's behavior and lifestyle since the beginning of his presidency to show that the president chooses to live like an ordinary Eritrean. In this respect, Isaias stands in contrast to many elites, especially the African leaders depicted so vividly by Achille Mbembe (1992) who demonstrate

Figure 7.1. Meme of Isaias Afewerki as Hitler from public Internet sources.

their claims to authority through extravagant lifestyles. The joke uses the theme of the president who is just like everybody else to speak to conditions of power and powerlessness. Even if Isaias subjects himself to the same conditions as citizens there is a major difference: Isaias (and not everybody else) has the decision-making power to decide what those conditions will be. The joke pokes fun at Isaias acting as if he is an ordinary citizen to whom something bad is happening, when in fact, he is the one making it happen. One could interpret the joke as suggesting a wider criticism of Isaias as a leader who refuses to take responsibility for the consequences of his policies.

One Isaias story about how the president chooses to act like an ordinary citizen rather than a person of authority and privilege was told to me by an older man during that same summer in Asmara. We were in the city on the day in July when the young people were required to board the buses for Sawa to begin their military training and national service. In the distance we heard shouting and cheering as the teenagers were seen off by their families and the buses pulled out. Despite the cheers we both knew it was a sad day as families complied with the government requirement and sent their children away from home to a year of hardship and severe discipline. To soften the melancholy atmosphere, the man said, "Isaias's children were sent to Sawa. Isaias went with everybody else like any parent to the bus to see them off."

There was a surprise ending, however, to this Isaias story. Whereas during earlier fieldtrips such a story would simply have ended there, a tale of an exemplary man of the people, in 2016 the story had a postscript. After a slight pause, the storyteller added: "But what good does that do? He should let the children stay at home with their families."

Both the joke about Isaias and the closed truck shops and the man's serious comment reveal something about how Eritreans are critically analyzing the status quo. A joke packages its message in a format that facilitates its circulation to new audiences and its entry into cultural discourse, while a critical comment like that of the older gentleman may not go beyond a private conversation.

The political significance of humor is an unresolved question. George Orwell wrote: "A thing is funny when—in some way that is not actually offensive or frightening—it upsets the established order. Every joke is a tiny revolution." A joke is not an actual revolution. Yet, a revolution like the Arab Spring or the fall of the Berlin Wall may come as a surprise, but it never comes out of nowhere. The processes through which subversive subjectivities and underground culture are produced are important to understand. The political potential of humor, like art, pop culture, graffiti, and other unconventional forms of expression, can easily be underestimated. Mbembe asserts that:

> The question of knowing whether humour in the postcolony is an expression of "resistance" or not, whether it is, a priori, opposition or simply a manifestation of hostility towards authority, is thus of secondary importance. For the most part, people who laugh are only reading the signs left, like rubbish, in the wake of the commandment. (1992: 8)

Villy Tsakona and Diana Elena Popa (2012) dismiss humor's political impact as a "myth," arguing that humor is a means of social control even when it expresses criticism of the status quo, since the invocation of dominant values serves to reinforce them. However, their key measure of political change (or lack thereof) is voting behavior, and this approach may obscure humor's political work. I suggest, for example, that when humor invokes dominant views, they become more distinct and humor, by decontextualizing or recontextualizing dominant views renders them more malleable in the public sphere. Humorous representations allow the status quo to become subject to new forms of reflection. While subversions can operate as safety-valves rather than threats to the dominant order, the border between these is fluid and has the potential to overflow. Considering humor as a form of cryptopolitics highlights its ambiguity and the complexity of its political effects.

One definition of humor explains that: "Based on the violation of what is expected or considered normal in given circumstances, humour emerges from two overlapping but opposed scripts" (Tsakona and Popa 2012: 4). Henri Bergson (1998) helpfully describes the comic as based on repetition, inversion, and what he calls "reciprocal interference" by which he means a setup where the same situation has the possibility of two entirely different meanings. These formulas for producing humor, I argue, have a distinctive resonance with the conditions of dictatorship.

Žižek writes that comedy entails an "attitude of self-estrangement" where "Hegelian 'reconciliation' works: not as an immediate synthesis or reconciliation of opposites, but as the redoubling of the gap or antagonism" (2005). This aspect of humor that doubles through alienation, widens gaps, and conjoins opposites while resisting synthesis may be especially important where powerful forces promote a dominant perspective. This is true of contemporary Eritrea where the state works tirelessly to saturate society with its narratives and to silence any other views. As Dominic Boyer observes, official discourses lend themselves to humor not least because "overformalization and monopolization [render] authoritative discourses and practices self-caricaturing" (2013: 276–77). Repetition is a central element of both comedy and propaganda.

Humor works by distorting the copy (through such means as caricature, parody, and recontextualization) and this carries political potential because it creates a gap between the original and its representation or between competing representations of the same thing. In this respect, humor, I argue, can be understood as a discourse about representation. Through producing estrangement and confronting audiences with "overlapping but opposed scripts" humor conjures an opening in the seemingly monolithic and impenetrable façade of power. Lisa Wedeen found in the Syrian context that "comedy and laughter can enable and enact an estrangement from the established order . . . allowing for penetrating diagnoses and, sometimes, political openings" (2013: 863). Perhaps as Angelique Haugerud suggests, "subversions of the status quo require humor as well as earnestness" (2013: 21). At the very least, humor is another tool in the political toolkit, and what needs to be explained is how it is used and what humor might accomplish that is different than what is done through serious politics. I next analyze conditions in Eritrea, showing why dictatorship fosters cryptopolitics in ways particularly suited to comedy.

Dictatorship and Duplicity

Overlapping but opposed scripts are a mechanism of humor, but also an apt description of the Eritrean national condition. A growing gap exists between President Isaias's autocratic, violent methods of governing and the regime's narratives of progress and national well-being (Connell 2011; Kibreab 2009). Hundreds of thousands have fled the country despite grave risks, yet the president claims everything is fine thanks to his leadership (Belloni 2019; Poole 2013). International reports documenting abuses and poverty present a dim view of life in Eritrea (Human Rights Watch 2021; U.S. Department of State 2021). But they may not capture the political culture as well as Mbembe's (1992: 4) description of "commandement":

> the commandement seeks to institutionalise itself, in order to achieve legitimation and hegemony (recherche hegemonique), in the form of a fetish. The signs, vocabulary and narratives that it produces are not meant merely to be symbols; they are officially invested with a surplus of meanings which are not negotiable and which one is officially forbidden to depart from or challenge. So as to ensure that no such challenge takes place, the champions of state power invent entire constellations of ideas; they adopt a distinct set of cultural repertoires and powerfully evocative concepts; but they also have resort, if necessary, to the systematic application of pain.

Eritrea's ruling party calls itself the People's Front for Democracy and Justice (PFDJ), but the Eritrean state is characterized by "arbitrariness, despotic modalities of governance, and erratic and unstable rules" (Bozzini 2013: 39). President Isaias, meanwhile, promotes an image of popular support and claims that grave threats to Eritrea necessitate the tight discipline and militarism he imposes. The regime's political tautology holds that no true Eritrean is critical of the regime; any Eritrean who does not support Isaias is aiding Eritrea's enemies as either a dupe or a collaborator. In his 2014 Independence Day speech, President Isaias repeated many of his familiar themes. Western powers, he said, especially the United States, seek to undermine Eritrea's sovereignty and have subjected Eritrea to "intense and unremitting acts of subversion comprising of military, political, diplomatic, economic as well as human-trafficking ploys that are accompanied by psychological warfare." Even so, he continued, "the progress we have achieved in laying the robust foundations for a sustainable economic order is substantial and that it is growing, sector by sector, with time in terms of quantity, quality, and capacity can be gauged easily by the facts on the ground." Concluding his speech, the president expressed appreciation for the people of Eritrea who are "engaged with the nation-building process day and night in a spirit of patriotic devotion to the homeland."[5]

Figure 7.2. Eritrean political cartoon from public Internet sources.

While Isaias conflates patriotism with loyalty to his regime, this cartoon upends that assumption.

Contradictions and ambiguities are embodied in the figure of President Isaias Afewerki. Isaias Afewerki is larger than life. He is not only Eritrea's leader; he symbolizes the nation. In this he may be like other powerful and long-lasting rulers who become synonymous with their nations (O. Woldemikael 2015). But in Isaias's case, this entanglement of man and the nation is particularly powerful because his life history as a guerrilla fighter allows him to embody the national history of sacrifice and struggle that have been established as the foundations of contemporary Eritrean political culture (Iyob 1995; Pool 2001; T. Woldemikael 1991). There is a Facebook group called "We Are All Isaias Afewerki." One of its members explained,

> We are because he is the embodiment of what Eritrea is all about. We are because he is and has been the face of Eritrea past, present and has set a precedent for the future. We are because he is what Eritrea is all about; grit, determination, perseverance, commitment and he is a finisher. We are because he is like every one of us; humble and determined to leave within his means while focusing on the future sacrificing a great deal.[6]

Isaias is also a ruthless dictator who has killed and disappeared perceived political enemies and caused a massive exodus from the nation.

> On the one hand, [Isaias] has become something of a semi-mythical figure, and his character and psychological makeup has become a favourite topic of awed conversation (necessarily subdued) in the bars and cafes of Asmara. At the same time, he has become the butt of so many jokes, particularly among the warsai [younger generation]. Many resent the power he has accumulated; yet he is also grudgingly admired as the only one capable of providing some measure of direction and leadership. (Reid 2009: 214)

On the Eritrean diaspora website Awate.com a poster called the domination of political culture by this one man, "Isaiasism" (or in his spelling "Iasaiasim"), which he describes as follows:

> Isaiasim—if we can call it that—requires a total surrender of individual rights; complete mistrust of the international community; vehement anti-Americanism; intolerance to dissenting views; hyper-nationalism, communism, nepotism, anti-intellectualism, militarism and the devaluation of human life. To defeat Isaias Afwerki is then to stand for the complete opposite of his traits and attitudes that are now part of the fabric that make up our society. Isaiasim may have been created by the dictator but it was cheered, cherished, applauded and cared for by the freedom fighters and a large portion of general public, be it knowingly or naively. (Awate, 10 June 2011)

As this post suggests, opposing Isaias requires rejecting the values and beliefs about him and about the nation that many Eritreans had embraced and absorbed over the course of decades. This produces a politics of ambivalence. Is Isaias a national hero or a ruthless dictator? President Isaias is both revered and reviled, sometimes by the same people. Eritreans generally cast Isaias as a hero in the early years of independence. Now, that view may be in the minority. On some Eritrean websites, for example, the shorthand reference PIA for President Isaias Afewerki has been replaced by DIA, Dictator Isaias Afewerki. Even today, however, President Isaias is not without support. On the website Dehai where pro-government sentiments remain strong, a post extolled "Eritre's President Admirable Personal Traits" (Dehai.org post May 2009; spelling and grammar original). Formatted like a poem or prayer in which each sentence began with the words "Our president," it asserts that "Our president has lots of sense of humor and sometimes helps us to see the funny side of politics." This, along with statements like, "Our president is honest, dedicated and adores his people, he lives it every single day" made me wonder if irony was intended. But the author ends by saying: "Above all our president is the leader of our fallen and alive heroes who continues to defy the CIA and western conspiracy striving to doom our existence." This line makes clear the author is serious because Eritreans do not joke about their "fallen heroes," the "martyrs" who have died for Eritrea. Despite everything, at least for some people, Isaias remains the revered leader and protector of Eritrea.

It would be easy to see the question of whether Eritreans see Isaias as a hero or a dictator as a matter of temporality—he was a hero when he led the Eritrean People's Liberation Front (EPLF) to victory and inspired Eritreans everywhere to support Eritrean independence. Later, Isaias became a dictator when Eritreans publicly criticized his regime (particularly after the disastrous 1998–2000 border war with Ethiopia), and he jailed critics, including top members of his own government. Alternatively, whether Isaias is a hero or a dictator might be seen as a matter of perspective: for loyal supporters like the poster quoted above, Isaias is a hero, while for others Isaias's actions make him a brutal dictator.

Yet the hero/dictator question cannot simply be answered in terms of a before and an after or an us versus them because Eritrean politics are shot through with ambiguity and ambivalence. Eritrean cryptopolitics are such that expressions of support are often compelled and criticism is silenced, while secrecy and censorship make it hard for those inside and outside the country to really know what is going on. Furthermore, even Isaias's supporters are troubled by the violent excesses of the regime and its constrained economy, while dissidents share the regime's concern to guard Eritrea's hard-won sovereignty and maintain national unity. In some ways, then, the figure of Isaias Afewerki can be understood as a double, both a dictator and a hero. This contradiction and joining of opposites I contend characterizes not only the president, but the political habitus of many Eritreans. Their political condition, thus, shares with comedy an underlying structure of doubleness. The concept of cryptopolitics offers the insight that such doubleness is much more complex than simply an issue of deception.

The most profound example of doubleness, or more specifically "reciprocal interference" to use Bergson's term, is the fact that the celebrated thirty-year long struggle that won Eritrea's independence also traumatized the population and dispersed and destroyed many Eritrean families and communities (Bernal 2017). National liberation, moreover, has not brought peace, prosperity, and freedom as promised. This conjoining of opposites, while tragic, is also ripe for humor. A parodic political subjectivity emerges because everything positive might contain its own negation, just as the overblown praise of the "Admirable Personal Traits" of the president could at first be read to mean the opposite of what it says. These conditions undermine sincere politics (whether for or against the regime) by engendering cynicism and conspiracy theories rooted in the profound understanding that nothing and no one can be trusted at face value. Here, then is another explanation for why humor is a response to extreme repression: because humor does not rely on truth claims to communicate its message, it is suited to a context where the trust on which such claims rests is absent.

Eritrean communications are fraught with self-censorship and infused with a sense of fear, distrust, and uncertainty about what it is permissible or safe to communicate to whom (Bernal 2014). As another scholar rather understates it: "There is tremendous sensitivity about what is said in Eritrea: government officials, researchers, and citizens are circumspect, and critiques of the government are veiled" (Riggan 2013: 751). Even in the ostensibly open context of an international conference in Asmara in 2016 in which I participated, the issues of political prisoners, press freedoms, the practice of keeping a large segment of the working population in indefinite national service, and the reasons why Eritreans are fleeing the country in droves were never discussed publicly. Uncertainty, suspicion, and pretense create a situation that is more complex than a dichotomy between public and hidden transcripts (Scott 1992). This is cryptopolitics territory.

There are ambivalences and contradictions at work. For one thing, there is no simple way of predicting a person's political position based on divisions of class, urban/rural origins, or ethnicity, though some opposition to the Isaias regime has deep roots in Eritrean Muslim experience and the history of the Eritrean Liberation Front as a largely Muslim-led movement that was marginalized by the EPLF. Isaias is known to imprison members of his own government, while government officials have been known to defect when sent abroad. Eritreans who escape illegally later seek rapprochement with the authorities, a practice that has become institutionalized with forms they can fill out stating they left only for economic rather than political reasons. Government insiders sometimes leak information to dissidents outside the country and warn individuals in the diaspora when it is not safe for them to enter the country. The fact that even those working in or for the regime may not be its supporters is one explanation of how, as happened in the Arab Spring, seemingly entrenched regimes can fall surprisingly rapidly, because the degree to which they already were hollowed out from the inside had not been fully evident.

Such conditions invite a parodic sensibility alert to the artifice and falsity by which people get by and through which the regime sustains its power. "[P]eculiar also to the postcolony is the way the relationship between rulers and ruled is forged by means of a specific practice: simulacrum (*le simulacre*)" (Mbembe 1992: 10). Lisa Wedeen's discussion of how people had to behave "as if" in Syria under Hafiz al-Asad helps to ground the notion of simulacrum in the everyday (2015: 6). In contrast to the Syrian experience where the performances were "transparently phony" to citizens and the regime, among Eritreans they remain ambiguous and tinged with some true feelings, perhaps because Eritrean nationhood is so deeply entangled with the only regime it has had since winning independence.

As Tekle Woldemikael observes regarding national rituals established by the PFDJ, real emotions are aroused even though participation is compelled (2008). Around Independence Day 2016, interlocutors on a diaspora website discussed whether it was hypocritical for opponents of the regime to celebrate Eritrean independence. Their desire is conflicted not only because the regime orchestrates the celebrations in the diaspora as well as in the homeland, but because Independence Day marks the EPLF's assumption of state power. Independence Day can be seen as yet another double—liberation and repression bound together so that to celebrate one can also mean to celebrate the other. The means of authentic political expression in such a context is unclear, as the online discussions indicate.

Dissimulation and simulacra are techniques of the ruler as well as the ruled. President Isaias repeatedly asserts bold, positive claims about conditions in Eritrea and denies all evidence to the contrary. Sometimes it seems he is not even trying to match his statements to any plausible reality. In a televised, widely circulated interview with Swedish journalist, Donald Bostrum in May 2009, President Isaias replied to the question of how he would describe the political and economic system of Eritrea by saying: "It is the best in the world. It is better than the system you have in Sweden." In a parody based on this interview, Swedes are so enticed by this that they seek asylum in Eritrea (see Bernal [2013] for an extended discussion). In another on-camera interview, this one with Al Jazeera journalist Jane Dutton, Isaias is asked to respond to critical reports and UN statements about conditions in Eritrea. His standard response is, "These are lies," and he comments several times, "This is a joke," finally adding, "When jokes are repeated it becomes boring." At one point, Dutton presses the president on the lack of political freedoms in Eritrea, confronting him with the facts that Eritrea jails more journalists than any other country and that the UN had reported 63,000 asylum cases brought by Eritreans. To this Isaias responds: "Lies, lies, lies. These are all your lies . . . Its undermining your credibility as a media outlet."[7]

One can surely question whose credibility is being undermined in such exchanges. The president's references to lies and jokes are interesting, however, given the cryptopolitics that make it difficult for Eritreans to know what or whom to believe. Everyday existence is predicated on innumerable public secrets that everyone knows but of which they must feign ignorance, including it seems the dictator himself. Rumors circulate, motives are called into question, and facts on the ground are hard to come by given the government's tight control over information. Eritreans can only speculate, moreover, to what degree President Isaias himself believes all of the things he says. It is intriguing that in the Dutton interview Isaias chooses to draw attention to the possibility of damaging one's credibility. Just when it would seem to many observers that his credibility has hit bottom, being publicly confronted on television with the documented abuses of his regime, Isaias performs another kind of doubling, a reversal through which his refrain of "lies, lies, lies" puts the journalist's credibility at risk, rather than his own.

Dutton's Al Jazeera interview of Isaias illustrates the limits of straight political responses to dictators since the journalist and President Isaias become stuck, in effect calling each other liars. This presents audiences with a simple either/or choice of whom to believe, rather than offering any stimulus to insight. Humor, in contrast, is structured in a way that breaks out of such deadlocks. As Gary Alan Fine explains, humor reflects "a contrast in meaning between two incompatible views of a scene. Humor results from the audience resolving these two conflicting images in a way that makes sense, given the distorted logic of humor. Humor is a puzzle, a problem that must be solved for mirth to result" (Fine 1983: 160). The agency involved in solving the puzzle, deciphering the joke in comedy's "distorted" logic has political potential, opening up new analytical avenues.

The potential for political play offered by the Al Jazeera interview was not lost on Eritreans and clips of the video were remixed to highlight the contradictions in his statements, literally disrupting the official narrative. One remix posted on the website Asmarino.com included footage of Eritrean children in refugee camps accompanied by a new soundtrack with the upbeat refrain "I'm alive" from the Celine Dion song of the same name. This made an exuberant, taunting response to Isaias's serious denials and deadpan expression. Examples like this attest to the pleasure in the production and reception of humor. Humor's entertainment value need not detract from its political impact, and may even contribute to it because the pleasure humor evokes helps fuel its circulation and consumption. The Al Jazeera interview also figured in a post on Awate.com titled, "Why Did the Chicken Cross the Road? (The Eritrean

Version; A Satire)." The author tacks between solemnity and humor in his introduction:

> With due regard to the seriousness of our discourse, I attempted to satirize, and caricaturize supposed dominant themes of our writers in an effort to lighten our mood and exact some humor along the way . . . May we (all the opposition) get to see and relish our beloved Eritrea again . . . For now, let us hear what some of our writers and notables answered when asked why the chicken crossed the road. (August 2010; parentheses original)

The post caricatures the styles and perspectives of government officials and supporters as well as critics. The parodic sensibility, as I suggest, is not merely something deployed against opponents, but forms part of a political culture characterized by ambivalence and ambiguity. When he gets to the president, the satirist titles the blurb "Issayas Afewerki: On Al Jezeera," thus referencing the interview with Jane Dutton. Isaias's answer to the proverbial question reads in part: "The chicken never crossed the road. I don't know what you are talking about. It is all lies, lies . . . Where is the evidence? It is boring. We know the chicken was made by CIA . . . Where is the chicken? This is CIA fabrications. Is there any evidence Eritrea has chickens?" The last line echoes Isaias asking Dutton for evidence, even in the face of the data she cited such as the number of Eritrean asylum cases. Chicken, moreover, is the main ingredient of a favored national dish, zighni dorho, that contains both chicken and eggs, making the question about the existence of chickens in Eritrea especially ridiculous.

This parody of the president substitutes the inane "chicken that crossed the road" for the troubling Eritrean circumstances raised in the interview such as the lack of press freedoms, indefinite national service, and the ongoing exodus of Eritreans who fear their own government. The parody presents the president as someone who habitually denies the facts, since the existence of chickens in Eritrea is obviously not in question and the answer to the riddle has no importance. The parody switches out tragedy for comedy in substituting road-crossing chickens for border-crossing asylum seekers, among other things. This substitution serves as a means of unmasking since, by altering the content of the statements, what becomes most visible is their form—blanket denials and accusations. In addition to suggesting Isaias's propensity to lie and to blame things on US conspiracies, the joke could also be interpreted as trivializing Isaias's power by engaging him in a senseless debate over a chicken.

A satirical Twitter account under the name H.E. Isaias Afewerki (H.E. can be assumed to stand for His Excellency) describes himself thus in the profile: "fulltime killer dictator father husband . . . " As these examples illustrate, Eritrean diaspora websites and social media platforms provide a space for carefully crafted satirical texts, cartoons, memes, and videos. Once posted online, they may be consumed and circulated by unknown audiences.

Shorter jokes circulate orally and pass through private channels. One theme of such jokes about Isaias concerns his militarism. One joke has Isaias convening ministers and generals to discuss Eritrea's economic problems. Isaias suggests that Eritrea should incite the United States to "invade us like Iraq and they will give us money for recovery." To this one of his generals replies: "That is a brilliant idea, but what should we do if we defeat them?" The humor here uses a preposterous premise—that Isaias would welcome a foreign invasion as a solution to Eritrea's problems—to criticize Isaias's leadership by depicting him as advocating war without regard to the lives that will be lost and the damage Eritrea will suffer. The joke echoes some Eritreans' view of Isaias' readiness to embark on the disastrous 1998–2000 border war with Ethiopia soon after independence. Since border hostilities continued to simmer until recently, some Eritreans feared that Isaias might propel the nation into war again. Ultimately, by proposing a US war as the solution to Eritrea's problems, the joke implies that Isaias will risk destroying Eritrea in order improve it. Since the general calls this outrageous plan "brilliant" there is also a dig here at the sycophancy that insulates Isaias from any criticism. The punch line is absurd—generals believing Eritrea could defeat the United States in war. But the serious message the punchline conveys is that the regime is far out of touch with reality. The mistaken optimism about Eritrea's prospects for victory over Ethiopia in the 1998–2000 border war caused much suffering that is not forgotten by Eritreans. The general's foolish optimism in the joke thus has multiple resonances.

Another joke has President Isaias commissioning his ministers to develop a nuclear bomb to "show the world what we are capable of and regain our dignity." When Isaias presses the button to launch it, however, nothing happens. Someone is sent to investigate and reports that it could not launch "because everyone in Asmara hopped on the bomb so that it can take them abroad." This joke, like the one above, contains a critique of Isaias's militarism, where here instead of an invasion, a nuclear bomb is what Eritrea needs. The joke is on Isaias, however, since what was to be his demonstration of power fizzles, thwarted by his own population. The ridiculous, yet macabre image of Eritreans trying to get out of the country by riding a bomb invokes the desperate, life-threatening lengths to which Eritrean migrants go to get to other countries. This joke can be interpreted as suggesting that Isaias's grandiose plans for Eritrea fail because they do not take the Eritrean people into account. It could be read as a parable of contemporary Eritrea: the state's efforts to create a strong nation and a militaristic citizenry through conscription is undermined as many thousands of citizens flee the country to avoid national service. The jokes depict a distorted version of a perverse reality, and thereby bring it into sharper focus.

Conclusion

Under dictatorship, official narratives and claims about how people benefit from the regime contradict citizens' everyday experiences and informal knowledge. Cryptopolitics is a survival strategy for the dictator, who must deny reality, and for the people, who must feign support, ignorance, or indifference to the conditions imposed by the regime. Humor that often operates by stating on the surface the opposite of what it means or combines contradictory narratives is well-suited as a response to such conditions. Eritreans' jokes about their president reveal a productive parallel between the duplicity of dictatorship and the mimesis of comedy. Comedic methods such as exaggeration, substitution, and recontextualization subject the contradictions at the heart of dictatorship to a distinctive kind of scrutiny. Rather than seeking to replace one truth-claim with another as sincere opposition attempts to do, comedy points to ambiguities and highlights the possibility of multiple interpretations and alternate realities. It encodes and decodes uncomfortable predicaments. The creativity and playfulness involved in humor is also a means of asserting one's humanity in the face of a regime like that of President Isaias that contrives to reduce people to mere subjects of power (Bundegaard 2004; Hirt and Mohammad 2013; Human Rights Watch 2009).

I argue that humor, moreover, is more than just another register through which to represent reality; it is a way of representing representation itself since its very structure involves the *open* deployment of artifice and distortion. This is an important source of its potential as a political intervention because it invites agency, foregrounding contradictions without resolving them. This stands in particular contrast to the didactic messages of dictators and state propaganda. It also contrasts with straightforward politics that can leave opponents deadlocked in an exchange of competing truth claims. Humor does more than simply replace one claim with another as earnest opposition so often does. Instead of seeking to offer closure with some definitive answer, humor opens up a conceptual space of imagination, exploration, and skepticism.

In this context, Michael Taussig's ideas about mimesis are stimulating. He argues that "in imitating, we will find distance from the imitated" (Taussig 1993: xix). Through humor, Eritreans create conceptual distance between themselves and the enveloping political culture of the Isaias regime. This distancing also may be politically important as a way to manage fear. To live in fear of Isaias is incapacitating, and a sober analysis of his brutal regime, however critical, could have the effect of further disempowering people. Humor, by creating distance, suggests a space in which some maneuvering is possible; it stands outside the totalizing worldview of dictatorship and provides a viewpoint from which to behold it. In these ways, humor as a political tactic accomplishes something distinctive compared to direct, literal critique. Here the representational gap or what Taussig calls "slippage" is significant. Taussig's (1993: 115) observation that we find in mimesis "not only matching and duplication but also slippage which, once slipped into, skids wildly" relates to how humor represents the familiar but with a twist that can change everything. Taussig could be describing political jokes when he writes: "It is the precariously contained explosion of the transgressive moment that allows for and indeed creates the 'mimetic slippage' whereby reproduction jumps to metamorphosis" (1993: 126).

Mimesis is a source of power because the making of a representation "gives one power over that which is portrayed" (Taussig 1993: 13). Seen from this perspective, Isaias jokes are, in part, a claim to power and may even be experienced as such by their subject. Indeed, I like to imagine Isaias Afewerki nervously googling himself every day to see what is being said about him. This may not be far from the truth as it is well known that the regime is extremely image-conscious and pays close attention to who is saying what about it, be they Eritreans in the diaspora, journalists, scholars, or international organizations. Perhaps the author of the post "Why I Am Optimistic" I quoted earlier is too optimistic about what humor portends for the Isaias regime, but his reference to "the public" reminds us that humor's political potential lies not only in the ways its form and content operate at an individual level to produce laughter, catharsis, and possibly new insights, but in its capacity to enter and alter cultural discourse by representing collective experience.

It may be useful to view humor as knowledge-producing. It is not simply that knowledge is necessary to create the joke as well as to get the joke, but that jokes can be knowledge-producing because humor works by suspending the normal rules where censorship and self-censorship operate. Humor is often subtle in structure if not in content, conveying messages indirectly, stimulating the audience to forms of interpretive agency to deduce the double meanings. This encouragement of intellectual agency runs counter to the stifling of thought under totalitarian regimes. Humor thus may be especially politically important under the conditions of extreme repression. The capacity for humor is part of what it means to be fully and socially human. Therefore, when Eritreans respond to human rights violations and state brutality by circulating jokes and satires, they are, in the process, resisting the dehumanization to which the population is subjected.

Humor, through its alienated, distorted logics hints at the existence of the elusive, that which can never fully be confined or defined, and therefore exceeds even a tyrant's reach. These are powerful political activities that stand in opposition to authoritarian practices. My reading of Eritreans' jokes suggests that humor communicates in distinct ways that afford it a special grip on autocracy and that comedy can serve as a special means to expose the flaws and expand the fissures of a totalizing system fraught with suspicion and distrust. Authoritarian rule and dictators who hold onto power for decades are not unique to Eritrea or to Africa, unfortunately. In revealing how the cryptopolitics of such power are represented through the distorted logics of humor, Eritrean political humor informs us in ways that resonate beyond its own peculiarities.

Victoria Bernal is a cultural anthropologist whose scholarship in political anthropology contributes to media studies, diaspora studies, gender studies, and African studies. Her work addresses questions relating to politics, digital media, migration and diaspora, war, globalization, transnationalism, civil society and activism, gender, development, and Islam. Dr. Bernal's research is particularly concerned with relations of power and inequality and the dynamic struggles of ordinary people as they confront the cruel and absurd contradictions arising from the concentration of wealth and political power locally and globally. She has carried out ethnographic research in Sudan, Tanzania, Eritrea, Silicon Valley and cyberspace. She is the author of *Nation as Network: Diaspora, Cyberspace, and Citizenship*, and *Cultivating Workers: Peasants and Capitalism in a Sudanese Village* as well as numerous articles. She is co-editor of the anthology *Theorizing NGOs: States, Feminisms, and Neoliberalisms.* Professor Bernal has received fellowships from the Fulbright Foundation, the Catholic University of Leuven, Belgium, the Center for Advanced Studies in the Behavioral Sciences at Stanford, the American Philosophical Society, and the Rockefeller Foundation.

Notes

1. "Eritrea Commits Crimes against Humanity, UN says." *Al Jazeera*, 9 June 2016. Retrieved 16 January 2023 from http://www.aljazeera.com/news/2016/06/crimes-humanity-eritrea-1991-160608100250646.html.
2. T.G. 2018. "Why Eritrea Is Called Africa's North Korea." *The Economist*, 14 August 2018. Retrieved 16 January 2023 from https://www.economist.com/the-economist-explains/2018/08/14/why-eritrea-is-called-africas-north-korea.
3. Abraham Zere. 2018. "Whatever Happened to Afwerki's Comely Face? Eritrean Music in an Age of YouTube." *African Arguments*, 13 February. Retrieved 16 January 2023 from https://africanarguments.org/2018/02/whatever-happened-to-afwerkis-comely-face-eritrea-music-in-an-age-of-youtube/.
4. Tsehaye Eyassu. 2017. "Isaias and His Tactics for a Quarter of a Century." Awate, 1 March. Retrieved 16 January 2023 from https://awate.com/isaias-and-his-tactics-for-a-quarter-of-a-century/.
5. "President Isaias Afewerki's Speech on the Occasion of the 23rd Independence Day Celebrations." *Ministry of Information: Eritrea*, 24 May 2014. Retrieved 16 January 2023 from https://shabait.com/2014/05/24/president-isaias-afewerkis-speech-on-the-occasion-of-the-23rd-independence-day-celebrations/.
6. Amanuel Biedemariam. 2016. "We Are All Isaias Afewerki and He Is Us." *Eritrea Madote*. Retrieved 16 January 2023 from http://www.madote.com/2015/12/we-are-all-isaias-afewerki-and-he-is-us.html.
7. Al Jazeera English. 2010. "President Isaias Afwerki | Talk to Al Jazeera." YouTube, uploaded 20 February. Retrieved 16 January 2023 from https://www.youtube.com/watch?v=O0uQwODNkTA.

References

Belloni, Milena. 2019. *The Big Gamble: The Migration of Eritreans to Europe*. Oakland: University of California Press.

Bergson, Henri. 1998. *Laughter: An Essay on the Meaning of the Comic*. Los Angeles: Green Integer.

Bernal, Victoria. 2013. "Please Forget Democracy and Justice: Eritrean Politics and the Power of Humor." *American Ethnologist* (40)2: 300–9.

———. 2014. *Nation as Network: Diaspora, Cyberspace, and Citizenship*. Chicago: University of Chicago Press.

______. 2017 "Diaspora and the Afterlife of Violence: Eritrean National Narratives and What Goes Without Saying" *American Anthropologist* 119: 23–34.

Boström, Donald, and Isaias Afwerki. News Morning, 2009. Accessed 6 January 2023 from https://www.tv4play.se/program/nyhetsmorgon/isaias-afwerki-vi-sl%C3%A4pper-inte-isaak/765021.

Boyer, Dominic. 2013. "Simply the Best: Parody and Political Sincerity in Iceland." *American Ethnologist* 40(2): 276–87.

Boyer, Dominic, and Alexei Yurchak. 2010. "American Stiob: Or, What Late-Socialist Aesthetics of Parody Reveal about Contemporary Political Culture in the West." *Cultural Anthropology* 25(2): 179–221.

Bozzini, David. 2013. "The Catch-22 of Resistance: Jokes and the Political Imagination of Eritrean Conscripts." *Africa Today* 60(2): 39–66.

Bundegaard, Christian. 2004. *The Battalion State: Securitization and Nation-Building in Eritrea.* Geneva: Graduate Institute of International Studies.

Carty, John, and Yasmine Musharbash. 2008. "You've Got to Be Joking: Asserting the Analytical Value of Humour and Laughter in Contemporary Anthropology." *Anthropological Forum* 18(3): 209–17.

Connell, Dan. 2011. "From Resistance to Governance: Eritrea's Trouble with Transition." *Review of African Political Economy* 38(129): 419–33.

Fine, Gary Alan. 1983. "Sociological Approaches to the Study of Humor." In *Handbook of Humor Research,* ed. Paul and Jeffrey Goldstein McGhee, 159–81. New York: Springer-Verlag.

Goldstein, Donna. 2003. *Laughter Out of Place: Race, Class, Violence and Sexuality in a Rio Shanty Town.* Berkeley: University of California Press.

Hasty, Jennifer. 2005. The Pleasures of Corruption: Desire and Discipline in Ghanaian Political Culture." *Cultural Anthropology* 20(2): 271–301.

Haugerud, Angelique. 2013. *No Billionaire Left Behind: Satirical Activism in America.* Stanford, CA: Stanford University Press.

Hepner, Tricia Redeker. 2009. *Soldiers, Martyrs, Traitors, and Exiles: Political Conflict in Eritrea and the Diaspora.* Philadelphia: University of Pennsylvania Press.

Hirt, Nicole, and Abdulkader Saleh Mohammad. 2013. "'Dreams Don't Come True in Eritrea': Anomie and Family Disintegration Due to the Structural Militarisation of Society." *The Journal of Modern African Studies* 51, no. 1: 139–68.

Human Rights Watch. 2009. *Service for Life: State Repression and Indefinite Conscription in Eritrea.* New York: Human Rights Watch. https://www.hrw.org/report/2009/04/16/service-life/state-repression-and-indefinite-conscription-eritrea.

———. 2021. "World Report 2021: Eritrea Events of 2020." *Human Rights Watch.* Retrieved 16 January 2023 from https://www.hrw.org/world-report/2021/country-chapters/eritrea.

Iyob, Ruth. 1995. *The Eritrean Struggle for Independence: Domination, Resistance, Nationalism, 1941–1993.* Cambridge: Cambridge University Press.

Kibreab, Gaim. 2009. *Eritrea: A Dream Deferred.* Suffolk: James Currey.

Kligman, Gail. 1998. *The Politics of Duplicity: Controlling Reproduction in Ceausescu's Romania.* Berkeley: University of California Press.

Mbembe, Achille. 1992. "Provisional Notes on the Postcolony." *Africa: Journal of the International African Institute* 62(1): 3–37.

Mole, Noelle. 2013."Trusted Puppets, Tarnished Politicians: Humor and Cynicism in Berlusconi's Italy." *American Ethnologist* 40(2): 288–99.

Pool, David. 2001. *From Guerillas to Government: The Eritrean Peoples Liberation Front.* Oxford: James Currey.

Poole, Amanda. 2013. "Ransoms, Remittances, and Refugees: The Gatekeeper State in Eritrea." *Africa Today* 60(2): 67–82.

Pype, Katrien. 2015. "Funerary Comedies in Contemporary Kinshasa: Social Difference, Urban Communities and the Emergence of a Cultural Form." *Africa* 85(3): 457–77.

Reid, Richard. 2009. "The Politics of Silence: Interpreting Apparent Stasis in Contemporary Eritrea." *Review of African Political Economy* 36(120): 209–21. http://www.roape.org/120/06.html.

Riggan, Jennifer. 2009. "Avoiding Wastage by Making Soldiers: Technologies of the State and the Imagination of the Educated Nation." In *Biopolitics, Militarism, and Development: Eritrea in the Twenty-First Century*, ed. David O'Kane and Tricia Redeker Hepner, 72–91. New York: Berghahn Books.

———. 2013. "It Seemed like a Punishment": Teacher Transfers, Hollow Nationalism, and the Intimate State in Eritrea." *American Ethnologist* 40(4): 749–63.

Scott, James.1992. *Domination and the Arts of Resistance: Hidden Transcripts.* New Haven, CT: Yale University Press.

Taussig, Michael. 1993. *Mimesis and Alterity: A Particular History of the Senses.* New York: Routledge.

Trnka, Susanna. 2011. "Specters of Uncertainty: Violence, Humor, and the Uncanny in Indo-Fijian Communities Following the May 2000 Fiji Coup." *Ethos* 39(3): 331–48.

Tsakona, Villy, and Diana Elena Popa, eds. 2012. *Studies in Political Humor.* Amsterdam: John Benjamins Publishing.

UN Office of the High Commissioner for Human Rights. 2015. "Report on the Commission of Inquiry on Human Rights in Eritrea." Retrieved xx from https://www.ohchr.org › A-HRC-29-42_en.

U.S. Department of State. 2021. "2020 Country Reports on Human Rights Practices: Eritrea." *U.S. Department of State,* 30 March. https://www.state.gov/reports/2020-country-reports-on-human-rights-practices/eritrea/.

Wedeen, Lisa. 2013. "Ideology and Humor in Dark Times: Notes from Syria." *Critical Inquiry* 39 (Summer): 841–73.

———. 2015. *Ambiguities of Domination: Politics, Rhetoric, and Symbols in Contemporary Syria.* Chicago: University of Chicago Press.

Woldemikael, Olivia. 2015. "Laughing with Redykulass: Critical Comedy in Moi's Kenya." Senior Honor's Thesis. New York: Columbia University.

Woldemikael, Tekle. 1991. "Political Mobilization and Nationalist Movements: The Case of the Eritrean People's Liberation Front." *Africa Today* 38(2): 31–42.

———. 2008. "The Invention of New National Traditions in Eritrea" In *Traditions of Eritrea: Linking the Past to the Future,* ed. Tesfa Gebremedhin and Gebre Tesfagiourgis, 263–86. Trenton, NJ: Red Sea Press.

———. 2009. "Pitfalls of Nationalism in Eritrea." In *Biopolitics, Militarism, and Development: Eritrea in the Twenty-First Century,* ed. David O'Kane and Tricia Redeker Hepner, 1–16. New York: Berghahn Books.

———. 2013. "Introduction: Postliberation Eritrea." *Africa Today* 60(2): v–xix.

Žižek, Slavoj. 2005. "The Christian-Hegelian Comedy." *Cabinet* 17. Retrieved 16 January 2023 from https://www.cabinetmagazine.org/issues/17/zizek.php.

CHAPTER 8

Regulating Refugees

Technologies, Bodies, and Belonging in Kenya

Lisa Poggiali

"The fingerprints will always pop up," lamented Aba, a young woman dressed in a long, colorful cotton dress that she curled around herself protectively as we spoke. We were seated on a mattress propped up on the floor of her small sitting room in an apartment in Nairobi that she shared with her two young children and a roommate who, like Aba, identified as a Somali refugee. Aba was from the port city of Kismayu, Somalia, a former stronghold of Somalia-based insurgent group Al-Shabaab that fell to government hands in 2012 following a battle led by the African Union Mission in Somalia (AMISOM)[1] and Somali government troops. Aba made her way down to Nairobi in 2010, following her brother who had migrated two years earlier, and settled in Eastleigh, a neighborhood widely known as the social and economic hub for Somalis in Kenya's capital city (see Carrier 2017). Migration patterns such as Aba's are common, as the border between Kenya and Somalia has been historically porous, and strong cross-border cultural, social, and economic links have long facilitated the flow of goods, money and people between the two countries (see Little 2003; Lochery 2012). Many Somalis have leveraged this fluidity as a survival strategy: they alternately claim Kenyan origins to avoid police harassment and claim Somali origins to receive food and medicine reserved for refugees. Since the Kenyan state adopted biometric technologies like fingerprint and iris scans to manage its refugee population, however, Somali-born refugees in Kenya like Aba have had more trouble maintaining these fluid identities. Once Aba's fingerprints had been recorded biometrically, they would, as she said, "always pop up." From the perspective of the Kenyan state, such fluid identities were a problem to be solved, and data-driven technologies were an important part of the solution.

This chapter narrates the experiences of people like Aba alongside an analysis of bureaucratic practices, procedures, and policies to highlight how new sociotechnical systems are reshaping the Kenyan state's techniques of territorial and social control, as well as the actions of the populations perceived to pose challenges to this control, in surprising and contradictory ways. While refugee management has long been a bureaucratic exercise for states and multilateral institutions like the United Nations High Commissioner for Refugees (UNHCR), the Kenya example foregrounds the datafication of refugee identity as an emergent element of this bureaucratic politics in an increasingly digital age.

Information has become a critical new currency for stateless peoples, serving as a key mediator between states, refugees, and technologies. In Kenya, for refugees to navigate the refugee status determination (RSD) process successfully and achieve their goal of being resettled in a third country, they must become adept at acquiring the information that will tell them which data points to include in their encounters with the state during the RSD process and how to structure that data. Well-informed refugees assume the de facto role of data scientist—collecting, recording, cleaning, structuring, and safely storing data points about their lives and journeys, curating them for and re-presenting them to the state. In more analog times, before bureaucratic offices in global capitals like Nairobi were outfitted with biometric fingerprinting, iris scanning, and Geographic Information Systems (GIS) technologies, refugees worked through extended kin and community networks to alternately leverage and evade forms of bureaucratic state regulation. Now, as the refugee experience becomes more intimately entangled with the politics of data management, social networks are most useful when they enable refugees to more effectively shapeshift to mirror the new digitally mediated demands of state regulation. As I will show, the stories refugees narrate to the state bureaucrats who have the power to christen them refugees or exclude them as "aliens" takes on a modular, abstract quality, conforming to the functionality of the mediating technology itself. At the same time, as I discuss below, refugees also leverage more flexible technologies like social media platforms WhatsApp and Facebook Messenger to form modular narratives of a different kind, for example, gendered romantic scripts that they activate in a hopeful effort to circumvent and subvert the state's exclusionary procedures—with varying degrees of success—in order to regain control over their lives.

The Government of Kenya's new digital methods of refugee regulation and refugees' attempts to navigate them are enmeshed in a sociotechnical system that includes biometric and geospatial technologies and the bureaucrats who deploy them; mobile phone and SIM card registration regulations and the shopkeepers and mobile network operators who enforce or ignore them; and social media platforms and the transnational groups that leverage them. In this chapter, I explore these intersections of the technological, social, legal, and bureaucratic to understand broadly how new technologies of population regulation encode and decode information about bodies, citizenship, and belonging; how they impact refugees' freedom of movement, legal status, and economic opportunities; and how they are used by refugees to attempt to circumvent state restrictions, creating alternative configurations of sociality and security in the process.

The empirical data that forms the basis of my claims was collected during six months of field research in Nairobi, Kenya, in 2018, and virtual follow up research in 2019.[2] Field research included surveys distributed to Nairobi-based refugees; social media data collection, primarily via WhatsApp; in-depth interviews with refugees, non-governmental organizations (NGOs), and government stakeholders; and participant observation at Refugee Status Determination interviews at the Refugee Affairs Secretariat at Shauri Moyo, as well as at various refugee-led community-based organization (CBO) meetings, government-led community events, and the World Refugee Day festivities.[3] Research participants were representative of the broader Nairobi-based refugee population and were chosen based on factors including national origin, age, gender, and neighborhood of residence. Other than in specific instances where I indicate otherwise, in this piece I employ a social definition of refugeehood rather than a legal one, that is, I use the term "refugee" to mean anyone who describes themselves as such. I do this because the process of conferring refugee status under the law, and the ways in which that process is shaped by emergent social technical systems in the context of broader regional and geopolitical histories, is the object of my analysis; I do not wish to reify the category as I interrogate it. Many of those whom I call "refugees" in this piece are legally classified as "asylum seekers."

Regional Political and Geopolitical Histories and the Securitization of Migration

Starting in 2012, powerful figures in the Kenyan government stepped up efforts to stymie the flow of refugees into the country, largely under the guise of enhancing Kenyan national security in the wake of a number of kidnappings of European nationals (tourists, Kenyan residents, and aid workers) and small-scale attacks claimed by, or attributed to,

Somalia-based group Al-Shabaab. While Kenya had been partnering with the United States (and to a lesser extent the UK and other allies) in some capacity to improve its counterterrorism capabilities since Al-Qaeda's attack on the US Embassy in Nairobi in 1998, US support increased dramatically after the rapid rise of Al-Shabaab, which by 2010 had became a powerful regional political force and by some accounts a legitimized (though not necessarily legitimate) government actor in the regions of Somalia it controlled, with a particularly impressive record of generating revenue by taxing the Somali population. By 2011, Al-Shabaab's attacks in Kenya had begun to seriously damage the nation's tourism economy[4] and the Kenyan government responded both militarily—by invading southern Somalia under Operation Linda Nchi (Kiswahili for "protect the nation")[5]—and politically, by calling for the restriction of refugees' rights.

Kenya's Department of Refugee Affairs (DRA), the body then responsible for refugee policy and administration, enacted such restrictions by threatening to enforce Kenya's "encampment policy" (Garlick et al. 2022), which requires all refugees and asylum seekers in urban areas to relocate to one of the country's refugee camps in the barren, economically depressed northern section of the country.[6] The DRA also administratively separated Somalis from other refugee populations, instructing Somali refugees to go to Dadaab refugee camp and all others to go to Kakuma refugee camp.

This policy generated intense criticism from human rights and civil society groups, and in July 2013, the Kenya High Court at Nairobi ruled it unconstitutional on the grounds of the freedom of movement clause and principle of nonrefoulement outlined in Kenya's Refugees Act (Garlick et al 2022). Nevertheless, the government doubled down on its enforcement of the policy in 2014. In March, Interior Cabinet Secretary Joseph Ole Lenku issued a directive (Press Statement 2014) ordering all refugees residing outside the refugee camps to go to them immediately and asked Kenyans and refugees to report those who were flouting this directive. To enforce this directive, he sent five hundred law enforcement officers to urban areas.

The government dubbed this plan Operation Usalama Watch (*usalama* means safety or security in Kiswahili), justifying it on both public and national security grounds. Refugees living in Nairobi at the time described it as a campaign of terror. Police officers beat down their doors in the middle of the night and forcibly took Somali Kenyans and sometimes refugees of other nationalities to Kasarani, a football stadium that had been turned into a makeshift detention facility where some were held for multiple days. The ethnic Somali neighborhood of Eastleigh was one of the main targets, though other areas with a large number of Somalis were also heavily impacted.

Abdul, a thirty-year-old Somali refugee who fled to Kenya as a teenager in 1999 and lived in Komarock, a neighborhood of mainly Somali and South Sudanese residents, describes his experience being detained:

> During [Usalama Watch] we spent most of the time hiding, moving from one place to another trying to escape the police. I was among those people who were arrested and taken to Kasarani. Without money, you can't get out, you have to bribe the police. If you're a kid, you pay 5,000 shillings (approximately US$50) and if you're an adult you pay 10,000 shillings (approximately US$100). If you have an ID that you got illegally, they might ask you for 20,000 shillings (approximately US$200).
>
> Some [without money were deported] to Somalia . . . I was lucky because a Kenyan friend of mine who is my neighbor paid 10,000 shillings for me and I was released. But after two days, the police came to my door and knocked again . . .

Abdul's story, a version of which was repeated by many refugees with whom I spoke, reveals the tension between protecting the nation and terrorizing portions of it, and the police's ability to profit from generalized insecurity.

At least 357 people were deported during Usalama Watch[7] (Freedom House 2015) in what would become a harbinger of things to come. The government continued to attempt to restrict the ability of Somali refugees to stay in Kenya, including by introducing amendments to the Refugees Act of 2006.[8] An attack by Al-Shabaab on Garissa University on 2 April 2015, in which almost 150 Kenyans were killed, prompted a fresh wave of anti-refugee sentiment, including threats made by the Minister of Interior to shut down the Dadaab refugee camp completely and repatriate all of its residents. He called Dadaab a "nursery for terrorists" and claimed that the Garissa attack, as well as the 2013 attack on the Westgate, the posh Nairobi mall popular with Western expatriates, had been planned from Dadaab camp (this has never been proven) (Rawlence 2016). Shutting down Kenya's refugee camps then became the rallying cry of Kenya's national security establishment.

Amid growing political pressure from the international community, Kenya's Ministry of Interior eventually ceased efforts to amend the Refugee Law, but never abandoned its overall goal of pushing refugees outside of Kenya's borders. Working in tenuous partnership with UNHCR, which had become skittish about Kenya's pronounced desire to abandon its commitment to protect refugees altogether, the government shifted its focus to procedural elements of refugee management: it limited refugee registration opportunities, enforced mobile phone and SIM card registration regulations, and incorporated biometric and geospatial technologies into the refugee registration and Refugee Status Determination (RSD) process.[9] Some of these decisions explicitly targeted refugees (like procedurally refusing Somalis the opportunity to register as refugees at registration centers), while others served broader national security goals (like enforcing registration requirements for all mobile money accounts). All resulted in the de facto restriction of refugees' ability to make a living or move freely throughout the country. Aba's lament about her fingerprints "popping up," mentioned at the outset of this chapter and explored in more depth below, is one example of this kind of de facto restriction in practice.

The Kenyan government worked with UNHCR to incorporate data-driven technologies more prominently in its RSD processes, symbolically casting the decision of who resides and thrives within Kenya's boundaries as an objective, technical one. New technologies were leveraged in the RSD process in myriad ways; for example, GIS technologies were used to verify the empirical accuracy of refugees' stories about their migration journeys. At the time, Kenya was admitting refugees from particular areas of the Great Lakes region (the Democratic Republic of the Congo, Burundi, and Rwanda) on a prima facie basis; if refugees could "prove" they were from one of the specified areas, they were granted legal refugee status (more below). Biometric data, meanwhile, which was collected at the time of registration, was used to verify refugees' identities and narratives over time. Each time a refugee was called to the RSD office for an interview, new data was added to the refugee's file and compared against data recorded in previous interviews; any perceived discrepancies were notated. Repeat visits were used to ascertain credibility, and data inconsistencies usually disqualified refugees from being resettled to a third country (most refugees' primary goal) as well from being granted refugee status to remain in Kenya. Utopian sentiment about digital technologies being vehicles of transparency were at an all-time high in Kenya at this time, as news about social media platforms' enabling role in the Arab Spring energized a nascent Kenyan technology sector that had risen from the ashes of Kenya's 2007/08 post-election violence on the grounds of increasing transparent and accountable governance and preventing future political violence (Poggiali 2016). Techno-utopianism became a surprisingly effective ideological alibi of Kenya's national security establishment, as digital technologies' strong symbolic association with objectivity, transparency, and accountability made any process that centered them difficult to attack on political grounds. Their power when invoked as a critical part of the RSD process was in their ability to render the profoundly political act of managing perceived threats to the body politic as an apolitical activity.

Out of all the refugee populations in Nairobi, Somalis posed a particularly robust challenge to digital methods of ordering and categorizing political identity, primarily because, as I mentioned at the outset, they had become accustomed to embodying a fluid, rather than a fixed identity. Much is at stake in these citizenship categories and their regulation. Prominent Somali Kenyans have benefited handsomely from the cross-border migration of people and money over the past decade—specifically through the trade in sugar, charcoal, and rice. They have garnered political support by controlling territories populated by ever increasing numbers of ethnic Somali migrants. Regulating the movement of ethnic Somalis in this context thus means regulating political and economic power.

Digital Surveillance, Social Control, and Somali Identity

"Because of security reasons we decided that it was good to screen [Somalis and Burundians[10]] so that we get the full information, the documents, like passports" said Maina, the head of security operations at Shauri Moyo, Nairobi's main site for RSD since the Kenyan government took over from the UNHCR in 2016. "It is for our *own* security, staff security," Maina emphasized, explaining why Somalis should receive extra security screening at Sharui Moyo. "Because you can't know how they operate," he continued. "You might think, 'this is just a person who is single, [but] we have seen even when they attack other countries, even America or Europe, they use young kids." This assumption that Somalis' allegiance to the Kenyan nation could not be trusted and that they were particularly effective at hiding sinister motivations and even terrorist proclivities was widespread among government bureaucrats. "They talk like you," a prominent government figure responsible for refugee management told me, speaking of the fact that many ethnic Somalis speak Kenya's national language Kiswahili and the local urban dialect *sheng*. "It's easy to lose track of them," he reiterated. "So it would be very easy for Somalis to just become Kenyan." If the government did away with the encampment policy, he continued, there would be no "refugees" because all Somalis would become Kenyan by falsely claiming Kenyan citizenship.

The deep-seated fear these men expressed about Somali integration was the product of decades of tense regional history—at Kenyan independence, ethnic Somalis living in what is now Kenya's northeastern province attempted to make the territory part of Somalia, resulting in a bloody conflict known the Shifta Rebellion. The northeastern province became an official part of the new Kenyan nation; resentment remained deep on both sides. Since the nation's founding, Somalis have had a tense relationship with Kenya's central government, often describing feeling like second-class citizens; they have had a particularly hard time gaining access to standard bureaucratic documents like ID cards. Biometric identification was a tool the Kenyan state could use to systematically track Somalis and make it more difficult for them to "become Kenyan." It enabled the Kenyan government to fix Somali identities in place, forcing them to choose whether to be Kenyan or Somali, but not both. For those Somalis who chose to register as refugees, after completing the enhanced security screening at Shauri Moyo, they would start the multiyear RSD process, claiming an exception to be able to stay in Nairobi rather than travel to live in Dadaab. They would often visit Shauri Moyo every few months for years for different interviews, but never receive the refugee ID: a laminated card, renewable every five years, that is the culmination of the RSD process. Many of those who qualified as refugees under the definitions of the 1951 or 1969 Conventions would never complete the RSD process because they did not have the transport funds for repeat visits to RSD headquarters, could not afford to take days off work that were required for each visit, and/or did not have the funds to bribe various gatekeepers to obtain the required documentation. Others simply got frustrated and tired with the slow-moving, often dehumanizing process, and saw little value in obtaining a refugee ID. "I have been [to Shauri Moyo] two dozen times and I still don't have the card," one young Somali man told me. "I decided to just leave it [i.e., stop trying]. [The Kenyan government] is just playing with us."

Many give up pursuing asylum through official channels, deciding that their best option for a stable life is, echoing Maina's fears, to register as a Kenyan. This was the case for Aba, the Somali woman I mentioned at the outset of this piece, who spoke about her fingerprints "popping up." Two years after Aba arrived in Nairobi, in 2012, she initially visited the UNHCR to register as a refugee. Her goal was to be resettled in Canada, where her brother lived at the time. He had agreed to be her sponsor, meaning that he would be financially responsible for her in Canada. She told the UNHCR she was underage (seventeen years old), a white lie which allowed her to quickly receive a mandate allowing her to remain in Kenya.

Armed with a mandate and confident that her brother's offer to sponsor her in Canada would enable her to move quickly through the resettlement process, Aba told me that she had "high hopes that [she] would leave the country." Shortly after registering, she met a Somali Kenyan man in her neighborhood, and they soon married. Unbeknownst to her, changing one's marital status during resettlement presented new bureaucratic hurdles in an already cumbersome, drawn-out process. New identities could not be transferred easily from one bureaucratic domain to another, as Aba learned when she was told she would have to start the resettlement process from the beginning: new documents needed to be collected and issued, new appointments needed to be made with the relevant officials, and new interviews needed to be conducted (Wirtz 2015).[11] Aba's brother became angry and frustrated with her for what he described as "creating these new roadblocks," and he stopped facilitating her resettlement. Her case stalled. She had two children in Kenya with her husband, but the marriage did not last. When I met her in 2017, Aba was single with few prospects of fulfilling her dream of leaving the country.

After making a few failed attempts to find a husband in Canada through Facebook, Aba did what so many Somali migrants before her have successfully done, attempt to become Kenyan. She took the over ten-hour bus journey to visit her friend, a Somali Kenyan whom she knew via social networks in Eastleigh, who worked at an ID processing center in Habaswein, a town in northeastern Kenya populated almost exclusively by ethnic Somalis. He offered to help her get a Kenyan ID, a process that would be tricky on her own, since she did not speak fluent Kiswahili nor have a tuberculosis vaccination scar, two telltale signs that she was not Somali Kenyan, but rather Somali (Balakian 2016). When Aba arrived at the ID center, however, her friend took her fingerprints and told her he could not help her as she had already registered as a refugee. Her fingerprints, he told her, had "popped up." "Biometrics," she told me, shaking her head as she recounted the experience. "If I did not have my fingerprints at UNHCR today, I would have a Kenyan ID." From the perspective of the Kenyan state, Aba's case is an example of the newly digitalized RSD process working as intended. Biometrics, in the state's view, were a bulwark against Somalis becoming Somali Kenyans—they were preventing the "enemy" from without from becoming the enemy within.

Social Networks and the Circulation of Identity: Mobile SIM Card Registration

Not all new techniques of refugee management led to such intractable results for Somali refugees. When the Kenyan government began requiring all mobile phone users to officially register their SIM cards in

2010, many refugees became disconnected from the network. As I will describe below, this meant they also lost access to their main way to get income. Because SIM card registration was not tied to the biometric system, however, refugees were able to circumvent these technological restrictions by leveraging their social networks and appealing to a more fluid, malleable expression of identity.

According to the Communications Authority of Kenya (2022), as of June 2022 there were over 64.7 million active mobile phone SIM card subscriptions in Kenya, a country with a population of 52.57 million. There were 37.2 million active registered mobile money subscriptions, resulting in value transfers of over KSh1.1 trillion (Kenyan shillings) (approximately US$9 billion). Most of these transfers were conducted via mobile phone company Safaricom's mobile money platform called M-Pesa (*pesa* means money in Kiswahili). A financial technology that allows users to store electronic currency—converted from cash—on their mobile phones, M-Pesa enables currency to be transferred to other M-Pesa users, used to pay for goods and services such as bread or electricity, and converted back into cash. The technology provides a significant service for the millions of Kenyans who do not have access to traditional banking structures and who primarily work in the informal economy. For refugees who are shut out of the formal labor market due to restrictive laws, and unable to legally open bank accounts, M-Pesa is a lifeline. This changed in 2010, when the Communications Commission of Kenya began requiring all M-Pesa SIM cards to be registered, giving users until October 2011 to produce national or foreigner IDs in order to keep their accounts operational.[12]

M-Pesa relies upon a network of agents who man both small kiosks and large storefronts; these agents—over 600,000 of them as of March 2022—change cash into electronic currency and load it onto a user's SIM card, and they can also change the electronic currency on a user's SIM card into cash. For the first time, Kenyan residents' ability to perform mobile transactions became linked to their identities and their official legal status as Kenyans or foreigners. In the years immediately following this new regulation, refugees could produce a document (called a "mandate") from UNHCR verifying that they were legally in the country. This changed in 2014, when Safaricom—M-Pesa's parent company—started quietly shutting down refugee accounts.

Salah, a Somali woman in her midtwenties, traveled from Mogadishu to Nairobi in 2015 after her brother was killed in crossfire. After relying on a chain of smugglers to shuttle her across the border and through a myriad of police checkpoints, she arrived in Eastleigh, the neighborhood with the highest concentration of Somalis in Nairobi. Once there, she started a small business reselling clothes that had been sent to her by her aunt, who lived in a refugee camp in South Africa. Selling inexpensive consumer goods is a common way that refugees make money in Nairobi. These goods include everything from clothes to peanut butter to car parts to snacks eaten by Muslims on Ramadan. Salah relied on M-Pesa to receive money from customers throughout Nairobi and even in other parts of Kenya. That is, until her account was mysteriously shut down.

Salah recalls no longer being able to send or receive money through M-Pesa and being told by her local M-Pesa agent that they did not know why she was being denied. They could not help her because the accounts were being shut off by Safaricom's corporate office. While it is unlikely that Safaricom specifically targeted refugees, and human rights organizations with whom I spoke suspected they did not,[13] the Kenyan government made clear in numerous public statements that the regulatory restrictions on SIM card registration was necessary to stem growing insecurity in the country. Such regulations, government figures said, would help them better track nefarious communication-based and financial transactions that were aiding and abetting terrorism. This decision was made after police reports were released claiming that the Al-Shabaab militants who planned and executed the attack on Westgate, the upscale mall frequented by foreigners, in September 2013, were communicating via unregistered SIM cards.

While her own account was no longer operable, Salah continued to receive money in exchange for her clothes by borrowing her Kenyan friend's ID and using her account. Almost all of the more than 160 refugees with whom I spoke reported having their M-Pesa accounts shut down, and almost all reported using the national IDs of friends, neighbors, and family members to register for SIM cards, move money, and withdraw and deposit cash. This was possible because unlike the RSD process, which relied on biometrics for verification, mobile money required one's identity to be verified by an agent who checked the ID against the account information. The agent could fail to recognize the discrepancy in appearance between the photo on the ID and the person standing in front of them, or they could choose to look the other way. Identities could circulate rather than being forced to remain fixed in place.

If the Kenyan government's aim was to use SIM card registration to better track digital identities and transactions—particularly those made by Somalis—this mode of digital regulation had the opposite effect. Somali refugees leveraged their historical social ties to Somali Kenyans in order to assume the identities of family members, friends, and other community members. Indeed, I noticed when sending research participants small amounts of money via M-Pesa—our mutually agreed upon compensation for their time and data—Safaricom's automated confirmation messages often displayed unknown Somali names. In using social ties to circumvent electronic regulation, refugees could continue to participate in the economic life of Kenya and sustain themselves financially despite the restrictions on refugee work and SIM card registration. Should SIM card registration ever become tied to biometric IDs in the future, however, refugees' ability to circumvent restrictions on moving money would be severely curtailed.

Becoming a Refugee in Kenya's Digital Age

The path to legal refugee status in Kenya is long and cumbersome. Those attempting to formally register for the first time need to arrive at Shauri Moyo during early morning hours and present themselves to a security guard stationed outside the building. They often wait for hours before passing through the turnstile and metal detector leading them to the interior of the drab indoor-outdoor space surrounded by high metal fences. They are then ushered into a sparsely decorated room with a wooden desk, a computer, and a chair, where they are asked to place their fingers on the surface of a machine that resembles a cell phone, and have their fingerprints recorded both biometrically and via the traditional ink method. They are asked to align their eyes with a device that resembles binoculars to have their irises digitally scanned. Finally, they are asked to provide biographical data points, including their name, nationality, date and place of birth, profession, the names of relatives with whom they were traveling, and the date when and place where they entered Kenya. This is the beginning of what is known as the Refugee Status Determination (RSD) process.

Biometric authentication became a formal part of the RSD process in early 2017 when the UNHCR introduced it to the Kenyan government as a way of more precisely recording refugee registrations. The Biometric Identity Management System (BIMS), as UNHCR called it, was created to "strengthen the integrity of existing processes and significantly improve efficiency for operations. Being able to verify identities," UNHCR (n.d.) argued, "is extremely important and a matter of human dignity." It was not lost on the Kenyans staffing the RSD office that BIMS was one more way, along with CCTV cameras, to mitigate the fraud that had long plagued the RSD system in Kenya (UNHCR 2017). Large scandals had engulfed UNHCR in Kenya in recent years, as staff members had been found to be selling fake IDs to refugees in exchange for money or sexual favors.

The Kenyan government attempted to adopt the technology as part of its domestic governance plans in January 2019, when it introduced the national ID called Huduma Namba ("service number" in Kiswahili),[14] claiming it would replace the national ID card system by December 2021 (Kimuyu 2020).[15] The Huduma Namba card captures citizens' personal data from government service delivery providers such as the National Health Insurance Fund, Kenya Revenue Authority, the National Social Security Fund, as well as national identification cards.

The program garnered criticism from Kenyan digital rights advocates and broader civil society for its lack of personal data protection regulation and concerns that it would exclude certain populations, including Somalis, from receiving essential goods and services. Kenya's High Court agreed, ruling on January 30, 2020 that the program needed a comprehensive legislative and regulatory framework to be able to continue (Open Society Justice Initiative n.d.). This debate is part of a continent-wide battle over new technologies and how they will impact the relationship between the public and the state. On the one hand, there is the allure of collecting standardized digital data in contexts in which paper recordkeeping has been logistically difficult, poorly managed, and ill-suited to an increasingly migratory population, and in which "digital" signifies transparency, development, and democracy. On the other hand, increasing concerns about data protection have emerged following an explosion of new forms of digital surveillance, from financial technologies that track consumer data to facial recognition technologies that attempt to reduce urban crime.

The Kenyan government's support for biometrics merged the discourses of security and science, presenting the image that biometrics would make Kenyans safer and healthier as a nation by fixing peoples' identities in place. By playing up associations with scientific transparency and objectivity, the government attempted to shift the discussion around biometric identity verification from a political one to a technocratic one. A Kenya Ministry of Interior Twitter post from 19 January 2021, for example, shows photos of what look like Kenyan doctors—outfitted in lab coats, gloves, masks, and clear plastic disposable hairnets—staring intently at a computer screen in one photo and large ID printing machines in another; the caption reads "UPDATE: Mass printing of Huduma Namba cards is underway. If you registered, you will soon receive an SMS notification prompting you when and where to collect yours." The experts decked out in full medical gear signal both the fear of a contaminate and a reasoned, scientific response to it. It is within this symbolic universe that refugees and other outsiders—those ineligible for a national biometric ID but forced to record their physiology just the same—are implicitly coded as vectors of disease, foreign viruses that through the biometric ID card could be appropriately expunged from the nation and the benefits of citizenship.[16]

Kenya's Ministry of the Interior has lauded biometrics more broadly for bringing transparency and objectivity to an RSD process that has long been criticized for being subjective and messy, rife with corruption and inefficiency. The Huduma Namba Secretariat is housed under this Ministry, the same government body that announced Usalama Watch and has repeatedly threatened to shut down Kenyan refugee camps. With biometrics and geospatial technologies, outsiders, the office has intimated, would no longer be able to hide. Yet while the Ministry claims biometric technologies will bring refugee identities to light, they are in fact creating "refugee identity" as a modular set of discrete data points, relegating refugees' actual experiences and narratives about them to the shadows.

New Information Economies: Refugees as Data Scientists and Geographers

This datafication of refugee narratives has spawned a new RSD information economy in Kenya; many refugees participate in multiple WhatsApp groups dedicated to sharing information about navigating the RSD process, including what to say—and not say—in your interview. Refugees test hypotheses about what stories work best for granting protection and resettlement and enlist geography tutors in order to be able to adequately answer questions about place and space asked by state bureaucrats. It is their social networks that enable refugees to meet the demands of the technologies, enabling them to reproduce the linear, consistent narratives demanded by the RSD process.

Many refugees differentiated between their "real story," the experiences they had before entering Kenya, and their "UN story," the narrative they crafted and repeated to officials throughout the RSD process. They called it their "UN story" because it used to be the United Nations and not the Government of Kenya that handled the RSD process. Many refugees told me that every time they visited Shauri Moyo, they would write down in detail what they were asked and what they said in their interviews. That way the information would be consistent for the next time. Jean, a Congolese man with dreams of immigrating to Australia, relayed how he kept copies of the narrative he told UNHCR during his interview on paper and on his computer so he "could not forget it . . . If your explanation to UNHCR is not clear," he said, "they'll reject your claim. Then you can't be assisted as a refugee."

New refugees arriving in Kenya are often advised to hire someone to coach them through this process and to help them compose a compelling story. A Congolese refugee named Paul described how his own narrative missteps led him to help other refugees write their RSD stories. "Other refugees used to tell me, 'if you've been waiting three years for your refugee ID, you told them a bad story! You should say this, and this, and this and it will go better,'" he recounted.

> Many people told me to create a story of ethnic conflict. To say, "my mother is a Munyamulenge from Congo [an ethnic group in Congo] and my father is a Mufulero [another ethnic group in Congo]. Rwandese don't like me, and Banyamulenge don't like me because I've spent a lot of time with my father. I'm seen as the enemy." You say things like that. Because it's known that many Banyamulenge say they've been kicked out of Congo by the Wafulero and the Wabembe. It makes your case go much more smoothly. That story of ethnic conflict has helped so many people.

Now Paul charges a small fee to help newly arrived refugees create clear, place-based narratives in which ethnicity maps neatly onto geography for their RSD interviews.

The most highly prized "coaches" are those who are able to access information crucial to aligning refugees' narratives with resettlement chances. For example, the priorities of nations who accept resettled refugees change from year to year—for example, one country might give preference to victims of gender-based violence one year, while another might give preference to LGBTQIA+ individuals. Those who learn this information first wield a tremendous amount of power, as the information helps new arrivals shape stories that will increase their chances of undergoing a quick RSD process and successful resettlement to a third country. This is one way entrepreneurial and savvy refugees close to the RSD process—translators, community leaders, and staff at implementing partner organizations that perform refugee service delivery—can make a small amount of money under challenging economic circumstances. The exchange of funds is not always blatantly contractual; as relationships develop, it is often expressed as a "thank you" for sharing helpful information with members of the community.

Rwandese are one of the groups that most commonly seek out this coaching. In 2013, the United Nations invoked the Cessation Clause, which stated that Rwandese refugees around the world should return to

Rwanda, as the country had been deemed safe (Executive Committee of the High Commissioner's Programme 1997). From this point on, they were prohibited from registering for refugee status in Kenya.[17] Banyamulenge—an ethnic group who live primarily in a section of the eastern Democratic Republic of the Congo and share cultural and linguistic traits with the Rwandese—were being resettled on a prima facie basis, based on their being targeted by other Congolese who claimed that, due to their historical relationship with Rwanda, they were not "real Congolese." As a result, it became common for Rwandese refugees who were unable to register to pretend to be Banyamulenge in order to receive a refugee ID. In order to succeed, they often hired other refugees to coach them on Congolese geography and customs. Knowing this, the staff administering the RSD interviews were particularly probing with those they thought might be Rwandese. The following story illustrates the importance of geospatial technologies in their decision-making and the kinds of refugee narratives determined to be credible or not credible as a result.

Charles, who had recently arrived from the Democratic Republic of Congo, entered Shauri Moyo looking like he had gotten dressed up for church, sporting a yellow golf shirt under a navy-blue sweater and a fitted wool blazer the color of sawdust. His beige pants were impeccably clean and ironed. He carried a pink plastic folder filled with documents. Charles was called into the RSD room first while his wife waited outside, a practice that was often used by RSD interviewers to see if the husband's and wife's stories aligned. Zaituni, the RSD interviewer, wore thick foundation and expertly drawn eyeliner, a black hijab, and a flowing buibui that nearly covered the black patent leather shoes whose pointed toes peeked out from underneath the fabric. She read the man a consent form and ran through the standard biographical questions that started all RSD interviews—his nationality, ethnicity, date and place of birth, the date he crossed the border into Kenya, the names of his relatives and his relationship to them. During this portion of the interview, Zaituni checked his responses against his case file, ensuring that the information he provided when he first registered was the same as he recounted that day.

Then she started entering new information into his file on her computer. "Where did you pass until you reached Kenya?" she asked him. Charles started narrating his experience, which started in 1996 in Congo shortly after his parents died and it became unsafe for him to stay in his village. He told a story that weaved together different elements: multiple national border crossings, first into Rwanda and then Burundi; the acquaintances and strangers who helped hide him at different crucial moments; government policies toward refugees and how they forced him into and out of refugee camps; and how he met his wife. Zaituni spoke with kindness, but was clearly frustrated with Charles's complex, meandering narrative. "You need to go in order," she interrupted, a common request in RSD interviews; "tell the story in terms of this happening, then that happening, then that happening."

Zaituni: In 1996, you fled Congo. Where were you living?
Charles: [gives name of a place]
Zaituni: You said your parents were killed. Who wanted to kill all the men there?
Charles: Interahamwe [a Rwandan militia composed of ethnic Hutu that helped carry out the Rwandan genocide].
Zaituni: Who were Interahamwe?
Charles: We don't know. They called themselves that. They were speaking Kinyarwanda [the main language of Rwanda].
Zaituni: Do you know why they wanted to kill you?
Charles: I don't know but they were saying that we were Banyamulenge [a Tutsi ethnic group in the Congo with historical ties to Rwanda]. That's what I think.
Zaituni: What are the ethnic groups of Interahamwe?
Charles: I don't know but they were speaking Kinyarwanda.[18]
Zaituni: If they're speaking Kinyarwanda and you speak Kinyamulenge, there's a similarity to the language?[19] What is the reason they wanted to kill you?
Charles: Because we were of the Tutsi clan, maybe that's why.
Zaituni seemed satisfied with this answer and moved on to another topic.
Zaituni: You said Rwandese helped you cross the river. What river was it?
Charles: [provides the name of the river]
Zaituni: Which place were you heading to?
Charles: [provides the name of the place]
Zaituni: Where in Rwanda were you staying?
Charles: [provides the name of the town]
Zaituni: How long did you stay in Rwanda for?
Charles: I cannot remember. If I guess, it was about one year.
Zaituni: What did you do on a daily basis in Rwanda for one year?
Charles: Nothing. I was living a very bad life. There was no food, I was sleeping badly.
Zaituni: Do you have documents from Rwanda, Congo, or Burundi?
Charles produces a large laminated document from his pink folder. It had UNHCR written on it and confirmed that he was living in a refugee camp in Burundi. He also produced a small laminated refugee ID card from Burundi. Zaituni indicated she would make a copy of both.

> Zaituni: When you were coming to Kenya, which places did you pass?
> Charles: [indicates a journey from Rwanda, to Uganda, to Kenya]
> Zaituni: Was there a way of coming to Kenya without passing through Rwanda?
> Charles: I don't know where I should pass. A person helped me come here.

Charles continued telling his story, including details of how he was captured by a pro-Burundian militia, and had been brought to a forest and watched people get killed and thrown into a pile of dead bodies. Charles's story demonstrated that he knew he should distance himself from Rwanda; he claimed to know very little about the country, its geography, and its political history, despite having spent a significant amount of time there. At the same time, however, Charles's narrative confounded the bureaucratic order of the RSD interview: from Zaituni's perspective, he provided both extraneous data points and ones that did not fit neatly into the RSD interview's bureaucratic logic.

In his landmark book *The Body Keeps the Score,* psychiatrist Bessel van der Kolk (2015) explains how trauma impacts memory, noting that humans organize traumatic memories differently from benign or happy ones. Van der Kolk (2015: 192–93) describes a study in which he asked participants to describe both positive events in their past, such as weddings, births, and graduations, as well as traumatic ones, such as rape, violence, and domestic abuse. The participants narrated the positive events "with a beginning, a middle, and an end. Nobody said that there were periods when they'd completely forgotten any of these events." When it came to the traumatic events, by contrast, their memories were "disorganized." "Our subjects remembered some details all too clearly (the smell of the rapist, the gash in the forehead of a dead child)," Van der Kolk recounted, "but could not recall the sequence of events or other vital details (the first person who arrived to help, whether an ambulance or a police car took them to the hospital)".

When read through the lens of van der Kolk's important research, the aims of the RSD interview worked at cross purposes with the brain's processing of traumatic memory. Zaituni's demand to Charles, that he narrate his story of fleeing death threats in his home country, witnessing the violent murder of friends and acquaintances, traversing challenging terrain and national borders without papers, living in and out of refugee camps, being captured by a militia, being separated from his wife, and attempting to evade surveillance and threats in Kenya "in order . . . in terms of this happening, then that happening, then that happening" flew in the face of a scientific understanding of how brains process traumatic memories. The demand for coherence and linearity conformed to a certain kind of bureaucratic ordering that at this time also included spatial information. Some refugees referred to this portion of the RSD interview as the "geography test," and savvy refugees provided data points they suspected the interviewer would find credible about the spaces and places they referenced.

Zaituni: Do you remember anything about the Congo where you were living?
Charles: I experienced a very bad life there.
Zaituni: Do you remember anything about where you were staying? The village? The features of it. I want you to tell me everything about the village. Tell me about it.
Charles: The village was in the hills. There were also rivers. One was called [name of river]. Another river was called [name of river]. Some neighboring villages. One was called [lists two villages]. Those were nearby villages. Also [names another village].
Zaituni: What about Rwanda? Tell me more about Rwanda.
Charles: I don't know it very well, just where I was staying in [village]
Zaituni: What used to stand out from [village]? Tell me something that stands out.
Charles: It was just near the border. There was a border between [village] and Congo.
Zaituni: [village] was a border town?
Charles: Yes, that's the only thing I can remember.
Zaituni: What was found in [village]?
Charles: I never liked that place. I used to sit at home. I can't say many things about [village].

Zaituni's questions were attempting to verify two main things: whether Charles was Rwandese, and whether his geographic knowledge demonstrated that he was from Congo. Charles's credibility was determined by measuring the place- and space-based information he revealed against the geographical, topographical and infrastructural features, and distances represented on the GIS mapping technologies that RSD officers like Zaituni had been instructed to use. Hailing from particular geographic regions of Congo granted you prima facie status in Kenya.

Mentioning his stay in Rwanda, as Charles had done in his interview, significantly complicated his case, despite the fact that he repeatedly tried to downplay his knowledge of the country. When pressed, he revealed information using tentative language: the "only thing he [could] remember" about the town in Rwanda in which he stayed for a year was that it was on the border with Congo. This is in stark contrast to the information he provided about the Congo, which was detailed and provided without qualifiers.

A "credible" interviewee described clear correlations between ethnicity, nationality, and geography as represented on GIS systems. Those whose stories did not fall neatly into established categories or patterns of movement faced additional hurdles to gain state protection. "Charles's case will be complicated by the Burundian wife," Zaituni told me after he had left the room, intimating that it was difficult to "place" Burundianness in his story. With so many additional hurdles to deal with, I left the room sensing that Charles's prospects for protection were dismal; he had likely entered a bureaucratic process of seemingly endless interviews. I thought about how many times he would likely return to Shauri Moyo in the same outfit. I wondered if he knew the narrative blunders he had made.

I often wondered what the Kenyan staff at Shauri Moyo thought about refugees' narratives given what they knew about how identity and circumstance mediated one's experience of a place. The rainy season might change a thirty-minute journey from school to home into a three-hour trek, and a local bus, which makes frequent stops and prioritizes keeping the vehicle filled to capacity, might transform what would be a fifteen-minute journey on an express bus into two hours. A Somali Kenyan might take thirty minutes longer to cross the city of Nairobi because of how frequently he would likely be stopped by the police. While the Kenyan staff knew that these contingencies would introduce variability into experiences of time and space, they had been trained to analyze refugees' stories against the maps using a set of uniform, mathematically calculable reference points, which presumed that transportation times remained the same regardless of the time of year and that all people experienced the same obstacles or lack thereof in moving from point A to B.

GIS technologies introduced a supposedly scientific, objective means of verifying the credibility of refugees' stories. Yet what these technologies verified was not refugees' credibility, but rather the correlation between their stories and the representations of space and place rendered on the digital maps. These representations were themselves filtered through understandings of distance, borders, and topography that were culturally and temporally contextual, despite the fact that they were imagined and articulated as global and universal. The technologies regulated refugees, rather than verifying their narratives.

Resettlement "The Legal Way": Reclaiming Agency via Online Romance

Leveraging social ties and technologies to find a romantic partner online was one way refugees circumvented the state regulation of the RSD process. I met Jean, a young, educated Congolese man, in the dark, damp two-room apartment in Kayole, an informal settlement in Nairobi, that he shared with his sister; the smell of dried fish, which he sold to members of his various WhatsApp groups, permeated the room. Jean had been in Kenya since 2012 and told me about his plans to get resettled in Australia. He recounted how he told a Congolese friend who had been recently resettled to "look for a lady for [him] over there" through one of the large networks of Congolese churches. His friend searched for women with children, as they are perceived as less attractive prospects for men and thus potentially more willing to engage a foreigner.

This arrangement was often seen as mutually beneficial due to the cultural cache a man from Africa was perceived to provide to a Congolese Australian woman. Jean explained: "If I'm in Australia, I can't take a Congolese girl from there to marry. But I can go to Congo to take her because the one in Australia, maybe she has been . . ." "Exposed!" my Congolese research assistant interrupted enthusiastically. "Exactly," Jean said. "So from [the West, Congolese] look for a husband or wife from Africa." Refugees like Jean capitalized on cultural stereotypes of Africans from the West as being "corrupted" by Western values in order to enhance their own eligibility.

The first woman Jean's friend proposed to did not pan out: she had three children from three different fathers, and said if she married Jean she would only promise him one additional child. They attempted to negotiate, with Jean offering to have two additional children with her, provided that they divorce once he reached Australia. She said if he did this, she would threaten to take Jean back to Africa; he moved on without making a deal.

Jean was soon introduced to another woman, Brigitte, with whom he started chatting regularly on WhatsApp. They had been talking for seven months when I met him, and Jean had started calling Brigitte's daughter, who had just turned two, his own, even changing his WhatsApp profile picture to a photo of the girl. He had been gaming out two different potential plans that involved Brigitte: go to Australia "the refugee way," which meant being resettled via an organization in Kenya, or "the legal way," which meant marrying Brigitte in Kenya and waiting for her to apply for family reunification so he could join her in Australia. The "legal way" was faster, he noted, as it would take only about a year after they got married in Kenya and Brigitte found lawyers in Australia to draw up the paperwork. "It would be better if she went back [to Australia] pregnant," he recounted to me. "That will make it easier. Then she can say, "I am pregnant by him, so he's coming to take care of the baby, he's the one who will be taking care of the baby once he is in Australia." "[The women] have to spend one or two months [in Kenya], so that they can go back [to Australia], and they're pregnant already."

"This is a very specific process!" I said, chuckling at the degree to which the process of family reunification seemed to mirror the Kenyan state and UNHCR's bureaucratic process of resettlement, with its own set of rules and procedures, and social relationships mediating the process in ways that could enhance or dampen one's chances. At the same time he was negotiating with Brigitte, Jean was in the final part of the refugee resettlement process through UNHCR. This involved first getting the appropriate document from Shauri Moyo, which he brought to the UNHCR offices.[20] There, he was asked to write a summary of his journey to Kenya, his biographic information, and his reason for leaving his country. Two months later, UNHCR called him for an interview to expound upon his story and provide his biographical data again. After the interview, they gave him an appointment to come back after six months. After returning six months later, he was given another paper asking him to come back in another six months. "If there's not a decision about your case when you go there, they just give you another paper," he clarified, repeating a process communicated by many other refugees. After two years of appointments every six months, Jean was given a "mandate" in 2014, the document stating that he had been determined as a viable refugee and could stay in the country legally. After receiving the mandate, Jean had to return again to Shauri Moyo to receive the refugee ID. Once he received the refugee ID, he was told he had a "protection case," meaning that his security was found to be compromised in Kenya, and he was invited to begin the resettlement process.

Many refugees developed an arsenal of strategies for getting abroad. It was common for refugees to have open resettlement cases with UNHCR, work hard to cultivate relationships with NGOs and CSOs (civil society organizations) that could recommend them for resettlement, and simultaneously establish relationships with Africans and/or Westerners abroad who could marry them and bring them abroad through the family reunification process.

Conclusion

The different forms of digital regulation I discussed in this chapter—biometrics, geospatial technologies, SIM registration, and social media—differently articulate and shape information about bodies, citizenship and belonging in Kenya. These technologies change the ground upon which citizenship claims can be made and policed, but not in ways that are predictable or uniform. Biometric technologies made embracing fluid identity categories—a Somali survival strategy in the face of long-standing state violence and exclusion—more challenging, forcing Somalis to consider whether they would rather be a "refugee" or a "Kenyan." Geospatial technologies and mobile money regulations, on the other hand, paradoxically created their own fluidity, as refugees were forced to claim or use false identities in mobile money and WhatsApp networks, as well as fabricate personal stories of their refugee journeys. These false identities also circulated in social networks that were mediated by technologies, like the marriages mediated by WhatsApp. These technological mediations made refugees' ability to circulate and access information, and articulate a proscribed constellation of data points, critical to their being able to claim a legal identity and resist the state's efforts to exclude them. Cryptopolitics was at the center of all of these dynamics, as digital regulation relied on and helped to produce shadow identities, systems, narratives, and relationships.

Technological surveillance has long been a way that states have managed and regulated populations they perceived to challenge their power—from lantern laws in antebellum America to facial recognition technologies in Xinjang, China. What makes contemporary sociotechnological systems different from their predecessors, however, is that they make possible ever more sophisticated forms of state social control. While introducing biometrics into the RSD process alone has not enabled the state to fulfill its stated desire to expel refugees from Kenya's borders, if biometric data were joined with other forms of data, for example, SIM card registration numbers and social media accounts, this kind of control would become more possible. Examining digital regulation and its effects invites us to consider the kind of relationship between states, citizens and stateless people we want to see, and the limits we may wish to place on state power, in an increasingly digital age.

Lisa Poggiali is a Senior Democracy, Data and Technology Specialist at USAID, where she works on strategy, policy, and programs to bring technology's global governance, development and use into alignment with democratic values and respect for human rights. Before joining USAID, she was a practicing anthropologist researching the impacts of emerging and established technologies on social cohesion and polarization, democratic governance, and national security in East Africa. She holds a Ph.D. in Anthropology from Stanford University.

Notes

I drafted this chapter in 2019 while I was a postdoctoral fellow at the University of Pennsylvania's Price Lab for Digital Humanities. I am grateful for the time and space the Price Lab afforded me to research, think, and write, and for the intellectual generosity of my colleagues. Big thanks, also, to the students who took my course "Mapping for Social Justice." Their efforts to creatively leverage technology to rectify inequity and injustice inspired and informed this research. My deepest gratitude goes to Francesco Bellafante, whose curiosity, compassion, and unwavering support made him an ideal sounding board for this work. He died by suicide before this research was published but his spirit infuses every word. I revised and edited this chapter in 2020 while I was a Science and Technology Policy Fellow with the American Association for the Advancement of Science in USAID's Africa Bureau. The opinions and views expressed are my own and not necessarily shared by USAID.

1. AMISOM is a peacekeeping mission in Somalia that was created by the African Union's Peace and Security Council in January 2007 and approved by the United Nations. The Kenyan Defense Forces were formally integrated into AMISOM in 2012.
2. This research was generously funded by a Facebook Protect and Care Grant. None of the raw data collected was distributed to Facebook, and the entirety of the research process—including research design, hiring and training of research assistants, procurement, budgets, operations and logistics, data collection, analysis, and dissemination—was conceived of and managed by me with support from my research assistants and no involvement from Facebook. I thank the British Institute of Eastern Africa (BIEA) for being the home institution for this research in Kenya and for assisting with remuneration for my research assistants.
3. I thank my three wonderful research assistants: Safari Eddy Ntachompenze, Halima Hassan, and Hassan Ibrahim Hassan for their dedication to this project and their openness to learning about and operationalizing new research methods and approaches. This research could not have been completed were it not for their skills, expertise, and tendency to embrace humor in the face of challenges.
4. The rise of piracy off the coast of Somalia was also hurting the Kenyan shipping industry, see Robert McCabe (2019). There were reports of pragmatic cooperation between pirates and Al-Shabaab.
5. Operation Linda Nchi led to retaliatory terrorist attacks by Al-Shabaab, including the high-profile multiday siege on Westgate, the upscale Nairobi mall, in September 2013 in which sixty-seven people were killed, and the attack on Garissa University in April 2015, when 148 people were killed and over seven hundred students held hostage.

6. Kenya's two main refugee camps are Dadaab, which is in Garissa County and houses mostly Somali refugees, and Kakuma, which is in Turkana county and is more diverse, but houses predominantly South Sudanese refugees.
7. At least three of those deported were registered as refugees. However, many more were likely unregistered Somali refugees, as Somalis had great difficulty at the time registering for refugee status in Nairobi. Some may have also been Kenyan citizens, as Somali Kenyans have notorious trouble obtaining official forms of documentation (see Lochery 2012).
8. On the grounds of it being unconstitutional, the Constitutional and Human Rights Division of the High Court of Nairobi struck down the December 2014 amendment to the Refugees Act of 2006, which stated that: "(1) The number of refugees and asylum seekers permitted to stay in Kenya shall not exceed one hundred and fifty thousand persons. (2) The National Assembly may vary the number of refugees or asylum seekers permitted to be in Kenya. (3) Where the National Assembly varies the number of refugees or asylum seekers in Kenya, such a variation shall be applicable for a period not exceeding six months only. (4) The National Assembly may review the period of variation for a further six months." (Security Laws [Amendment] Act No. 19 2014)
9. States often employ procedural regulations in concert with more conventional, straightforward methods of national exclusion such as enforcing borders, enacting deportations, and/or changing citizenship laws.
10. While Burundians were also asked to undergo a second security screening, this appeared circumstantial and time-bound, related to a recent prison break near an area that many Burundians passed on their journey to Nairobi. Somalis, by contrast, were consistently described by the Shauri Moyo staff as a persistent security threat.
11. Elizabeth Wirtz analyzes how these bureaucratic requirements kept women in abusive relationships with spouses despite wanting to leave, because they did not want to compromise their resettlement process by getting divorced.
12. The Kenya Information and Communications Act of 2013 made it a criminal offense to fail to register one's SIM card, with a fine of up to KSh100,000 (Kenyan shillings) (approximately US$1,150) and/or up to six months of imprisonment. Nevertheless, the deadline to register was pushed back multiple times, most recently to 15 October 2022.
13. People speculated that refugee accounts were getting shut down because the numerical system used for official refugee IDs is different from the system used for Kenya national IDs. In other words, if this is true, it would mean that Safaricom's algorithm only recognized information corresponding to valid Kenya national IDs and would disconnect others, flagging them as potentially suspicious.
14. Officially called the National Integrated Identity Management System or NIIMS.
15. This date has been delayed as Huduma Namba has been mired in controversy, but as of November 2022 the government still planned to move forward with this plan.
16. This is part of a broader discourse that links viruses, both medical and computer, with foreignness and illegality (see Helmreich 2000).
17. Refugees who revealed to me that they were from Rwanda reported being surveilled and threatened inside Kenya, varying their movement patterns to avoid being "disappeared" like Rwandese friends and acquaintances they had known.

18. It is highly unlikely Charles would not have known that Interahamwe was an ethnic Hutu militia group.
19. Kinyamulenge is the language spoken by the Banyamulenge (Congolese with historical ties to Rwanda). It is nearly indistinguishable from Kinyarwanda.
20. At that time, UNHCR and the Government of Kenya did not yet have integrated refugee status determination processes.

References

Balakian, Sophia. 2016. "'Money Is Your Government': Refugees, Mobility, and Unstable Documents in Kenya's Operation Usalama Watch." *African Studies Review* 59(2): 87–111.

Carrier, Neil. 2017. *Little Mogadishu: Eastleigh, Nairobi's Global Somali Hub.* Oxford: University Press.

Communications Authority of Kenya. 2022."Operators Deactivate 287,214 SIM Cards Registered with Wrong IDs As 15th October Deadline Looms." *Communications Authority of Kenya,* 22 September. Retrieved 14 October 2022 from https://www.ca.go.ke/operators-deactivate-287214-sim-cards-registered-with-wrong-ids-as-15th-october-deadline-looms/.

Executive Committee of the High Commissioner's Programme; Standing Committee. 1997. "Note on Cessation Clauses." UNHCR, EC/47/SC/CRP.30. *Refworld,* 30 May. Retrieved 14 August 2020 from https://www.refworld.org/docid/47fdfaf1d.html.

Freedom House. 2015. "Freedom in the World 2015—Kenya." *Refworld,* 28 January. Retrieved 26 February 2021 from https://www.refworld.org/docid/54d0d7b215.html.

Helmreich, Stefan. 2000. "Flexible Infections: Computer Viruses, Human Bodies, Nation-States, Evolutionary Capitalism." *Science, Technology, & Human Values* 25(4): 472–91.

Kenya Law. "Kituo Cha Sheria & 8 Others v. Attorney General." Retrieved 8 January 2022 from http://kenyalaw.org/caselaw/cases/view/84157.

Kimuyu, Hilary. 2020. "Huduma Namba Cards to Replace ID Cards by End of 2021." *Nairobi News,* 18 November. Retrieved 14 May 2021 from https://nairobinews.nation.co.ke/news/huduma-namba-cards-to-replace-id-cards-by-end-of-2021.

Little, Peter D. 2003. *Somalia: Economy without a State.* African Issues. Bloomington: Indiana University Press.

Lochery, Emma. 2012. "Rendering Difference Visible: The Kenyan State and Its Somali Citizens." *African Affairs* 111/445 (2012): 615–39.

McCabe, Robert. 2019. "Lift for Maritime Sector in Kenya and Djibouti after Fall in Piracy." *The Conversation,* 15 December. Retrieved 26 Dec 2019 from https://theconversation.com/lift-for-maritime-sector-in-kenya-and-djibouti-after-fall-in-piracy-128073.

Open Society Justice Initiative. n.d. "Nubian Rights Forum et al. v. the Honourable Attorney General of Kenya et al ('NIIMS case')." *Open Society Foundations.* Retrieved 4 December 2022 from https://www.justiceinitiative.org/litigation/nubian-rights-forum-et-al-v-the-honourable-attorney-general-of-kenya-et-al-niims-case.

"Press Statement, Cabinet Secretary for Interior and Coordination of National Government, Refugees and National Security Issues." *Human Rights Watch*, 26 March. Retrieved 8 January 2022 from https://www.hrw.org/sites/default/files/related_material/PRESS%20STATEMENT%20BY%20CABINET%20SECRETARY%20FOR%20INTERIOR%20%20COORDINATION%20OF%20NATI%20%20%20.pdf.

Poggiali, Lisa. 2016. "Seeing (From) Digital Peripheries: Technology and Transparency in Kenya's Silicon Savannah." *Cultural Anthropology* 31(3): 387–411.

Rawlence, Ben. 2016. *City of Thorns: Nine Lives in the World's Largest Refugee Camp*. London: Picador Press.

"Samow Mumin Mohamed and Nine Others v. Cabinet Secretary, Ministry of Interior Security and Co-Ordination & 2 Others." Retrieved 8 January 2020 from http://kenyalaw.org/caselaw/cases/view/99326/.

"Security Laws (Amendment) Act No. 19." 2014. Retrieved 9 January 2020 from http://kenyalaw.org/kl/fileadmin/pdfdownloads/AmendmentActs/2014/SecurityLaws_Amendment_Act_2014.pdf.

UNHCR. n.d. "Biometric Identity Management System." *UNHCR*. Retrieved 21 August 2021 from https://www.unhcr.org/en-us/protection/basic/550c304c9/biometric-identity-management-system.html.

———. 2017. "UNHCR Refers Kenya Staff to Police after Internal Investigation Finds Fraud at Kakuma Camp." *UNHCR*, 30 May. Retrieved 8 January 2022 from https://www.unhcr.org/en-us/news/press/2017/5/592dcf644/unhcr-refers-kenya-staff-police-internal-investigation-finds-fraud-kakuma.html.

van der Kolk, Bessel. 2015. *The Body Keeps the Score: Brain, Mind, and Body in the Healing of Trauma*. London: Penguin Publishing Group.

Wirtz, Elizabeth. 2015. "Bureaucratic Bindings: Refugee Resettlement and Intimate Partner Abuse." In *Applying Anthropology to Gender-Based Violence: Global Responses, Local Practices*, ed. Jennifer R. Wies and Hillary J. Haldane, 29–44. Lanham, MD: Rowman and Littlefield.

Conclusion

Studying Cryptopolitics

Daivi Rodima-Taylor, Katrien Pype,
and Victoria Bernal

Cryptopolitics thrives on difference, and the boundaries of information distribution, giving rise to hidden realms of meaning, intention, and action. People build layers of obscurity and opacity in order to avoid the transmission of knowledge. Yet, those who want to expose the workings of cryptopolitical agency do the opposite: they seek to uncover the hidden, decode the ambiguous, and enlarge the group of "those who know."

Conspiracy theories work ambiguously with cryptopolitics. On the one hand, some of their basic aesthetics and ethics are the exposure of hidden truths. Yet, on the other hand, these theories often lead to new cryptopolitics: first and foremost because they fabricate layers of power, action, and intention that are far removed from factual, observable realities; and second, because they stimulate feelings of fear, anxiety, anger, and sometimes disgust, generating new configurations of hiding and exposing.

It is to these cryptopolitics—social, economic, and political—that our contributors have drawn attention. Every interaction between human beings, or between humans and institutions, is characterized by some degree of opacity. In some situations, people manipulate and mobilize that possibility for ambiguity. The rise of digital communicative platforms can be seen as central to contemporary activities of obfuscation and revelation—offering new possibilities for the empowerment of the marginal, but also creating new mechanisms of surveillance and control.

Cryptopolitics are intimately entangled with power and difference. Secrecy and decoding are used to draw and redraw the boundaries of exclusion and inclusion. Our focus on cryptopolitics casts light on the emerging dynamics of digital platforms in Africa that are often characterized by ambivalent implications to power and agency—the ability of individuals to make their own choices and act upon them. Various social media and internet search platforms, including Twitter, Facebook, WhatsApp, and Google, increasingly feature as an arena for construction and negotiation of alternative meanings and strategies of resistance, as our case studies demonstrate.

Our anthology reveals the role of the new digital publics that emerge on diverse global and local social media platforms to question and contest the political legitimacy and narratives of the state. For example, among Eritreans, the double meanings and ambiguities of humor both mirror and decode the cryptopolitics in the narratives of the authoritarian state, and expose these to public scrutiny. The chapters also draw attention to important continuities in political cultures, and the ways long-standing cryptopolitical understandings and practices are adapted to digital media. As we saw, social media in Burundi draws on the patterns of selective concealing that are part of the cultural repertoire in Burundian politics, while providing citizens with new avenues to combat the machinations and violence of the state. In post-conflict Somalia, the enduring struggles to reify and strategically manipulate otherwise fluid and contextual clan identities have been transferred to the digital world of algorithmic search engines. Communication on Congolese digital platforms is shaped by a locally specific aesthetic of ambiguity that foregrounds socially conditioned modes of concealment and revelation, forming an important strategy for managing personal relationships. New digital technologies of identification aimed at regulating and surveilling migrants in Kenya give rise to new strategies among Somali and Burundi refugees who evade and manipulate the state authorities, while providing them with informal ways to draw on their customary ties of sociality and mutual security.

The chapters of this book use cryptopolitics as a tool to illuminate the underlying discourses of power and powerlessness that are mediated by the novel technologies. Enabling new strategies of concealing and revealing information and intentions, the digital technologies are shown to disrupt and reconfigure people's communicative practices and lifeworlds. However, the chapters also show that the emerging virtual public sphere that allows people to connect through a variety of new media should not be seen as always enabling free speech and empowerment but is shaped by complex interaction between a variety of actors—individual and collective, public and private. We can therefore see how cryptopolitical practices are anchored in local cultures and social norms, but also interlink online and offline, public and intimate socialities.

Several case studies of this book demonstrate that while the digital media may render participation in political and economic governance more accessible to the masses, the outcomes remain contested and ambiguous. Thus, for example, digital platforms such as Twitter have disrupted the control of the state over the circulation of information in Kenya and introduced new, participatory practices of engaging with institutional politics. However, digital platforms also entail new opportunities for the state to strengthen its repressive information regime. Similarly, the restrictions and freedoms produced by the engagement of the users with Western-owned BigTech platforms that often dominate the digital economy landscape in Africa are also ambivalent and context-dependent. In South Africa and Kenya, for example, WhatsApp-mediated informal savings groups have emerged as an alternative to digital group accounts offered by commercial banks and dedicated FinTech platforms. While they build on vernacular templates of mutuality and allow broader financial access to the masses, they have also given rise to rapidly spreading scams and data capture by technology companies. Fundraising campaigns increasingly combine WhatsApp with offline contribution networks and mobile payment channels, demonstrating the continued importance of integrating existing offline and online modes of livelihood management.

As the chapters show, digital publics in Africa are thus constituted through multiple materialities and communicative forms. These spaces are shaped by a variety of actors that include individual users as well as governments, civil society organizations, diasporas, and increasingly, technology companies and investors. Many of the social media platforms are owned by BigTech companies originating from the Global North, profiting from monopoly power and user data extraction, and expanding foreign-based forms of governance and developmental paradigms (see also Friederici, Wahome, and Graham 2021). Increasing numbers of such platforms integrate various modes of digital payment and credit, becoming part of the FinTech platform political economy with its rapid scaling and multisided value creation while consolidating and transforming existing market infrastructures (see Langley and Leyshon 2020; Langley and Rodima-Taylor 2022). These old and new inequalities and exclusions shape the digital public sphere in many African countries. Our focus on the cryptopolitics of these encounters between the powerless and powerful enables novel and nuanced perspectives on the developing inequalities, digital divides, and opportunities for resistance and empowerment in Africa's rapidly evolving digital landscape—and suggests new trajectories for the study of new media and civil society in Africa.

Studying Cryptopolitics in the Era of New Media and Big Data

One of the biggest challenges for ethnographers, rarely trained in IT (information technology), resides exactly in understanding the imbrications of digital infrastructures in cryptopolitics. New centralized systems for managing information may conceal more than reveal, with transparency featuring as a commodity serving the interests of governments and private capital (Nutall and Mbembe 2015). A considerable expansion in data production and quality has occurred with the advent of software-powered machine learning that mines data, detects patterns, and builds predictive models (Kitchin 2014). Computational data management is increasingly central in consumer credit scoring, predictive policing systems, processing job and immigration applications, organizing social media newsfeeds, and managing search autocomplete features of internet platforms, to name a few. Private information is sold for profit, facilitating new markets and modes of accumulation. Big Data may also reveal more than private information about the users, casting light on their "unconscious secrets" of statistical behavior patterns and preferences (Jones 2014: 58). Digital technologies have fostered new surveillance and security measures used by states and private companies. These stockpiles of data are powerful public secrets that are known yet hidden from citizens, a form of cryptopolitics.

While software-powered information management introduces new areas of invisibility and secrecy, it also has important epistemological implications. It has been often argued that Big Data introduces a "new era of empiricism, wherein the volume of data, accompanied by techniques that can reveal their inherent truth, enables data to speak for themselves free of theory" (Kitchin 2014: 3). However, neither technology design nor research are neutral, and there is an inherently political dimension to the ways data is analyzed and interpreted (Kitchin 2014: 9). Algorithms contain significant areas of the unknowable, due to proprietary secrets of corporations and software companies, but also because of the complexities of machine learning that allow developing new procedures directly from the data, without relying on predetermined procedures or equations. Instead of following the formalized definitions of software experts, Nick Seaver (2017: 10) suggests that social studies of algorithms should approach them as empirically situated and enacted through diverse practices—as "heterogeneous and diffuse sociotechnical systems" constituted by procedures as well as people, institutions, and the intersecting contexts of algorithm use and sensemaking.

The complexities of studying the political dimensions of the hidden and the occult in the current era of neoliberal globalization can be illustrated with the example of the "occult economies" of post-apartheid South Africa (Comaroff and Comaroff 1999). As the impoverished masses witness vast wealth passing to the elites through the hidden speculations of the neoliberal market, people resort to the pursuit of novel magical means for the desired ends. Their practices, often parodying the free market, find expression through a variety of contemporary media—including "dial-in-diviners" and multimedia ritual technologies. The proliferation of "mystical arts" in post-independence Africa should not be viewed as a retreat to the traditional past, however, but rather as employing culturally familiar tropes and technologies for producing new ways of coping with contemporary inequalities: a "new magic for new situations" (1999: 284). Populations are disenfranchised or marginalized politically as well as economically and seek sources of power in the occult while also suspecting that elites use such powers to achieve the positions they hold.

Fieldwork and Cryptopolitics

Cryptopolitics is not only a topic to study in the lifeworlds of our research subjects. Collecting ethnographic data and publishing research involves strategies of exposing, concealing, and obscuring as well. As anthropologists, we have sometimes failed to acknowledge the politics of ethnographic research and scholarship, and the local and global power relations that shape our engagement with the people we write about. In the field, we may reflect on how much private information to disclose to various interlocutors, and sometimes we deliberately hide or distort the truth while presenting ourselves to interlocutors, state officials, NGOs, and other people and institutions. Ethnographers may decide that lying about or revealing their sexual orientation or their religion could hamper the fieldwork; while our interlocutors also weigh how far they are open to the researcher, perhaps deciding it is wiser to fabricate stories or only tell partial truths. While performances of hiding and obscuring do not hint at the fact that there is something hidden, sometimes it may be socially significant to allude at the performance of duplicity. Duplicity can become discretion. This may sometimes have socially rewarding consequences. For example, when preparing to record dirges at a funeral on Crete, Michael Herzfeld (2009: 147) was advised by one of his interlocutors not to take a big audio-recorder along but to "use the small cassette recorder—but make sure that it pokes out of your pocket, said he, so that people will realize that you are trying to be discreet."

In academic writing we may feel pressure to omit from our account the various missteps, misunderstandings, and even more serious events that marked our field experiences. Our usage of pseudonyms or the alterations of various idiosyncratic characteristics are also practices of cryptopolitics, of producing layers of meaning, of hiding and obscuring so that our interlocutors or our relationships with them are not harmed. These processes of anthropological research are well known. Yet, with the ubiquity of social media, practices of data collection, contacting interlocutors, and maintaining relationships with them are constantly being transformed. Our interlocutors themselves and interested others also now have easier access to public and private data about the researcher and their work that is available online (Fabian 2008), as well as other anthropological research done on those topics and locations.

In addition, data protection measures are by now a standard requirement in grant proposals and human subject review protocols. Scholars rightly need to reflect on how digitally stored ethnographic material will be protected from risks such as data hacking, theft of devices carrying data, and unintended publication online. Just as citizens are not always fully in control of the flow of data they consciously produce or inadvertently generate, neither are researchers. This points to a need for new approaches and perspectives in the discipline that would allow for more balanced disclosures in an environment of mutual dialogue and respect, to replace the old, extractive modes of knowledge-making.

Daivi Rodima-Taylor is a social anthropologist and researcher at the African Studies Center of the Pardee School of Global Studies of Boston University. Her research focuses on African informal economies, financial technology and social media platforms, and migration and remittances. She has conducted longitudinal research in East Africa and published in journals including *Africa, African Studies Review, Global Networks, Social Analysis, American Ethnologist, Journal of International Relations and Development, Environment and Planning: Politics and Space, Geoforum, Global Policy,* and *Review of International Political Economy.* Her recent publications include the co-edited volume *Land and the Mortgage: History, Culture, Belonging* (Berghahn Books, 2022) and the co-edited special issue *Fintech in Africa* (*Journal of Cultural Economy,* 2022).

Katrien Pype is a cultural anthropologist, mainly interested in media, popular culture, and technology. She has written about the production of television serials, television news programs, TV dance shows, and long-distance communication, all in the context of contemporary Kinshasa. Her work is published in edited books and journals such as *Africa, Ethnos, Journal of the Royal Anthropological Society, Journal of Modern African Studies; Journal of Africa's Media Studies,* and others. Her monograph, *The Making* *of the Pentecostal Melodrama: Religion, Media, and Gender in Kinshasa*, was published with Berghahn Books (2012). Pype also co-edited, with Jaco Hoffman, *Aging in Sub-Saharan Africa: Spaces and Practices of Care* (Policy Press, 2016).

Victoria Bernal is a cultural anthropologist whose scholarship in political anthropology contributes to media and IT studies, gender studies, and African studies. Her work addresses questions relating to politics, gender, migration and diaspora, war, globalization, transnationalism, civil society and activism, development, digital media, and Islam. She is Professor of Anthropology at the University of California, Irvine. Bernal's articles and chapters have appeared in various collections as well as in anthropological, African Studies, and interdisciplinary journals, including *American Ethnologist, Cultural Anthropology, American Anthropologist, Global Networks, Comparative Studies in Society and History, African Studies Review*, and *Political and Legal Anthropology Review.*

References

Comaroff, Jean, and John Comaroff. 1999. "Occult Economies and the Violence of Abstraction: Notes from the South African Postcolony." *American Ethnologist* 26(2): 279–303.

Fabian, Johannes. 2008. *Ethnography as Commentary: Writing from the Virtual Archive.* Durham, NC: Duke University Press.

Friederici, Nicolas, Michel Wahome, and Mark Graham. 2020. *Digital Entrepreneurship in Africa.* Cambridge: MIT University Press.

Herzfeld, Michael. 2009. "The Performance of Secrecy: Domesticity and Privacy in Public Spaces." *Semiotica* 175: 135–62.

Jones, Graham. 2014. "Secrecy." *Annual Review of Anthropology* 43: 53–69.

Kitchin, Rob. 2014. "Big Data, New Epistemologies and Paradigm Shifts." *Big Data & Society* April–June: 1–12.

Langley, Paul, and Andrew Leyshon. 2020. "The Platform Political Economy of FinTech: Reintermediation, Consolidation and Capitalisation." *New Political Economy* 26(3): 376–88.

Langley, Paul, and Daivi Rodima-Taylor. 2022. "FinTech in Africa: An Editorial Introduction." *Journal of Cultural Economy* 15(4): 387–400.

Nuttall, Sarah, and Achille Mbembe. 2015. "Secrecy's Softwares." *Current Anthropology* 56 (S12): S317–24.

Seaver, Nick. 2017. "Algorithms as Culture: Some Tactics for the Ethnography of Algorithmic Systems." *Big Data & Society* July–December: 1–12.

Index

www.ingramcontent.com/pod-product-compliance
Ingram Content Group UK Ltd.
Pitfield, Milton Keynes, MK11 3LW, UK
UKHW021850250826
8166IPUK00004B/62

9 781807 581046